# RADICAL MARKETS

# Radical Markets

## Uprooting Capitalism and Democracy for a Just Society

Eric A. Posner and E. Glen Weyl

**PRINCETON UNIVERSITY PRESS**

PRINCETON AND OXFORD

Copyright © 2018 by Princeton University Press

Published by Princeton University Press,
41 William Street, Princeton, New Jersey 08540

In the United Kingdom: Princeton University Press,
6 Oxford Street, Woodstock, Oxfordshire OX20 1TR

press.princeton.edu

Jacket design by Karl Spurzem

All Rights Reserved

ISBN 978-0-691-17750-2
Library of Congress Control Number: 2017964479

British Library Cataloging-in-Publication Data is available

This book has been composed in Adobe Text Pro and Gotham

Printed on acid-free paper. ∞

Printed in the United States of America

10 9 8 7 6 5 4 3 2

*To the memory of William S. Vickrey*

# CONTENTS

# ACKNOWLEDGMENTS

Economic production and development are fundamentally social, not individual, processes, or so we argue throughout this book. Intellectual products such as this book are no different. The social milieus in which we developed and the wide range of communities to which we have belonged shaped our ideas and, if this book has the impact we aspire to, the *zeitgeist* will doubtless be far more important than our intellectual exertions. Yet there are many people among these broader forces who especially contributed to this work.

While we identify many of our most important intellectual influences in the course of the book, each of us had personal intellectual mentors who go less noted there, but merit our thanks. Gary Becker and especially José Scheinkman played critical roles in encouraging Glen to pursue his boldest ideas, despite the costs to his professional standing and the difficulty publishing this work. Jerry Green, Amartya Sen, and especially Jean Tirole were central to shaping Glen's view of mechanism design as a force for social transformation. Jennifer Chayes, Glen's supervisor at Microsoft, gave him the professional space, interdisciplinary environment, and personal inspiration he needed to believe in and pursue this project. Eric is grateful for the support of his colleagues at the University of Chicago, and to the Russell Baker Scholars Fund for financial support. Glen is grateful to the Alfred P. Sloan Foundation for financial support through his fellowship.

We owe a special debt to Soumaya Keynes, whose interest in and enthusiasm for the merging of our various ideas helped stimulate us to write this book.

The many co-authors and collaborators on projects that contributed to our vision here are cited throughout, but a few deserve explicit mention here: Anthony Lee Zhang pioneered the idea of the common ownership self-assessed tax with Glen; Steve Lalley proved the fundamental theorems about Quadratic Voting with Glen, and Nick Stephanopoulos together with Eric devised the practical vision of egalitarian election law based on it; Fiona Scott Morton devised the 1% rule for institutional investors with us; and Jaron Lanier has been Glen's partner every step of the way in Data as Labor.

Our editor Joe Jackson and his colleagues at Princeton University Press made this book a reality. Susan Jean Miller did a superb job helping us hone our prose. We are also grateful to a talented team of research assistants. Graham Haviland, Eliot Levmore, Stella Shannon, Han-ah Sumner, and Jill Rogowski provided invaluable assistance.

A conference on our manuscript hosted by the Cowles Foundation at Yale University and supported enthusiastically by its director Larry Samuelson helped shape our thinking. Seven discussants (Ian Ayres, Dirk Bergemann, Jacob Hacker, Nicole Immorlica, Branko Milanovic, Tim Shenk, and Matt Weinzierl) provided us vital feedback. Tim was particularly helpful in shaping our understanding of the relevant history of ideas. We also received comments from many friends and colleagues, including Anna Blender, Charlotte Cavaille, Patrick Collison, Adam Cox, Richard Eskow, Marion Fourcade, Alex Peysakovich, Greg Shaw, Itai Sher, Steve Swig, Tommaso Valetti, and Steve Weyl. Steph Dick and Chris Muller provided thought-provoking reactions that shaped our revisions. Richard Arnott, Bill Vickrey's archivist, shaped our understanding of his ideas and beliefs. Dionisio Gonzalez, Tod Lippy, and Laura Weyl supported us in thinking through the aesthetics of the book. We also appreciate the collaboration of the members of the "Radical Economics" and "Social Life of Data" reading groups at Microsoft, especially Nicky Couldry, Dan Greene, Jessy Hwang, Moira Weigel, and James Wright.

Encouragement from Satya Nadella and Kevin Scott, business leaders at Microsoft, and Atif Mian and Ken Rogoff from the academic side, has also been important to the development of this work.

Glen is grateful to his wife, Alisha Holland, more than anyone. She suffuses this book from start to finish; as only she will recognize, this book doubles as a sort of love letter. She was the one who brought Glen to Rio and got him thinking about favelas, and it was she who encouraged him to develop the ideas of the epilogue. The spirit of the city and the migrant, and the passion to improve the lot of both, that animate so much of our work come from her. Glen and Alisha's two-person writing group transformed much of our writing. Without Alisha's support of Glen's professional risks and iconoclasm he would not have dared write this book; without the empathy and appreciation for beauty she taught him, he never could have had the vision to do so. Every day Glen discovers more how interwoven and inseparable their ideas and emotions are. Building that bond, starting as isolated and nerdy adolescents, has not always been easy or comforting. But just like a society, a partnership that can radically reform itself in the face of crisis, and thus foster rather than constrain equality, growth, and cooperation, is a partnership that deserves to last.

# The Auction
# Will Set You Free

> The nineteenth-century liberal was a radical, both in the etymological sense of going to the root of the matter, and in the political sense of favoring major changes in social institutions. So too must be his modern heir.
>
> —MILTON FRIEDMAN, *CAPITALISM AND FREEDOM*, 1961

The seed of this book was planted during a summer one of us spent in Rio de Janeiro. Rio is the most naturally beautiful city in the world. Lush tropical hills, which roll down to an island-laden bright blue bay, afford unrivaled views. Yet these same hills are covered with *favelas*, squalid jerry-rigged slums that lack basic sanitation and transportation.

Leblon, possibly the wealthiest neighborhood in all of Latin America, lies at the base of the hills. There your money can buy, at wildly inflated prices, the luxury watches and cars that are leading status symbols. Yet the citizens of Leblon don't dare wear their watches on the street, nor stop their cars at red lights at night, for fear of the violence looming from the favelas above. Rio is one of the most dangerous cities in the world.

*Cariocas*, as the people of Rio call themselves, are relaxed, kind, creative, and open. They perceive race more subtly than we do in the United States, with our sharp line between white and black. Both countries have long histories of slavery, but in Brazil, everyone is of mixed heritage. Even so, variations in skin tone convey gradations of class, an omnipresent force in Brazilian society.

Economically, Brazil is the most unequal country in the Western hemisphere. While it overflows with natural abundance, a few families control much of its wealth and almost 10% of Brazilians live below the global poverty line. The last president was ejected for abusing her power, her predecessor is in jail for corruption, and corruption investigators are closing in on the current leader, whose approval rating is in single digits. He will probably be jailed by the time this book is published. Living standards in the country have stagnated for long periods. Entrepreneurship is sparse.

Why has this paradise fallen? How can its potential be fulfilled? The debate is familiar.

> LEFT: The government should tax the rich to supply homes, medical care, and jobs for the poor.
>
> RIGHT: Yes, and you end up with Venezuela or Zimbabwe. The government needs to privatize state-owned industries, enforce property rights, lower taxes, and reduce regulation. Get the economy going, and inequality will take care of itself.
>
> TECHNOCRATIC MIDDLE: We need an economy carefully regulated by internationally trained experts, targeted interventions that have been tested by randomized controlled trials, and political reform that protects human rights.

People in rich countries, where inequality is rising, will recognize Brazil in their own countries. In the rich countries, economies are also stagnating and political conflict and corruption are on the rise. The long-standing belief that a "develop*ing* country" like Brazil will eventually end up as a "devel-op*ed* country" like the United States is under scrutiny, and people are beginning to wonder if things are moving in reverse. Meanwhile, the standard prescriptions for reform are the same as they have been for the last half century: increase taxes and redistribute; strengthen markets and privatize; or improve governance and expertise.

In Rio, these prescriptions are palpably stale. Poverty, tight and concentrated control of land, and political conflict seem to be intimately linked. Wealth redistribution has made few inroads on inequality. Improvement of property rights has not done much to foster development. Slum dwellers hang on to property that could instead be a public park, a nature preserve, or modern housing. Land in the city center, where favela dwellers could live decently and have access to public services, is monopolized by the wealthy, who are too fearful of crime to enjoy it. The same concentrated control of wealth that breeds inequality seems to corrupt politics and restrain business initiative: Brazil is in the bottom 10% of countries in terms of ease of creating a business, according to the World Bank.

The case of Rio demands an answer to the question: Is there no better way? Can this city not escape inequality, stagnation, and social conflict? Does Rio foreshadow the fate of New York, London, and Tokyo, except without the pleasures of samba and beaches?

## Auctions as Radical Markets

The problem stems from ideas, or rather the lack thereof. The arguments of both the Right and the Left had something to offer when they originated in the nineteenth and early twentieth centuries, but today their potential is spent. No longer bold reforms, they box us in. To open up our social possibilities, we must open our minds to radical redesigns. To get to the root of the problem, we must understand how our economic and political institutions work and use this knowledge to formulate a response, which is what we do in this book.

Our premise is that markets are, and for the medium term will remain, the best way of arranging a society. But while our society is supposed to be organized by competitive markets, we contend the most important markets are monopolized or entirely missing, and that by creating true competitive, open, and free markets, we can dramatically reduce inequality, increase prosperity, and heal the ideological and social rifts tearing our society apart.

Like those on the Right, we think that markets must be strengthened, expanded, and purified. Yet we perceive a fatal flaw in the Right: it has been timid and unimaginative in its vision of the social changes necessary to make markets flourish. Many on the Right support Market Fundamentalism, an ideology they assume to have been proven in economic theory and historical experience. In reality, it is little more than a nostalgic commitment to an idealized version of markets as they existed in the Anglo-Saxon world in the nineteenth century. (We will use the term *capitalism* to refer to this idealized historical version of markets, in which governments focus on protecting private property and enforcing contracts.) We contrast Market Fundamentalism with Market Radicalism, which is our own commitment to understand, restructure, and improve markets at their very roots.

We share with the Left the idea that existing social arrangements generate unfair inequality and undermine collective action. But the Left's flaw has been its reliance on the discretionary power of government bureaucratic elites to fix social ills. Imagined by the Left to be benevolent, ideologically neutral, and committed to the public good, these elites are sometimes arbitrary, corrupt, incompetent, or, perceived that way whether they are or not, distrusted by the public. To harness the radicalism we believe is inherent in markets, we must decentralize power while spurring collective action.

The Radical Markets we envision are institutional arrangements that allow the fundamental principles of market allocation—free exchange disciplined by competition and open to all comers—to play out fully. An auction is the quintessential Radical Market. Because the rules of an auction require people to bid against each other, the object on the block winds up in the hands of the person who wants it most—with the caveat that differences in bids may represent differences in wealth as well as desire.

Although most people do not think of auctions outside the realm of estate sales, fine art, and fund-raisers, they are commonly conducted on the Internet, away from the public eye. But in what follows we will show how spreading them throughout our society could save Rio—and the world.

## Rio for Sale: A Thought Experiment

Suppose the entire city of Rio is perpetually up for auction. Imagine that every building, business, factory, and patch of hillside has a going price, and anyone who bids a price higher than the going price for an entity would take possession of it. Auctions might extend to some kinds of personal property like automobiles, or even to what is normally determined through the political process, like the amount of pollution that factories are permitted to discharge. Much of this book is devoted to figuring out how such a system might work.

As a thought experiment, however, let us assume for the moment that the auctions are conducted via smartphone apps that automatically bid based on default settings, eliminating most of the need for people to constantly calculate how much to offer. Laws ensure that the obvious sorts of disruptions don't occur (for example, coming home to find your apartment is no longer yours). Incentives are in place to care for and develop assets, and ensure that privacy and other values are also preserved. All of the revenue generated by this auction would be returned to citizens, equally, as a "social dividend," or used to fund public projects, which is how revenues from oil sales in Alaska and Norway are used.

Life under this auction would transform Rio's society and politics. First, people would think about their property differently. The stark distinction between owning a house and occupying a spot on the beach would erode. Private property would become public to a significant extent and the possessions of those around you would, in a sense, become partly yours.

In addition, perpetual auctioning would undo the tremendous misuse of lands and other resources. The highest bidder for the most scenic hillsides would never be someone planning to build rickety and dilapidated slums. The highest bidder for central city land would not be the developers of small, ritzy condos but the builders of skyscrapers for the new, vast middle class auctioning would create.

A third result would be the end of the primary source of economic inequality. Although at first blush you might assume that the auction would allow the rich to buy up everything of value, reflect for a moment. What do you mean by "the rich"? People who own lots of businesses, land, and so forth. But, if everything were up for auction all the time, no person would own such assets. Their benefits would flow equally to all. Chapter 1 explains how.

Fourth, the Rio auction system would limit corruption by taking many major political decisions away from politicians and placing them in the hands of citizens. With an improved public life, crime would be reduced, street life would be restored, and the retreat into private communities would cease. Far from the usual image of markets substituting for and undermining the public sphere, Radical Markets would bolster trust in public life. Chapter 2 explains how an auction could organize politics.

## Radical Heroes

Our argument draws on an intellectual tradition that goes back to Adam Smith. Smith is frequently invoked by conservative thinkers these days, including Market Fundamentalists. But Smith was a radical—in the two ways highlighted by our epigraph. First, he dug deeply into the roots of economic organization and proposed theories that remain influential today. Second, he attacked the prevailing ideas and institutions of his day and presented a series of daring propositions and reforms. People regard these ideas as "conservative" today simply because they were so successful in reshaping policy and thinking at the time.

Market Fundamentalists draw a line from Smith to people like Friedrich Hayek, Milton Friedman, and George Stigler—midcentury conservative idols and Nobel laureates who took from Smith an idealized notion of markets based on private property. They put this vision to work in support of libertarian economics and politics. The Fundamentalists ignore those economists who share Smith's radical spirit, such as Henry George, whose ideas helped launch the Progressive era and who may have been the most widely read economist of all time, but whose vision was lost in the Left-Right battles of the Cold War. George was more concerned about inequality than were the conservative followers of Smith, and he recognized that private property could stand in the way of truly free markets. To remedy this problem, he proposed a tax scheme that would create a system of common ownership for land.

The most important "Georgist" economist, to whose memory we dedicate this book, is a mid-twentieth-century professor named William Spencer Vickrey. Vickrey, pictured in figure P.1, was the Master Yoda of the economics profession: silly, carefree, reclusive, absent-minded, and a fount of often inscrutable yet world-changing insights. He roller-skated from the train to class and wore his lunch on his shirts. He might wake from a nap in the middle of research workshops to comment, "This paper would benefit from . . . Henry George's principle of taxing land values." He mentioned George's scheme so often that a colleague who was eulogizing him quipped, "I imagine by now he has mentioned it to God, too."[1] Also aloof, arrogant, and private, Vickrey often failed to publish academic articles that contained his best ideas.

The inspirations of Vickrey's research closely resembled ours. He focused during most of his career on the organization of cities and the tremendous waste of resources in most urban forms. He was particularly fascinated by cities in Latin America, where he advised governments on urban planning and taxation. It was while he was designing a fiscal system for Venezuela that he produced the paper that finally undermined his best efforts at ensuring his obscurity.

That paper was published in 1961. Its title, "Counterspeculation, Auctions, and Competitive Sealed Tenders," seemed to ensure it would soon be forgotten. But it was rediscovered a decade later. Vickrey's paper was the first to study the power of auctions to solve major social problems, helped found a field

FIGURE P.1: William S. Vickrey (1914–1996), Nobel
Laureate in Economics, father of mechanism design, and
quiet hero of our drama. Photo by Jon Levy, permission
granted by Getty Images.

of economics called "mechanism design," and earned him the
Nobel Prize in 1996.

Vickrey's ideas have transformed economic theory and had
an impact on policy. Governments around the world use auctions based on Vickrey's ideas to sell licenses to use radio spectrum. Facebook, Google, and Bing use a system derived from
Vickrey's auction to allocate advertising space on their web
pages. Vickrey's insights about urban planning and congestion
pricing are slowly changing the face of cities, and they play an
important role in the pricing policies of ride-hailing apps like
Uber and Lyft.[2]

However, none of these applications reflects the ambition
that sparked Vickrey's work. When Vickrey won the Nobel
Prize, he reportedly hoped to use the award as a "bully pulpit"
to bring George's transformative ideas and the radical potential

of mechanism design to a broader audience.[3] Yet Vickrey died of a heart attack three days after learning of his prize. Even had he lived, Vickrey may have struggled to inspire the public. In 1996, economies were booming around the world and a new era of global cooperation seemed to be dawning. No one wanted to tinker with success and Vickrey's approach faced daunting practical obstacles.

Today, however, the outlook for economic and political progress is no longer sunny, while, thanks to developments in economics and technology, the practical limits on Vickrey's approach can now be overcome. This book, therefore, tries to act as Vickrey's lost bully pulpit, fleshing out the vision he might have shared with the world had he lived.

# RADICAL MARKETS

# Introduction

## THE CRISIS OF THE LIBERAL ORDER

The ideas of economists and political philosophers, both when they are right and when they are wrong, are more powerful than is commonly understood. Indeed the world is ruled by little else. Practical men, who believe themselves to be quite exempt from any intellectual influence, are usually the slaves of some defunct economist.

—JOHN MAYNARD KEYNES, *THE GENERAL THEORY OF EMPLOYMENT, INTEREST, AND MONEY*, 1936

The Berlin Wall fell when one of us was just starting preschool and the other was beginning his career, that moment was crucial in shaping our political identities. The "American way"— free markets, popular sovereignty, and global integration—had vanquished the Soviet "evil empire." Since then those values— which we will call the liberal order—have dominated intellectual discussions. Leading thinkers declared "the end of history."

The great social problems that had so long been the center of political drama had been solved.[1]

Both of us came of age intellectually in an unprecedented era of global intellectual consensus, confidence, and complacency. Nowhere was this atmosphere clearer than in the policy world in which we each ended up—one of us in law, the other in economics. Ironically, economics, more than any other field, took on the mantle of leadership in a world where debates over economic systems had disappeared. Economists, who at one time had helped define the extremes of the political spectrum (remember Karl Marx?), saw themselves as mainstream voices of reason, entrusted by the public with policy decisions.[2]

In universities and professional associations, economists focused on centrist policy analysis, which, being highly mathematical and quantitative, appeared to be ideologically neutral. Meanwhile the field marginalized those on the radical left (Marxists) and right (the so-called Austrian school).[3] Most of the work done by academics in the areas of economics, law, and policy were devoted to justifying existing market institutions or offering moderate reforms that, in essence, preserved the status quo.

With few exceptions, mainstream economists of this era assumed that the prevailing design of market institutions was working about as well as possible. If markets "failed," the theory went, moderate regulation, based on cost-benefit analysis, would pick up the slack. Questions about inequality were largely ignored. Economists believed that because markets generated so much wealth, inequality could be tolerated; a social safety net ensured that the worst off didn't starve. One of us ended up working at Microsoft, pursuing his interest in extending the standard approach to modern technology platforms, and the other focused on questions of legal reform. Meanwhile, the ground was shifting beneath our feet.

The financial crisis of 2008 and the subsequent recession were the first tremors. Yet even though the economic downturn was the worst since the Great Depression, for a time it seemed to be no different from most recessions. People lost their homes, jobs, and access to credit, but this had happened many times before and the economy had recovered. Only in 2016 did it become clear how dramatically things had changed.

It turned out that a great deal of the economic progress that had taken place before the recession was illusory—it had benefited mostly the very rich. Ballooning inequality, stagnating living standards, and rising economic insecurity made a mockery of the old style of policy analysis. The angry political reaction to the recession—exemplified in the United States by the Occupy Wall Street and Tea Party movements—did not subside as the economy recovered. The public lost faith in the mainstream policy analysis of elites who had supported financial deregulation and then the unpopular bailouts. With the old ways of doing things in doubt and new directions unclear, public opinion polarized. And because of long-simmering controversies over cultural issues, especially immigration, anger at the elites took an ugly nativist turn. Xenophobia and populism at a level not seen since the 1930s erupted across the world.

Unfortunately, ideas have not kept up with the crisis. Capitalism is blamed for increased inequality and slowing growth, yet no alternative has presented itself. Liberal democracy is blamed for corruption and paralysis, but authoritarianism is hardly an appealing substitute. Globalization and international governance institutions have become favorite scapegoats, yet no other sustainable path for international relations has been proposed. Even the best-run governments of the most advanced countries rally around the mainstream technocratic approach of the past despite its many failures.

In searching for a way out of this impasse, we have thus found ourselves rereading the works of the founding fathers of modern social organization: a group of self-styled "political economists" and "Philosophical Radicals" of the late eighteenth and nineteenth centuries, including Adam Smith, the Marquis de Condorcet, Jeremy Bentham, John Stuart Mill, Henry George, Léon Walras, and Beatrice Webb.

Although these thinkers—whose ideas we will explore in later chapters—lived in a world different from ours, they faced some similar challenges. The economic and political system they had inherited from the eighteenth century could not keep up with changes in technology, demographics, the globalization of the time, and the larger cultural environment. Entrenched privilege blocked efforts to promote equality, growth, and political reform. Believing the intellectual resources of the day were insufficient to provide a way forward, the Philosophical Radicals developed new ideas that have played an enormous role in the development of our modern market-based economic system and of liberal democracy. Their vision and reforms combined the libertarian aspirations of today's right with the egalitarian goals of today's left and are the shared heritage of both ends of the standard political spectrum. This is the common spirit we seek to revive.

## Inequality

The most significant problem of our time is the rising inequality within wealthy countries. Figure I.1 shows the evolution of the share of income earned by the top 1% of the income distribution in the United States from 1913 to 2015.[4] The figure

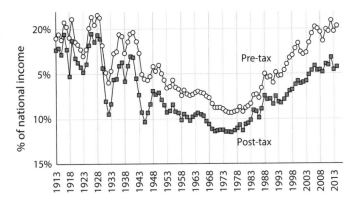

**FIGURE I.1:** US income shares of top 1% households, including capital gains, before and after taxes.
*Source:* Thomas Piketty, Emmanuel Saez, & Gabriel Zucman, Distributional National Accounts: Methods and Estimates for the United States, *Quarterly Journal of Economics* (Forthcoming).

shows this share both before and after taxes. Focusing on the after-tax figure most relevant to final consumption, we see that the share of income taken by the top 1% of earners has roughly doubled from its trough of 8% in the mid-1970s to its recent peak of 16%. A similar pattern, though less dramatic, prevailed in many other Anglo-Saxon countries during this period. Income patterns were more muted in some continental European and East Asian countries where government redistribution is more generous.[5]

Is this growth in inequality simply the price of a dynamic economy, as suggested by many "neoliberal" economic arguments? Some economists have argued that growing inequality reflects the diverging skills and opportunities of the talented, skills that will go to waste if not rewarded by rising income. Yet rising inequality does not reflect only diverging wages, but the shift of national income away from wages entirely. Figure I.2 shows the share of national income that accrues to all labor, from factory workers to CEOs, what economists call the "labor

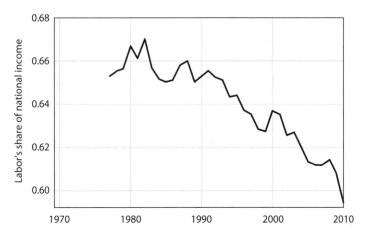

FIGURE I.2: Labor's share of US National Income over time.
*Source:* David Autor, David Dorn, Lawrence F. Katz, Christina Patterson, & John Van Reenen, The Fall of the Labor Share and the Rise of Superstar Firms (MIT Working Paper, 2017), https://economics.mit.edu/files/12979.

share." There has been a nearly 10% drop over this same period in the share of national income in the United States that rewards work, bringing the United States closer to developing countries where labor's share is far lower than has traditionally been the case in rich countries.

Where has the money that used to pay workers gone? If it were rewarding saving, that might not be so worrying. After all, any citizen can choose to save, and rewarding saving can stimulate growth. Yet increasing evidence suggests that the reward to saving is itself falling (as evidenced by falling interest rates) and instead an increasing fraction of national income is being absorbed by market power—what we later call the "monopoly problem."[6] Figure I.3 illustrates the trend.

The top panel of figure I.3 shows the share of US national income accounted for by "economic profits" above what would be expected under perfect competition, profits attributable to monopoly power. Such excess profits have risen roughly four-

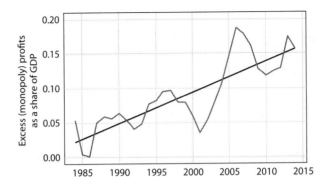

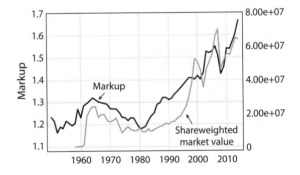

FIGURE I.3: Above—competitive profits as a fraction of national income in the United States over time. Below—markups over cost (black) and average share-weighted stock market value (gray).
*Sources:* Simcha Barkai, Declining Labor and Capital Shares (2017), http://home.uchicago.edu/~barkai/doc/BarkaiDecliningLaborCapital.pdf, and Jan de Loecker & Jan Eeckhout, The Rise of Market Power and Macroeconomic Implications (2017), http://www.janeeckhout.com/wp-content/uploads/RMP.pdf.

fold just since the early 1980s, in tandem with rising inequality and declining labor share.[7] These profits are overwhelmingly claimed by the extremely wealthy. As we argue below, the rise in inequality and the fall in labor's share are both fueled by and fuel a rich-get-richer dynamic. Sixty percent of the income of the top 1% of earners comes from such profits or returns on capital (as opposed to wages), four times as large a fraction as for the bottom 90% of income earners. The bottom panel of the figure shows the co-evolution of another measure of market power (the excess price or "markup" firms charge over cost) and the stock market value of corporations.[8] The close coincidence of these series, and the tight correlation the authors found between market value and markups across companies in a given year, strongly suggest that falling labor's share and rising inequality are not simply the necessary consequence of accelerated growth. Instead, they are close correlates (symptoms, causes, or likely both) of increased market power.

The trajectory of inequality *across* countries is a different story. Figure I.4 shows the fraction of global inequality, measured by the common "mean logarithmic deviation" (discussed further in chapter 3), that prevailed between, rather than within, countries from 1820 to 2011. From 1820 to 1970, inequality between countries grew nearly tenfold; in contrast, inequality within countries declined by about a fifth. This pattern has reversed since 1970; international inequality has fallen by about a fifth and domestic inequality within wealthy countries has risen.

Again, if this international inequality were an outgrowth of dynamic international markets, it might be worth its price. Yet, the fact that international inequality began to fall just as globalization began to accelerate and decolonization was completed suggests that international inequality may be attributable to colonialism and closed international markets rather than to free markets.

## Stagnation

The last significant shift in economic philosophy took place in the 1970s, when "stagflation" (simultaneously high inflation

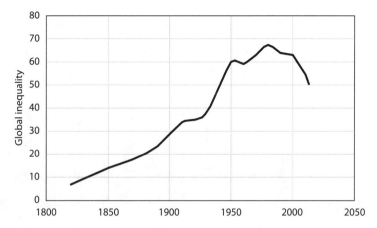

FIGURE I.4: Global inequality that is across as opposed to within countries from 1820 to 2011, measured by the mean logarithmic deviation (see chapter 3).
This series is based on a merger of the data of François Bourguignon and Christian Morrisson, Inequality Among World Citizens: 1820–1992, 92 *American Economic Review* 4 (2002), and Branko Milanovic, Global Inequality of Opportunity: How Much of Our Income Is Determined by Where We Live?, 97 *Review of Econonomics & Statistics* 2 (2015), performed by Branko Milanovic as a favor to us.

and unemployment) undermined the then-accepted Keynesian argument that inflation was a cost worth paying for full employment. The neoliberal and "supply-side" ideas that grew up in response promised that allowing greater play of capitalism (lower taxes, deregulation, privatization) would unleash economic growth. Even if capitalism might cause some inequality, wealth would eventually "trickle down" to ordinary workers. Yet not only has the promised wealth failed to trickle down; it has not materialized at all. In fact, productivity growth has dramatically fallen over this period. For example, in the United States, the growth in labor productivity from the end of World War II until 2004 was around 2.25% annually. Since 2005, productivity growth has slowed by a full percentage point, to around 1.25%.[9]

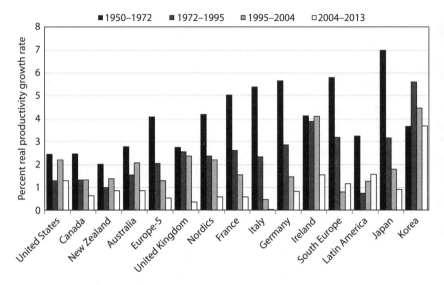

FIGURE I.5: Average annual real productivity growth around the world for various regions or countries and time periods, 1950–2013.
*Source:* OECD.

This phenomenon has been less dramatic in the United States than in other wealthy countries. Figure I.5 shows productivity growth in countries around the world beginning in 1950.[10] Overall, productivity growth has dramatically fallen since midcentury, with the exceptions of the 1995–2004 period in certain wealthy countries and the different trend observed in developing countries. In many wealthy countries, such as France and Japan, productivity growth fell by a factor of 10, from 5% to 7% during the period from 1950 to 1972 to just a fraction of a percent in the last decade. Recent data paint an even more discouraging portrait.[11]

A related problem concerns the key economic resources of labor and capital, which are marked by widespread unemployment (in the case of labor) or misallocation (in the case of capital). This aspect of sluggish economic growth has independent significance because unemployment and low wages cause social and political conflict. Unemployment and misemployment differ from country to country, depending on the treatment of the long-term unemployed. In Europe, unemployment rates have risen, while in the United States, prime-aged males are dropping out of the labor force. For example, the labor force participation rate of prime-aged US men fell from 96% in 1970 to 88% in 2015. In most countries in Europe, unemployment has risen from rates of 4% to 6% midcentury to a persistent 10% or higher rate.[12] And it is not only labor that is underused in today's economy. Recent research indicates that capital assets are misallocated across firms as well, in the sense that capital is not employed by the firms, sectors, or cities that could make most valuable use of it.[13] This suggests that reallocating capital and employment from less productive entities to more productive ones could dramatically increase aggregate output.[14]

Together, the trends of rising inequality and stagnating growth mean that typical citizens in wealthy countries are no longer living much better than their parents did. Economist Raj Chetty and co-authors found that while 90% of American children born in 1940 had a higher living standard than their parents, only 50% of children born in 1980 did.[15] Similar figures are not yet available for other wealthy countries, but these patterns likely characterize them as well.

These trends pose the same problem for the neoliberal economic consensus that stagflation posed for the Keynesian consensus before it. We were promised economic dynamism in exchange for inequality. We got the inequality, but dynamism is actually declining. Call it *stagnequality*—lower growth combined with rising inequality rather than inflation. It is no surprise, then, that the public has rejected conventional economic wisdom.

## Conflict

Given that leftists have long criticized "trickle-down economics," it would be natural to expect a leftist populist backlash to stagnequality and a subsequent move to redistribute income. To some extent this prediction has been confirmed by recent events, as summarized in table I.1. Bernie Sanders nearly won the US Democratic primary despite identifying as a socialist earlier in his life and running for president as a social democrat. In the UK, Labor Party leader Jeremy Corbyn is the most left-wing leader of Britain's Labor Party with a serious chance of victory since World War II, and left-wing movements in France and Italy have achieved unusual political success.

However, history has shown that fascist or ultranationalist movements have come to power when the social fabric is fraying. Promising to claim wealth for the masses, not from the rich, but from an external enemy or from an internal "other," a vulnerable minority group, reactionary movements often turn their fury outward, threatening international stability. Although discredited for a time by the Holocaust and World War II, there are troubling signs of their revival.

As table I.1 shows, rightist movements have gained greater traction at ballot boxes and in achieving political goals than have leftist movements. [16] In the United States, the UK, and Russia these movements have either taken control of government, achieved significant influence over government, or achieved concrete political ends. In France and Italy, they have come close. One has to reach far back in the history of the countries they affect to find a precedent for them. Japan, France, Germany, Italy, and Australia have not seen such movements gain this level of success since World War II. While the United States has a rich populist tradition, Donald Trump is

**TABLE I.1:** Anti-establishment, illiberal, and populist movements in the ten largest economies in the world with above-average living standards, ordered in descending size, by 2016 International Monetary Fund nominal Gross Domestic Product

| Country | Leftist movement | Recent electoral standing | Rightist movement | Recent electoral standing | Historical precedents |
|---|---|---|---|---|---|
| United States | Bernie Sanders | Near-victory in Democratic primary | Donald Trump | Won Presidency | Unprecedented since at least Civil War |
| Japan | None | | Nationalism and militarism within ruling party | Prime Minister has close ties to far Right | Unprecedented since WWII |
| Germany | None | | Alternative for Germany (AfD) | Third largest party | Unprecedented since WWII |
| United Kingdom | Jeremy Corbyn's Labor Party | Near victory in 2017 general election, leads in polls | Brexit, UK Independence Party, Theresa May | Won national referendum, swayed Conservative party close to their views | Unprecedented since WWII |
| France | Unsubmissive France | Fourth place in first round of presidential election | National Front (FN) | Second place in presidential election | Unprecedented since WWII |
| Italy | Five Star Movement | Leading recent opinion polls | Five Star Movement, Northern League | Leading, third in recent opinion polls | Unprecedented since WWII |
| Canada | None | | None | | |
| South Korea | None | | None | | |
| Russia | None | | Vladimir Putin | Control of state since late 1990s | Leonid Brezhnev in early 1980s |
| Australia | None | | Pauline Hanson's One Nation | Fourth largest party | Unprecedented |

the first true populist president, a man with no experience in political or military office. Trump attacked fundamental political institutions with incendiary language on the campaign trail and in office, something no other president has done, with Andrew Jackson as the arguable exception.[17]

Right-wing populist movements appeal to historically dominant population groups that have been left behind economically relative to their expectations: the poorly educated, those who live in rural areas, and workers who have lost jobs because of international trade.[18] Arguments made by the leaders of right-wing populist movements for trade barriers and immigration restrictions fall on willing ears. But rather than explicitly appeal to class identity or distributive justice, the leaders of right-wing populist movements appeal to the ethno-nationalist creed of "blood and soil." These groups look nostalgically back to a past when people like them enjoyed greater economic security and higher status.

Right-wing populist movements bring out into the open the underlying problems with the systems they challenge. They simultaneously reflect and further heighten the high levels of political polarization, threatening the political stability of democratic countries.[19] The movements offer little in terms of realistic policy proposals that would benefit their members as well as the general public; they are protesting against the failures of existing political systems rather than acting as a positive force.[20] The rise of these movements, then, reflects a failure of democratic institutions to advance the public interest and resolve conflicts between different social groups.

Today's right-wing movements come into conflict with those who do not share their narrowly defined identity. White, male, working-class earnings are stagnating in wealthy countries, while women, ethnic and racial minorities, and people in developing nations are enjoying relative advances.[21] Rightist leaders blame the economic success of minorities for the problems that are oppressing working-class white men and promise that "taking back" the increased wealth of poor countries will solve them.

Within wealthy countries, movements assert rights for women and a variety of minorities. In developing countries, nationalistic movements of another sort have been gaining strength. Many rising powers (China, India, Turkey, Mexico) have seen an increase in authoritarian and nationalist sentiment, driven in many cases by leaders accusing Western-dominated international institutions of holding back their countries. A collision seems to be looming between the demands for economic progress in developing countries and the increasingly nationalistic politics of wealthy countries.

Many of these domestic and international political conflicts relate to the difficulty of democratically resolving issues that pit the fundamental concerns of minority groups against the less pressing interests of majority groups. These issues have important economic foundations but are often formulated in social and cultural language that clearly marks the right-wing leader as being on the side of a particular group.

In the United States, for example, gun rights, religious liberty, and the right of the wealthy to contribute to political campaigns animate the Right, while the identity politics of minority groups and civil liberties inspire the Left. Attempts to resolve these issues often end up in the hands of the judicial system. But judges are members of the elite and tend to be out of touch with what life is like for many ordinary citizens. Their decisions often inflame rather than settle cultural disputes.

On the international stage, institutions, such as the World Trade Organization and the European Union, which were designed to help resolve the tensions between national sovereignty and international order, are increasingly seen as illegitimate, unresponsive, and unable to balance the interests of richer and poorer countries. In short, governance institutions around the world face a crisis of legitimacy.

## The Markets and Their Discontents

The heroes of our story, the Philosophical Radicals, came to prominence in the face of a constellation of woes closely related to those we are seeing today. They saw aristocratic privilege restraining markets as the problem. Their goals were to free markets from the control of feudalistic monopolists whose hoarding of land impeded productivity and concentrated wealth; to create political systems responsive to popular sentiment and able to resolve internal conflict; and to establish an international system of cooperation that would benefit the general population of countries and undermine traditional elites. This is precisely the sort of movement that our present crisis calls for.

The spirit of the market form of organization appears most famously in the late-eighteenth-century writings of Adam Smith. Smith saw markets as settings where "It is not from the benevolence of the butcher, the brewer, or the baker, that we expect our dinner, but from their regard to their own interest."[22] While now a cliché, the notion that self-interested behavior led to the public good was shocking at the time because it contrasted so sharply with common experience.

In the past, most individuals lived their lives within small, tight-knit communities where moral impulses, social shame, gossip, and empathy provided the primary incentives for individuals to accommodate themselves to the common good. Economists and sociologists sometimes call these communities "moral economies."[23] Self-interested behavior was of course common and unavoidable but was regarded as an unfortunate consequence of the fallen nature of human beings rather than as a source of prosperity. Religion served to constrain such deviance at every turn. The virtuous were farmers, craftsmen, soldiers, and valiant aristocratic warriors, who followed an age-old way of life for its own sake or to please God. Merchants, financiers, and others who amassed wealth from "commerce" were regarded with suspicion well into the nineteenth century.

Even today, moral economies flourish in approximate form outside the cities and govern our relationships with close friends and family. An idealized portrait of such a society is Frank Capra's 1946 classic film *It's a Wonderful Life*. George Bailey (played by Jimmy Stewart) is a banker motivated less by profit than by the needs of his small community, which he is able to serve thanks to his intimate knowledge of his fellow townsfolk. When trouble comes with the onset of the Great Depression, the community reciprocates his altruism and saves him and his bank from ruin. Smithian capitalism—embodied by a greedy, amoral competitor, Mr. Potter, who finances slums and exploits his customers—is portrayed as a threat to the community. The sense of mutual support between Bailey's bank and the town attests both to the economic efficiency of the moral economy and its intrinsic value.

Smith's critics have emphasized the real advantages of moral economies over markets.[24] Market prices cannot detect, account for, reward, or punish the many ways in which individual actions affect others. In a market economy, if a homeowner beautifies her house, she raises the value of her neighbor's property, but the market rewards her only for the increase in her own home's value, not for the benefits to her neighbor. In a moral economy, the same homeowner would be rewarded by her greater standing in town and the appreciation of her neighbors, who will reciprocate in some way. In a market economy, a business that sells defective products may eventually suffer some reputational costs, but usually will profit for years. In a moral economy, the business owner would be run out of town. Governments try to step into the shoes of the village gossip, but the regulations and rulings their bureaucrats and judges hand down are never as responsive to local conditions as community members are.

Despite these advantages, moral economies break down as the scope and scale of trade expand. We benefit from mass production and global supply chains because fixed costs of production are spread over millions of people and we can draw on diverse skills and inputs from around the world, resulting in delightful products at very low prices. But if millions of people worldwide consume a product, it is impractical for them to coordinate a boycott—except in unusual cases—if the product is hazardous or of low quality. Moreover, mass production requires merchants to trade over long distances, with strangers, and this means that personal reputation cannot ensure that contracts are kept. A modern market economy—which combines government support for trade (contract and property law) along with government protection against abuses (tort law and regulation)—generates value far beyond the capabilities of a moral economy. Because of these limitations, moral economies can feel constraining and antiquated when confronted with large-scale market societies. Unable to account for the needs of those far away, they may become hostile to outsiders and intolerant of internal diversity, fearing it will erode group values.

From *The Scarlet Letter* to *Sister Carrie*, a dystopian vision of moral economies has been a fixture of American literature. The 2017 video adaptation of Margaret Atwood's novel *The*

*Handmaid's Tale* depicts the reestablishment of a strict moral economy in the United States, where fertility rates have drastically fallen. The small minority of women who remain fertile are held in reproductive slavery and ritualistically raped by ruling-class men who are perverted and degraded by this arrangement and the strictures intended to prevent them from abusing their power. Diversity of opinion and lifestyle is ruthlessly suppressed as the enslaved women and their male counterparts are forced to constantly monitor one another.

These cautionary tales have not quashed the ideal of moral economies for the far Right, and even for certain nostalgic leftists. But since the era of mass production started in the nineteenth century, only a handful of idiosyncratic and religiously based communities, such as the Amish, have managed to sustain moral economies, which operate mostly outside of the market.

The major alternative idea, and the force behind the politics of the far Left, is central planning, as we discuss in the next chapter. Marxists believed that state ownership of capital and control of industry were the only paths out of "wage slavery,"[25] but central planning ultimately proved a failure. The Soviet Union did manage to turn out weapons and build factories but produced drab apartments, dull cars, and shortages of even basic goods. Its central planners could not account for diversity and tastes of individual consumers. All told, the market faces no serious contender as an approach to organizing large-scale economies.

## The Rules of a True Market

If the market economy is left with no rivals, we still must ask how markets should be organized. The standard view on the Right is that the government needs only to "get out of the way." There is a kernel of truth in this argument. When communist countries fell in 1989 and the early 1990s, it initially seemed that the removal of the heavy boot of centralized planning was all that it took to yield a flourishing market. Yet any sophisticated, large-scale market depends on well-designed and well-enforced rules of the game without which rampant theft, constant breaking of contracts, and the rule of the physically strongest would prevail. These rules can be boiled down to three principles: freedom, competition, and openness.

In a *free* market, individuals may purchase any goods they want as long as they pay a price sufficient to compensate sellers for the loss of those goods. They also must receive from others for work they do or products they offer just the value that these services create for other citizens. Such a market gives every individual the maximum freedom consistent with not infringing on the freedom of others. As the prominent Philosophical Radical John Stuart Mill put it, "The only purpose for which power can be rightfully exercised over any member of a civilized community, against his will, is to prevent harm to others."[26] Unfree markets deprive individuals of opportunities for gain through trade. A vivid example of restrictions on the freedom of trade is the rationing system imposed in many countries during World War II. While arguably a necessary expedient and social glue in such times, rationing resulted in bland uniformity and gave rise to black and gray barter economies that allowed individuals to trade away, for example, cigarettes they did not smoke for baby food that their children needed. The celebrations in Trafalgar Square and burning of ration books that greeted the UK's final abandonment of rationing in the 1950s testify to how much people value the flexibility and diversity allowed by free market exchange.

In a *competitive* market, individuals must take as a given the prices they pay and get paid. They have no ability to manipulate prices by exercising what economists call "market power." *Uncompetitive markets* turn self-interest from a productive engine into a destructive scourge by allowing individuals or groups to obstruct trade and reduce production to shift prices in their favor. The struggle against monopolies has been with us at least since the American colonists' fight against the East India Company's monopoly on the tea trade. In the late nineteenth century, a popular antimonopolist movement fought against the great cartels of the era, roiling politics and spawning parties such as the Bull Moose party in the United States, the "new Liberal" party in the United Kingdom, the Radical Party in France, and the Radical Liberal party in Denmark. Monopolists deliver low-quality goods at high prices. For instance, in most places in the United States there is only one cable service available, but many types of electronic devices to connect to cable. We thus pay high prices for low-quality Internet service, while we can choose from a plethora of high-quality, reasonably priced devices, from computers to phones.

In an *open* market, all people, regardless of nationality, gender identity, color, or creed, are allowed to participate in the process of market exchange, maximizing the opportunity for mutual benefits. Markets that are closed reduce the opportunity for exchange and unfairly cut some people off from the benefits of these exchanges. Opening markets to trade across nations brought pasta to Italy. Opening labor markets to new participants brought the contributions of women into the boardroom. Opening markets for apps brought us the cornucopia of ways in which we now use our smartphones. Open markets embody the idea that by cooperating as broadly as possible, we can all benefit from each other.

Smith saw the markets blossoming around him as not only a productive force, but also a profoundly egalitarian one. He famously argued that in a well-functioning market, "The rich . . . are led by an invisible hand to make nearly the same distribution of the necessaries of life, which would have been made, *had the earth been divided into equal portions among all its inhabitants*; and thus, without intending it, without knowing it, advance the interest of the society."[27] The portion of this quotation we have italicized is usually neglected in discussions of Smith, perhaps because it originates from a book that preceded his most famous *Wealth of Nations*. Yet Smith passionately believed that inequality was mainly the result of legal and social restrictions that favored the aristocracy and were incompatible with a market economy.

Smith did not think that free, competitive, and open markets were automatic or inevitable. He observed that "people of the same trade seldom meet together, even for merriment and diversion, but the conversation ends in a conspiracy against the public, or in some contrivance to raise prices" and declared that "law . . . ought to do nothing to facilitate such assemblies, much less make them necessary."[28]

The central theme of the Philosophical Radicals was the struggle against a society dominated by the aristocracy. The Radicals complained that the aristocracy controlled the government, causing it to protect the aristocracy's monopolies by restricting markets and closing borders to trade. They understood that economic privilege and political privilege were two sides of the same coin and thus fought with equal vigor for competitive democratic elections through the expansion of the franchise and for open borders to international trade.

These pioneers won many victories, but they soon came to realize their initial proposals did not go far enough. At the same time as markets for land and labor advanced, industrial capitalism showed a tendency toward new forms of monopoly power over factories, railroads, and natural resources. Expanding the franchise weakened the landed aristocracy, but newly empowered majorities tyrannized minorities of all sorts and capitalists used their resources to corrupt politicians and control the press. The expansion of free trade across borders went hand in hand with international power politics. The leading free trader—Great Britain—exploited its colonies for slave labor and natural resources.

The next generation of liberal reformers in the late nineteenth and early twentieth centuries, individuals such as Henry George, Léon Walras, and Beatrice Webb, sought to address these problems. The effects of their handiwork, which built on the legacy of the Philosophical Radicals, remain with us today. Antitrust policies and legal support for labor unions restrained the power of monopolies. Social insurance, progressive taxation, and free compulsory education enhanced competition by expanding access to opportunity. Systems of checks and balances, protection of fundamental rights, and increasing judicial power to protect minority rights addressed the tyranny of the majority. International institutions, free trade, and human rights treaties were designed to pave the way to greater international cooperation in a liberal order.

Following World War II, these reforms helped usher in an unprecedented period of economic growth, declining inequality, and political consensus in wealthy countries. This great success for liberalism transformed practical politics and academic economics in similar ways. In both spheres, leaders decided that more or less perfect markets had been achieved. Ideas for further breakthroughs in expanding trade or eliminating monopoly power were largely abandoned. Economists came to believe that differences in individuals' natural talents are the main source of inequality. They agreed that progressive taxation and welfare systems are needed to ensure a fair distribution, but that they must be limited lest they come at a cost to the size of the total economic pie.

This tradeoff fragmented the liberal coalition. Those who had led the second generation of reforms coalesced into the modern political Left, known as liberals in the United States and social democrats in Europe. They prioritized equality within nations and opening of markets to domestic minorities and women, groups previously excluded from market exchange. During the 1960s and 1970s they won victories in the US Civil Rights movement and the feminist movement throughout the developed world.

Those liberals who prioritized free markets and efficiency over equality formed the modern political "Right" and came to be known as libertarians in the United States and neoliberals in Europe. Beyond fighting government intervention, the Right also played a crucial role in pushing for more open markets for goods and capital internationally. Their great victories came during the 1980s and 1990s, as countries sold off nationalized industries, deregulated the economy, and opened to foreign trade. Yet, while inequality across countries, and between dominant identity groups (white men) and other groups (women, African Americans), declined, inequality within wealthy countries expanded. Growth rates declined and never returned to their midcentury levels. With economic stagnation and rising inequality within countries—stagnequality—politics have become fractured and poisoned.

While some commentators believe that stagnequality is the result of broad economic and demographic forces that are beyond people's control, we believe that it is the result of a failure of ideas. The economic wisdom of left and right did not cut to the core of the tensions in the basic structure of capitalism and democracy. Private property inherently conferred market power, a problem that ballooned along with inequality and that constantly mutated in ways that frustrated efforts by governments to solve it. One-person-one-vote gave majorities the power to tyrannize minorities. Checks, balances, and judicial intervention limited such tyranny, but did so by handing power to elites and special interest groups. In international relations, efforts to enhance cooperation and cross-border economic activity empowered an international capitalist elite that disproportionately benefited from international cooperation and faced nationalist backlash from the working class.

The ideological and military victories of World War II and the Cold War, accompanied by economic and political achievements of the second half of the twentieth century, thus bred arrogance, which led to complacency and internal division. The radical reformers of the nineteenth and early twentieth centuries became the squabbling technocrats of today.

## Perfect Competition: Opium of the Elites

The intellectual basis of this bind was economists' increasing assumption that markets are "perfectly competitive,"[29] meaning that there are a small number of homogeneous commodities, and no individual holds or buys a large fraction of any of them. All are forced to vigorously compete to sell their products and to purchase the things they need from others. Grain is the classic example of a perfectly competitive market. No producer of grain owns a large share of the market and thus no one producer can affect the price much. In addition, because so many millers, ranchers, and bakers buy grain, no one buyer can hold down its price by withholding purchases. All must accept whatever price the market offers them.

Yet few markets in the real world work this way, as pioneering economic theorists like Joan Robinson realized.[30] Consider the process of buying a home. The housing markets that come closest to being perfectly competitive are those in large cities where houses frequently become available and many people are looking to buy. Yet as anyone who has bought or sold a house in such a place knows, the system is far from perfect. Houses differ in location, amenities, views, light, and so forth. They are far from homogenous, nothing like grain (whose homogeneity is itself the result of careful market design).[31] The failure to reach a deal can mean months of delay while buyers look for other houses that might meet their needs.

This means that buyers and sellers both have significant bargaining power. Each party works hard to ascertain what the other would be willing to pay or accept and jockeys for the best price possible. Such strategic behavior often causes trades to fail. Even when they succeed, huge amounts of time and effort have been wasted in the process. These problems are magnified in complex business transactions. For example, in land development schemes, where many contiguous pieces of land must be bought up to build a factory or a mall, the existing homeowners have the upper hand in bargaining because the stakes are so high for the developer. Many homeowners will hold out for a large payment, delaying or even stopping the project.

Most markets in which individuals and businesses participate are more like the housing market than the grain market. Factories, intellectual property, companies, paintings—all are highly idiosyncratic, one-of-a-kind assets. In these and many other cases, the assumption of perfect competition makes little sense. The same holds true for labor markets, since all workers have different talents and dispositions and live in different places. Even in many markets for relatively homogenous commodities, such as Internet services or airplane flights, a few dominant firms prevail. And even when there appear to be many such firms, they frequently share owners or they collude. From bottom to top, market power—the ability of companies and individuals to affect prices in their favor—permeates the economy. We claim that market power is omnipresent and intrinsic to the current institutional structure of capitalism and that it is one of the two dominant sources of stagnequality and political conflict.

The other primary problem, we believe, is that, at the same time that some markets are clogged with market power, many areas of human life are lacking in markets that could vastly improve people's well-being. This problem is most acute for goods and services usually provided by governments, like policing, public parks, roads, social insurance, and national defense: what is needed is a market for political influence.

A market for political influence? That sounds preposterous. If money were allowed to purchase political influence, wouldn't politics be controlled by a few plutocrats? The history of political corruption in the late nineteenth-century United States bears this out. Local politicians were commonly bought off by political machines, railroad men, and oil barons.

Yet the alternative model, that every citizen should have an equal voice and thus that every issue is determined by majority rule, has its own severe weaknesses. Once the majority rules, what happens to those in the minority? They may care deeply about an issue—say the right of transgender people to use a restroom, or preventing abortions—but there is no way for them to exert influence in proportion to the importance of that issue for them. One-person-one-vote stops compromise among groups of people and leads to wild swings of power between ideological blocs.

Politics is not the only realm of contemporary life in which markets are almost entirely absent. Severe restrictions on migration halt cross-border trade in labor, creating a hole in the labor market. Data, one of the most valuable commodities in the digital economy, are collected and monetized by companies such as Google and Facebook, but the users who create these data receive no direct compensation. A much-needed market in data simply does not exist. Our supposedly perfectly competitive market economy, so it would seem, is actually plagued by monopolized and missing markets.

These observations cast doubt on the rosy assumptions of standard economic rhetoric, yet they also reveal missed opportunities. If we face the fact that markets are hampered by market power and often are even absent, then perhaps we can escape polarization between left and right, and renew the Radicals' fight against prejudice and privilege.

## Imagining Radical Markets

Our solution to the present crisis is to radically expand markets. Chapters 1 and 2, which present the central ideas in this book, describe how this can be done in the economy and in politics. Chapter 1 shows how a simple tax can greatly reduce the incentive to abuse market power and limit competition by converting the market in private property into a kind of market in "uses." Chapter 2 describes an efficient market for "public goods" shared by many people and normally created by governments. The other chapters have narrower foci: chapter 3 advocates policies to create a more efficient and politically sustainable market in migrant labor; chapter 4 argues for a limit on financial holdings that would break the stranglehold of institutional investors on the corporate economy;

chapter 5 demonstrates how market forces can be extended to the digital economy. The ideas in these chapters have the power to solve the crisis of our time. They can advance equality and economic growth, while promoting public order and the spirit of compromise.

Any agenda that aspires to such sweeping changes faces enormous barriers to its adoption. Our proposals will require years of testing, improvement, and gradual scaling up before they are ready for full implementation.

To help readers grasp how radical these ideas are, we begin each chapter with a fictional vignette that illustrates how they might work in a future society. We then examine the history behind the institutions we propose to uproot, highlighting the accidents, paradoxes, and missteps that have led us to the present crisis. Next come our proposals, laid out in simple terms, followed by a defense of them in which we address common objections. Finally, we offer some ways that our ideas could be tested and refined.

Each chapter can stand on its own, but the conclusion ties the proposals together and discusses how much they would achieve if implemented together. An epilogue imagines what will take place when the gains from radical markets are exhausted.

Even if we don't sell you on all our ideas, we hope this book will open your mind to a new way of imagining the economy and politics. This challenging moment, when long-held assumptions are being overturned, is ripe for radical rethinking.

# 1

# Property Is Monopoly

## CREATING A COMPETITIVE MARKET IN USES THROUGH PARTIAL COMMON OWNERSHIP

As a child fascinated by Elon Musk's Hyperloop, Alejandro Espinosa often pictured himself in the cab of the first supersonic train, sitting side by side with the conductor. It never occurred to him that these trains would have no conductors. Yet the topographic and economic maps displayed in the holographs he was peering at clashed even more powerfully with his childish dreams.

Espinosa grew up to be the head of OpenTrac, a new venture that would fulfill his lifelong ambition. The company was making plans for its supersonic train to run between Los Angeles and San Francisco, but before tubes could be installed, magnets laid down, and vacuums prepared, a route through the Central Valley had to be selected. The other sections of the train's full route, those through the East Bay and the San Fernando Valley, offered very limited choices, but there was a wide range of potential ways through the Central Valley.

Espinosa wanted to move fast. If landholders in the Central Valley heard about the project, some of them might be tempted to raise the price of their property. Doing so, however, would be a risky gamble: a price increase would impose a higher tax burden on the owner, while the probability of being on the selected route would be low.

Narrowing down the large number of possible routes was a headache, even with the Cadappster app displaying the listed value of each plot—every plot's value is posted there for anyone to see. It made Espinosa's head spin to imagine what planning a project like his must have been like before the institution of the common ownership self-assessed tax. He would have had to choose a route before he had any idea what landowners along it would be willing to accept as payment, and then he probably would have had to endure years of negotiations and court fights to obtain all the property. He knew he was lucky that finally there was a transparent, liquid, and honestly priced market for property. He would not have to endure the guilt and the public relations disaster of having to force an elderly woman off land that had been in her family for generations. These days any such resident could post a high price and deter the purchase, or sell and be richly compensated.

To find feasible routes, OpenTrac's computer scientists used many approximations. They focused on the number of topographical obstacles that would confront the engineers, such as the rockiness of the area and the heights and depths of its hills, mountains, or gorges, and used simple rules of thumb to narrow the selection. Espinosa instructed them to generate the five most promising routes.

All five selections had roughly similar land prices and offered reasonable tradeoffs in engineering cost and speed. Back when trains ran at slower speeds, the views along each route might have influenced the decision, but nowadays, even if the tubes were transparent, passengers would see only a blur. After a meeting with several of his top engineers and one marketing expert, the group settled on the route with the cheapest land costs, and felt confident that they made the best choice.

Espinosa's treasurer immediately opened Cadappster and confirmed OpenTrac's willingness to purchase each property along the route at its posted price. This automatically secured OpenTrac's ownership: having just raised a new venture round, OpenTrac was flush with cash and made all payments on the spot. With residents scheduled to move out within three months, ground-breaking could begin by the end of the year. As the new holder of the land, Espinosa merged the whole route into one plot and posted a value several times the sum of the purchase prices to ensure the security of the route.

Developers today face great challenges. When asked what the largest barrier is to implementing Hyperloop One, co-founder Josh Giegel replied, "We really need a right of way." The interviewer responded, "Some constituencies, such as private landowners ... could see holding this up for quite some time."[1] There is an obvious incentive for a landowner to hold out for a high price when such a valuable project is coming through.

Suppose that each of 2,000 landowners along the route would normally be willing to accept $100,000 ($200 million in total) to cede right of way. Giegel believes that, net of other costs, Hyperloop can yield $500 million of operating profit. Now suppose that after the developer has bought the right of way on 1,999 pieces of land, the two-thousandth landowner learns of his plan. Rather than sell for $100,000, that home-owner might insist on a much higher price. Giegel would have no choice but to pay up: if he does not buy, he has lost his $199.9 million investment in the first 1,999 pieces of land. In principle, the landowner could hold out for nearly the entire $500 million. Even if she set the price at $400 million, the de-veloper would do better by accepting the offer than by turning it down since $100 million is better than nothing. But if the developer anticipates holdout, he would not embark on the development in the first place. And remember that the devel-oper has to contend with all 2,000 individual landowners, any of whom might decide to hold out for a high price. Several holdouts would quickly squash the project.

At present, developers minimize the holdout risk by taking costly precautions when they buy up land—for example, by acting secretly through shell corporations. But they still must engage in lengthy and expensive negotiations with individual sellers, which can cause delays and increase risk to intolerable levels. That is why governments often take the lead, using the power of eminent domain to create new commercial or resi-dential districts. But eminent domain is often unfair and al-ways politically controversial.

Large-scale land development controversies receive public attention, but bargaining problems like those faced by developers affect ordinary people and small businesses every day and cause trillions of dollars per year of losses that are hidden from public view. This challenge—which we dub the "monopoly problem"—turns out to be inherent in private property. It has preoccupied economists and philosophers since the birth of the modern economy.

## Capitalism and Freedom, or Capitalism and Monopoly?

Modern capitalism evolved out of a system of feudal land ownership, which put significant restrictions on people's freedom to sell land and labor. As Adam Smith explained, a defining feature of capitalism is the right to trade. Capitalism advanced in tandem with the scientific and technological innovations that made trade a valuable and significant part of the economy. A fiefdom in a valley in, say, thirteenth-century Europe, might have occasionally traded with itinerant merchants. But most goods—including foodstuffs and textiles—were produced in the community for community members. When improvements in navigation made long-distance trade cheaper, it became more efficient for the community to specialize in one commodity (say, wheat or textiles) while buying the goods it needed from other communities. It was the harnessing of steam and electric power in the late eighteenth and nineteenth centuries that allowed for a massive expansion in trade.[2]

Making the system more efficient also required adapting communities to serve the broader market by allowing extensive trade within communities and local areas as well. For example, a lord could sell his game park to an entrepreneur, who might use it for more modern intensive farming or for the premises of a factory. A lone craftsman makes far fewer pins per person than a factory where workers are assigned to specialized tasks. To set up a factory, however, an entrepreneur might have to acquire land from several feudal estates and hire a large number of workers who were bound as serfs to different feudal lords. Industry thus depended on ending the system of entailments, which kept land in the hands of a single family, and on peasants freeing themselves from bonds of fealty. At the same time, a great deal of property was held communally, such as common pastures where peasants grazed their flocks. Peasants could not buy or sell rights to graze and could not acquire plots of this shared land.

Smith and other Radical reformers in Britain (such as Jeremy Bentham and James Mill) saw these privileges and traditions as barriers to achieving the most efficient use of property, or what came to be known as *allocative efficiency*. To support such allocative efficiency, Radicals promoted clearer and freer property rights and the enclosure of common areas (including pastures and forests), which turned them into private property. These changes are closely associated with the rise of capitalism. In the American West, the conversion of open pastureland into family farms was a first step to industrialization.

Yet the justification for private property goes back well before capitalism, at least to Aristotle, who realized that people care best for things they own. If you own a plot of land, which no one can take from you without your permission, you will be compensated for any investment you make by either your enjoyment of that land or the high price that you can charge a future buyer. In contrast, a common pasture will be overgrazed, a shared kitchen neglected, and a group project usually put on the back burner. We will refer to this beneficial feature of private property as *investment efficiency*.

When put into practice, however, the Radicals' vision of capitalism did not run as smoothly as they had hoped. At first, events seemed to bear out their optimism. The nineteenth century saw an unprecedented period of economic development. Previously, economic growth was largely in line with population growth, which in turn proceeded slowly. Income per person, an important measure of social progress, had been stagnant for nearly all of human history. The nineteenth century was the first time that national productive capacity steadily grew. The fruits of invention and development abounded. Factories opened in enormous numbers. Steam carried passengers across continents. Goods from around the world became available in many countries.

However, these gains were concentrated among the *bourgeoisie*, a small class of rich city-dwellers. The former peasants who became the working class lived under miserable conditions like those depicted by Charles Dickens. Despite the early industrial revolution, workers' wages in Britain remained flat from 1750 to 1850.[3]

Nor did the new capitalist order even seem to be as productive as hoped. Some aristocrats allowed large swaths of their lands to lie idle or be used unproductively. The "Long Depression" of the 1870s in the United States inspired self-trained political economist Henry George to write his 1879 masterpiece *Progress and Poverty*. In that book, George summed up the paradoxes of nineteenth-century capitalism:

> The nineteenth century saw an enormous increase in the ability to produce wealth. Steam and electricity, mechanization, specialization, and new business methods greatly increased the power of labor ... Surely, these new powers would elevate society from its foundations, lifting the poor-

est above worry for the material needs of life . . . Yet we
must now face facts we cannot mistake. All over the world
we hear complaints of . . . labor condemned to involuntary
idleness; capital going to waste . . . Where do we find the
deepest poverty, the hardest struggle for existence, the greatest enforced idleness? Why, wherever material progress
is most advanced . . . This relation of poverty to progress is
the great question of our time.[4]

George's concerns echoed a growing chorus of socialist critics.
They shared Smith's aims of efficiency but doubted that private
property would achieve it.[5]

It is useful to remember that many people in nineteenth-
century Britain inherited their land. Rather than investing in it
or selling it, they would lazily collect rental payments from
tenant farmers. Even after early reformers succeeded in eliminating many feudal restrictions on property, owners often refused to sell their land to people who wanted to put it to more
productive use except at absurd prices, thus impeding industrialization.[6] Aristocrats gave scant attention to their properties, preferring to spend their time in high society or in politics.
Many depictions of this period focus on the social lives of the
aristocracy; little attention is given, or was given by the aristocrats, to the hard work of managing their properties. Even
those who did sell them would waste the money they raised on
the indulgent entertainments depicted in Jane Austen's novels
rather than investing the money in new ventures.

Caring for the land was left to the peasants, slaves, and tenant farmers. Yet even the most fortunate of these, the tenants,
had little reason to invest in land because it could be expropriated by their shiftless landlords. So farmers allowed it to
decay, with poor results for output. As the population grew

and productivity increased, aristocrats charged ever more for their land, inhibiting further progress and leaving even less to tenant farmers. Land lay idle and neglected, and the growth of cities was stunted.

The wealthy were rewarded for doing nothing. Poor people who needed land had to pay vast prices to obtain it or else starve. Critics attacked these circumstances as perverse, and portrayed the rich, in fiction and nonfiction alike, as parasites (sometimes literally, as in Bram Stoker's *Dracula*).

The problem critics identified we label the monopoly problem (as did many of them), though our use is somewhat broader than is common these days for reasons we discuss later. We normally think of a monopolist as a person or company that owns all of a good and can charge a price higher than the normal market price by withholding some of the supply. However, a landowner can also be regarded as a monopolist because land is so often unique in its character and location.

Like a monopolist, the landowner can earn higher returns on the sale of her land by holding out for a generous offer (effectively withholding supply from the market) rather than selling to the first person who offers a fair price. In the meantime, the land is unused or underused. Thus, private ownership may actually hamper allocative efficiency. And this is the case not just for private ownership of land: private ownership of any asset, except homogenous commodities, may hamper allocative efficiency. Think of business equipment, automobiles, art, furniture, airplanes, intellectual property. The amount of money we are talking about is not small. Because of the ubiquity of private property in our economy, empirical research suggests that the misallocation of resources due to monopoly and related problems we discuss below may be reducing output by 25% or more annually—trillions of dollars per year in the United States alone.[7]

The capitalist system created by Radical reforms, it thus seemed, had loosened the restrictions inhibiting the free flow of land and labor in order for them to be put to their best uses, but had not eliminated them. Monopoly power blocked the path of progress.

## Central Planning, Corporate Planning

Some socialist critics imagined that this "irrationality" of capitalism could be solved through state ownership and central planning. After all, they reasoned, if the government owns all the land and employs all citizens, it can simply order the land to be improved and used in the best way. So long as the government is benevolent and operated by well-informed experts, there can be no monopoly problem because no private person enjoys the right to exclude others from the land. This central planning approach is closely identified with the ideas of Karl Marx, though Marx ultimately soured on centralized planning, seeing it as too open to abuse.[8]

Yet planning wound up being as important to capitalism as it was to any dream of a socialist utopia. Social critics were not the only ones increasingly frustrated with the way landowners, small-business people, and other property owners stood in the way of economically valuable projects. As many economists have pointed out, creating large-scale enterprises consistently requires putting together a variety of moving parts, each controlled by a local monopolist.[9] Entrepreneurs were frustrated by monopoly problems at every turn. If they tried to expand their factories, a landowner would hold out. If they tried to build a railroad, thousands of local politicians tried to extract a pound of flesh. Every small supplier of oil, coal, or parts would waste endless hours bargaining with them or trying to take advantage of them.

Nobel Laureate Ronald Coase called these frustrations the "transaction costs of the market."[10] He explained that to avoid this chaos, business people formed large corporations that would own many assets, such as factories and parcels of land, and employed many workers whom the head of the corporation could centrally direct to accomplish its goals without constant negotiation. Corporations rapidly took over the business landscape during the nineteenth and early twentieth century. Standard Oil, for example, came to dominate oil production and the railroads were managed by similarly large corporations.

Yet corporations eventually reached their limits, becoming unwieldy and decaying as they overextended themselves, like a restaurant chain whose quality peters out as it builds more and more outlets. Corporate managers were often insensitive to local conditions and new opportunities, and were constantly threatened by new entrants to the market. As we will discuss in chapter 4, corporations did overcome some monopoly problems, but their large accumulations of wealth and power also allowed them to hold down wages, raise prices, and retard economic development, causing political and social backlash. So, while corporate planning played an important role in the economy, and helped overcome many local monopoly problems, it never supplanted markets as the primary means of organization.

## Markets without Property

Political economists concerned about the monopoly power created by private property therefore continued to search for alternatives to central planning. One formulation was for the government to own land and other "gifts of nature," but to allow them to be competitively managed. "Artificial capital"— useful things produced by humans—would remain privately owned to reward those who create it.

The government would rent out the land to those it deems most likely to use it productively and could terminate the lease when it finds someone who is willing to pay more to use the land than the current tenant. In these schemes, people rent land but do not own it; private property in land is abolished.

This idea came to be called competitive common ownership and was a core dogma for many of the figures who shaped twentieth-century economic thought. Two of the three fathers of the great advance in economic thought known as the "marginal revolution" (William Stanley Jevons, Léon Walras, and Karl Menger) were deeply skeptical of private property. Jevons wrote, "Property is only another name for monopoly."[11] In his treatise on the social economy, Walras stated, "Declaring individual land ownership . . . means . . . thwarting the beneficial effects of free competition by preventing the land from being used as is most advantageous for society."[12] Walras believed that land should be owned by the state and the rents it generated should be returned to the public as a "social dividend," either directly or through the provision of public goods.[13] By ending "individual landownership and monopolies" he aimed to "suppress" the "true causes . . . of . . . feudality."[14]

Walras described his approach as a form of socialism, what he called "synthetic socialism." However, Walras was hostile to central planning, fearing that planners would themselves become monopolistic feudal lords. He wanted landed property to be controlled by society through a process of competition and wanted returns on that property to be enjoyed by society. As these widely divergent ideas of socialism indicate, "society" can manage resources it controls in many ways. In the late nineteenth century, socialism was a rather amorphous term and was not always associated with central planning. Socialists agreed on only one point: that traditional private property and the inequality of its ownership posed significant challenges to prosperity, well-being, and political order.

Henry George, whom we met earlier, proposed what was perhaps the most prominent idea among economists for solving the monopoly problem. He argued that the "simpler, easier and quieter way" to achieve common ownership than state ownership would be to "appropriate land rent for public use, by taxation."[15]

George's land tax differed from today's property taxes, which are charged at a low rate, usually 1–2%, but take as a base the full value of a home, which is usually determined by a government appraiser. On the one hand, George's land tax would have been much higher: the full value of the rent one would have to pay to occupy the land. On the other hand, it would have completely exempted the value of structures built on the land. Assessors would have to determine how much of the house's value arose from the unimproved land lying beneath the house (that is, how much the property would be worth if the house were knocked down) based on recent sales of nearby vacant lots. This full land value would be taxed away, but the homeowners would keep any extra value created by the structures on the land.

Taxing away all such "land rent" would mean that while owners could enjoy the full value of anything they built on the land, they would have to pay to the government any value of the land itself, just as someone who leased the land would. "Land monopolization would no longer pay. Millions of acres, where others are now shut out by high prices, would be abandoned or sold at trivial prices."[16] If the government imposes a tax on ownership of land, then people who can use their land productively will do so and be able to pay the tax, while those who would otherwise be happy to let it sit vacant will sell the land in order to avoid the tax.

George's proposals quickly captured the public imagination (see figure 1.1). Monopoly, perhaps the most popular board game ever, was originally titled The Landlord's Game. Elizabeth Magie designed it in 1904 as a way to educate the public about George's ideas. According to the rules we are now familiar with, each player tries to monopolize properties in order to bankrupt the other players and drive them out of the game. However, the original game (which one can purchase from Folkopoly Press on eBay) had different rules under which a tax on land rents (though not on the houses built upon them) funds public works, giving players free access to the utilities and railroads, and paying out a social dividend that augments the wages earned when passing what is now called "Go."[17] These rules make domination by one player impossible and ensure that as every player develops her properties, all players benefit.

By 1933, American philosopher John Dewey estimated that George's *Progress and Poverty* "had a wider distribution than almost all other books on political economy put together."[18] Many eminent politicians and thinkers were Georgists, including the aristocratic Winston Churchill, the radical progressive Dewey, and the Zionist visionary Theodore Herzl.

Yet Georgism had some serious defects. Because the tax would expropriate all the value of land lying beneath any structure, it provided no incentive for possessors to invest in, or even care for, the land. This is the problem of investment inefficiency. At the time, investment inefficiency for land was not considered a problem, because people thought that land did

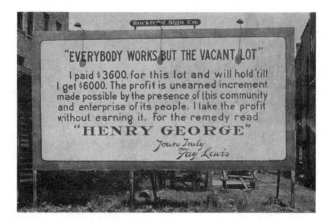

FIGURE 1.1: Billboard promoting Henry George's ideas. The New York Public Library, https://digitalcollections.nypl.org/items/510d47de -036a-a3d9-e040-e00a18064a99.

not need maintenance and the only value that could be added to land was through above-ground structures like houses. But these assumptions ignored environmental damage. As ecologist Garrett Hardin observed many years later, land without a single owner often becomes overgrazed, eroded, and polluted in what he labeled the "tragedy of the commons."[19] George's scheme ran into even greater problems with natural resources that can be depleted, like metal from mines or oil from wells. If all the value of land is taxed away, the possessor of such a resource will remove the oil or ore as quickly as possible, leading to waste.

In addition, George's scheme would have been an administrative nightmare. George distinguished between naturally occurring land, which should be taxed, and everything built on top of it or using it—what he called artificial capital—which should not be taxed. This distinction was, well, artificial. Factories are built from metal drawn from mines and, once built, may be monopolized just as much as land may be. Also, a factory cannot be easily moved about, and it may help develop a neighborhood, which increases the value of the land. This would have made it fiendishly difficult to distinguish between the value arising from the land and the value of the structures built on top of it.

Consider, for example, the Empire State Building. What is the pure value of the land beneath it? One could try to infer its value by comparing it to the value of adjoining land. But the building itself defines the neighborhood around it; removing the building would almost certainly change the value of the surrounding land. The land and the building, even the neighborhood, are so tied together, it would be hard to figure out a separate value for each of them. The same would hold true for many neighborhoods, defined less by their purely physical location than by many other factors, such as the look and feel of their architecture and the relationship among buildings, streets, parks, and paths.

### The Battle for the Soul of "Socialism"

George's ideas gained popularity in the early twentieth century, a period of social upheaval and intellectual ferment. Growing inequality and industrial tensions strained the social fabric of wealthy countries. The Social Democratic party in Germany, the Labor Party in England, the Progressive movement in the United States, and the French Section of the Workers International rose to prominence. Colonies increasingly chafed under the domination of the empires. Two world wars threw the established social order into question and destabilized many governments. In the 1930s, the first truly global depression undermined confidence in traditional laissez-faire capitalism.

Revolutions erupted. In 1911, Chinese Nationalist forces led by Sun Yat-sen overthrew the Qin Dynasty and worked to establish a new republican government free from foreign control. While Sun's ideas drew on many sources, George's philosophy was the economic pillar of his *Three Principles of the People*. Sun wrote, "The teachings of . . . Henry George . . . will be the basis of our program of reform."[20] Yet Sun failed to form a coherent government as China disintegrated into warring fiefdoms.

In Russia, Vladimir Lenin learned from Sun's mistakes and ruthlessly suppressed dissent. He was inspired by early Marxist dreams of central planning, the zeal of the French Revolution, and the rising power of bureaucratic corporations. Wielding an iron fist, Lenin formed a powerful government, which not only controlled Russian territory, but also exported revolution to other countries, including to China. There, with Russian assistance, Mao Tse-tung's Chinese Communist Party eventually defeated Chiang Kai-shek, who had taken over the anti-Communist branch of Sun's Nationalist organization. Chiang fled to Taiwan. However, by this time the world was largely divided into capitalist and communist camps. The Georgist ideas of the Nationalist revolution withered under anti-communist dictatorship. Soon, two major economic systems subsequently vied for dominance—capitalism in the West, now moderated by regulation, redistribution, and anti-monopoly laws, and Communist state planning in the Soviet Union and its allies.

Although the eventual victory of capitalism makes it hard for us to imagine the allure of central planning, during the Great Depression and even well after World War II, capitalism was on the defensive. In 1942, the prominent conservative economist Joseph Schumpeter predicted that socialism would ultimately replace capitalism.[21] His view was that most economic activity in capitalist economies took place in corporations and that a corporation is just a bureaucracy in which "management" at the center issues orders to various workers. From this vantage point, it was a small step to an economy in which each industry was dominated by one or two gigantic corporations, with government regulation to ensure that they do not abuse their monopoly power, an outcome not much different from the central planning of socialism.

Many economists, inspired by the success of large corporations and of wartime planning, went further and embraced the Soviet system. One of the most extreme cases was Oskar Lange, a Polish economist who taught at the University of Chicago in the 1930s and '40s. After a trip to Soviet-occupied Poland, he renounced his US citizenship, and became the ambassador to the United States of the Soviet-aligned Polish communist government. For the next two decades he served in leading roles in Polish government. Our epilogue describes his case for central planning in greater detail.[22]

Ludwig von Mises and Friedrich Hayek, who were students of the third marginal revolutionary, Carl Menger, pointed out the flaw in central planning: those who undertake it lack the information and analytical capacity to make the best allocative decisions.[23] People's valuations are private information; the genius of the market is its capacity for disseminating this information from consumers to producers through the price system. Central planning, in contrast, results in massive misallocation of resources—the production of goods no one wanted—that was characteristic of real-world socialist economies like that of the Soviet Union.[24] Moreover, centralization of the economy opened the way to political abuse, which Hayek memorably called the "road to serfdom."[25]

Reacting to these horrors of central planning, Western liberals concluded that capitalism, whatever its limitations, was the superior method of economic organization. The best approach to monopoly was antitrust law (see chapter 4), regulation, and limited state ownership in the most important industries. In the United States, the government subjected "natural monopolies" like electricity to price regulation, and in Europe, major utilities and other large companies were often owned by the government. Amid the postwar economic boom, the fundamental problems with private property faded from view.

The intellectual deep freeze into which the monopoly problem had been placed was sealed by the misinterpretation of Coase's classic 1960 article, "The Problem of Social Cost." Coase argued that if transaction (that is, bargaining) costs are low, the allocation of property rights is irrelevant from the standpoint of efficiency, because property will be transferred from lower-valued to higher-valued uses through bargaining.[26] Imagine that a quiet doctor's office and a noisy music teacher's office are separated by a thin wall in an office building. The doctor is disturbed by the noise and wants the teacher to leave or install soundproofing. One legal rule would give the music teacher the right to make as much noise as he wants. Another would give the doctor the right to be free of noise.

Coase argued that under ideal conditions, the bargain the two sides would reach would be the same: in one scenario the doctor would pay the music teacher to be a bit quieter, and in the other the music teacher would pay the doctor to accept some noise. If bargaining is perfect, the law does not determine the level of noise; it affects only who pays whom.

Coase's point was more complex than is often understood, but the subtlety was lost in the hands of zealous defenders of capitalism, such as the University of Chicago Nobel Laureate George Stigler.[27] In his 1966 edition of *The Theory of Price*, he promoted the "Coase Theorem" as a justification for the simplistic idea that private bargaining that takes place under any set of strong and clearly defined property rights will usually lead to efficient outcomes. This misinterpretation assumes away the monopoly problem, implying the superiority of private property because it enhances investment efficiency.[28] Most mainstream economists even today continue to assume that bargaining eliminates the monopoly problem.

## Competitive by Design

Not all thinkers followed Stigler's lead, however. Vickrey recognized the monopoly problem, admired George's vision of common ownership, and offered as his own solution the ideal of the auction. We laid out a fanciful version of this approach in our preface: an auction where all property—every factory, house, and car—is held in common and the right to rent and use it is constantly auctioned. The citizen who offers the highest bid (in the form of a rental payment) possesses the object until outbid by another citizen. Each factory, house, or car would have a standing highest bid placed on it, representing the rent that the current possessor agreed to pay to the government for using the asset. Anyone could beat this bid and claim the object. The money collected from rents is used to finance public goods (see chapter 2) and fund a social dividend. While Vickrey never directly spelled out this utopian vision, it connects so many of his ideas that we imagine it was part of the sweeping vision he hoped to bring to the world just prior to his death. We thus label it the *Vickrey Commons*.

Most novel concepts initially seem farfetched. A decade ago, renting out an apartment online to strangers seemed a very odd idea. Later in this chapter, we will address an objection that surely has already occurred to you—that the stability of everyday life would be upended by the Vickrey Commons. Yet bear in mind that his idea is already used to assign the advertising slots of Web and Facebook pages all of us visit every day. Every few seconds, these slots are reallocated to the highest current bidder via an auction design proposed by Vickrey.[29]

Governments also use auctions. Coase persuaded the Federal Communications Commission (FCC) to auction off the rights to use the broadcast spectrum instead of giving it away or selling it at a price determined by the government.[30] In response, economists Robert Wilson, Paul Milgrom, and Preston McAfee developed Vickrey's work into an auction design to sell off the spectrum.[31] But this design only temporarily solved the monopoly problem. Spectrum auctions occurred infrequently and gave winners the chance to hold onto the spectrum for years or even decades at a time. A company that won an auction for a portion of the spectrum years ago might no longer be its highest-valued owner. If a new company would like to buy that portion, its owner may decide to hold out for an excessively high price, which is precisely what has happened, as we discuss below.

Vickrey's most prominent followers, Roger Myerson (who also won the Nobel Prize for his work on the topic) and Mark Satterthwaite, used his ideas to deepen Jevons and Walras's insight about the monopolistic nature of property.[32] They showed mathematically that the simplistic interpretation of

Coase's results will never hold except in the unusual case that the buyer and seller are both absolutely certain that the buyer values the asset more than the seller does. Otherwise there is no way for bargaining to overcome the monopoly problem and ensure that assets consistently flow to their best (highest-value) users. This work helped explain why spectrum markets had so stubbornly failed to reallocate spectrum to new uses and why auctions for Internet advertising slots worked so much better. Only a true, continuous auction in uses can solve the monopoly problem and hence produce allocative efficiency.

But continual auctions also may create a problem—for investment efficiency. If possessors know that their possessions can be taken by others at any time and that they will not receive the proceeds of any bid, they will be discouraged from taking care of and improving their property. In this situation, you might well let your house fall into disrepair. Like George's tax proposal, the Vickrey Commons does not give people good investment incentives.

A response could be to use private property rights where investment incentives are more important than allocative efficiency (George's "artificial capital"), and common property (with uses distributed through auctions) where allocative efficiency is more important than investment efficiency (George's "land"). Indeed, the current system of ownership in the United States vaguely echoes this formulation. The private property system prevails in most cases, but the government owns vast resources—including a huge fraction of the nation's land—which it rents out, allows people to use for free, or occasionally auctions, as in the case of spectrum. But forcing every form of property into one of these extreme molds is wasteful, as it always leads to extreme inefficiency along either the investment or allocative dimension. Most types of property benefit from investment, and most types of property will, and should, move from one person to another over the course of their useful life.

A better approach is to find a way to balance the demands of investment efficiency and allocative efficiency. We will call this approach "partial common ownership"—a halfway house between common ownership and traditional private property. Partial common ownership optimizes allocative efficiency and investment efficiency within a single property regime, as the common ownership can deter monopoly power while the private ownership encourages investment. In the late 1980s, economists Peter Cramton, Robert Gibbons, and Paul Klemperer presented a way to share property rights, which was refined by Ilya Segal and Michael Whinston, among others.[33]

Consider a start-up company whose two founders got into an argument and now want to go their separate ways. Dissolution of a partnership is normally a messy business. Each partner must give her consent to break up, but they inevitably disagree about who should get the larger share, or how valuable the partnership is, leading to impasse—just another version of the monopoly problem. Under the Cramton et al. proposal, also known in legal circles as a Texas shootout, each person submits a bid for the value of the company and the higher bid wins. The winner must buy out the share of the other partner at the average of the two prices.

This scheme works best when the shares owned by each partner exactly equal the chance that she is the best eventual owner for the company.[34] Let's consider why, in this case, both partners will find it in their interest to bid their true value for keeping the company.

Let's say partner A owns 60% of the partnership and B owns 40% of it. They agree to use a Texas shootout to determine which partner will become sole owner. Each partner makes a bid; the partner who makes the higher bid wins the partnership; and the value of the partnership is set by the average of the two bids. The winner must then buy the loser's share based on that value. So, if A wins, A gains B's 40% share but must pay B 40% of the average of the two bids. Because of our assumption that shares are proportioned to the chance of each partner being the best owner of the company, if each bidder is truthful about her bid, A will win 60% of the time and B 40%.

Now suppose that A considers raising her bid above her true value. If she wins, which happens roughly 60% of the time, she will now have to pay more for the 40% share of the company she is forced to buy from B. Thus, whatever amount she increases the price by, she will have to pay on average 60% times 40% equals 24% of that amount on average. On the other hand, in the roughly 40% chance she loses, B will have to pay more to her for her 60% stake, so she will gain 24% of this amount on average. It is no coincidence that these two numbers cancel out: this says, precisely, that A has no incentive at all to raise her bid. The same goes for lowering her bid.

However, A does have an incentive to keep her bid honest for two reasons. First, if she raises her bid above her true value, there is a chance B will have bid above her true value, but below her new bid, and thus that she will end up having to buy the company while paying above her true value. This is bad news for A. On the other hand, if she lowers her bid below its true level, there is a chance that B has bid below A's true value but above A's bid. This would lead to B winning but paying A less than the company is worth to A. Again, this is bad news for A! To reinforce this point, when A raises her bid, this increases the chances of her winning and paying the new higher price she has created, while if she lowers it she increases the chance she will lose and be paid less. All these forces mean that A has a very strong incentive to honestly bid her value and an analogous logic applies to B.

Even if the shares do not perfectly line up with the chances of each party winning, any degree of shared ownership will dampen each partner's incentive to either exaggerate or understate her value. Each partner knows that either overbidding or underbidding runs the risk of putting her on the wrong side of the deal. If she overbids in the hope of being paid more, she will risk winning and overpaying, but if she underbids to pay less, she risks being bought out below her value.

An important advantage of this system over the Vickrey Commons was suggested by one of us in research with Anthony Lee Zhang: it largely preserves investment incentives.[35] An individual with a 90% ownership stake in a partnership still has 90% of the incentive to invest that an individual with a 100% stake does. If she ends up winning the bidding process, she retains the good (and thus the return on the investment) and must pay only 10% of it to her partner for the right to enjoy this value. If she loses the process, her partner pays her 90% of the value of the investment as a settlement. Thus, while the Vickrey Commons gives no one any incentive to invest in the asset, the Cramton et al. procedure gives all individuals an incentive to invest in proportion to their ownership shares.

Partnerships are a form of common ownership that people undertake voluntarily. This means that they can arrange by contract the most efficient method for dissolving them. For that reason, the Cramton et al. scheme cannot be applied to land and other everyday assets that are held privately. However, a simple idea with ancient roots makes it possible to extend this logic to a wide range of settings.

## Name Your Price—and Your Tax

Most of us think of the *liturgy* as the words chanted by members of a religious community. But the term originated in ancient Athens where it meant roughly "public works" and referred to the responsibility of the roughly 1,000 wealthiest citizens to fund the operations of the state, particularly the army and navy. How did the Athenians determine which citizens were the wealthiest? According to Demosthenes, any member of the liturgical class could challenge any other citizen he believed was wealthier to *antidosis* or "exchange."[36] The person being challenged would have to either assume the liturgical responsibility or exchange all possessions with the challenger. The system gives everyone an incentive to be honest despite the burdens of the liturgy. If you falsely claimed to be poorer than the top 1,000 so as to avoid the liturgical burdens, then you could end up being forced to exchange your possessions with someone who is poorer than you are.

This is the first historical example we know of a "self-assessment" system. In such a system, individuals (rather than a bureaucratic authority) are required to declare the value of their possessions for the purpose of a transaction or public project, but also must stand ready to "prove" that the declared value is correct. Self-assessment systems are still in use. In the type of horse race called "claiming stakes," you can put forward a horse for any race, even one for which the horse might be overqualified, but you must stand ready to sell the horse for the cost of the prize (the "stakes") for winning the race to anyone willing to buy (or "claim") it at that price.[37] This deters owners of extremely fast horses from putting them up for races against much slower horses, where the stakes are usually low. Instead, an owner would put up a fast horse only for a race valuable enough for him to be willing to lose his horse for the prize.

In an Andorran mutual fire insurance arrangement, *la crema*, individuals declare how valuable their property is. If a house burns down, this is the amount the owner will be paid by the other members of the group, who are charged according to their own self-assessments. Owners of very valuable houses pay a correspondingly large share of the compensation if someone else in the community is affected by a fire.[38] This burden deters people from declaring a value for their house that is higher than it is actually worth.

To enforce Georgist land taxation, China's Sun proposed self-assessment.[39] Normally, a homeowner pays a property tax equal to a percentage of the assessed value of his home, which is determined by officials known as appraisers. Under Sun's system, individuals self-declare the value of their land and pay a tax equal to a percentage of that self-declared valuation, but the state could at any time take the land at the self-assessed price. When Chiang's government, which saw Sun as the "Father of the Nation," retreated to Taiwan, it implemented Sun's scheme. Unfortunately, the government was rarely willing or able to take possession of undervalued land and the scheme largely failed.[40]

In a 1962 speech in Santiago, Chile, University of Chicago economist Arnold Harberger proposed an ingenious variant of Sun's scheme as a solution to the problem of enforcing property taxes in corruption-ridden Latin America. Following up on Vickrey's concerns about the Venezuelan fiscal system, Harberger worried that appraisers were frequently bribed by homeowners to understate the value of property so as to minimize the tax burden. While he was apparently unaware of the historical precedents, his solution has a timeless elegance:

> If taxes are to be levied ... on ... the value of ... properties ... it is important that assessment procedures be adopted which estimate the true economic value ... The economist's answer ... is simple and essentially fool-proof: allow each ... owner ... to declare the value of his own property, make the declared values ... public, and require that an owner sell his property to any bidder ... willing to pay ... the declared value. This system is simple, self-enforcing, allows no scope for corruption, has negligible cost of administration, and creates incentives, in addition to those already present in the market, for each property to be put to that use in which it has the highest economic productivity.[41]

While Harberger designed his scheme as a way to raise government revenue, it offers an inspired solution to the monopoly problem we highlighted above. Harberger's tax, later also proposed by the Nobel Prize–winning economist Maurice Allais, makes it costly to declare a high valuation and thus deter the purchase of assets. Therefore, it penalizes any attempt to exercise monopoly power over an asset.[42] The higher the price the possessor demands, the more tax she must pay.

Harberger's tax closely resembles the partnership scheme of Cramton et al. Suppose that the annual tax rate is set equal to the probability that a buyer who values the asset more than the seller materializes within a period of, say, a year. Anastasia owns a house, and likes it. But there is a certain probability that someone else will show up who likes the house more than Ana does, and is willing to pay more for it than Ana's valuation or reservation price (we call this probability the "turnover rate," meaning the rate at which assets of this sort typically move into another person's hands). Suppose that the tax rate and the turnover rate are both 30%. If Ana raises her sale price above her reservation (that is, actual) value, she benefits from the higher sale price 30% of the time—when those higher-value buyers turn up. Her benefit from raising the price would thus be $.3\Delta P$, where $\Delta P$ is the increment in the sale price. On the other hand, as long as she remains in possession of the house she must pay the tax of 30%, which, applied to this incremental value, forces her to pay an additional $.3\Delta P$. Thus, the benefit from increasing the price above the reservation price is exactly offset by the cost. This stops owners from holding out for a high sale price by setting a price higher than their reservation value.

At the same time, Ana also wants to ensure that the asset is not taken from her at less than her reservation value. So, she will, of course, not declare a price below her actual valuation. This means that she can do only one thing: set a price exactly equal to her reservation value, ensuring that exactly the buyers willing to pay more than her reservation value will end up taking the asset. Full allocative efficiency is achieved: every asset passes to the hands of the person best able to use it and invest in it.

For any tax rate below the turnover rate, the possessor will always set a price above the amount she is willing to accept.[43] When the tax rate is zero, the possessor is free to set any price she wishes at no cost and thus would set the monopoly price.

When the tax rate equals the turnover rate, she has to reveal her true value. For intermediate tax rates, she will still be discouraged by the tax from setting a very high price, but she will not have a full incentive to report her exact value. Instead, she will set a price intermediate between her true value and the monopoly price that she expects a buyer to be willing to pay. As the tax rises from zero to the turnover rate, the price she quotes will gradually fall from the monopoly price to her true value.

What of investment efficiency? Remember that George's original proposal failed because of the concern that people would not invest in their property if they must pay confiscatory taxes on the rents it produces. At first glance, Harberger's tax also seems vulnerable to this problem. Suppose that the asset (which, for the sake of simplicity, let us suppose lasts only this year, like a machine that wears down from use) is currently worth $100,000 to its possessor, and that by investing $75,000 she can increase its value for her to $200,000 and also increase the value that any potential future buyer will place on it by $100,000 as well. Assuming the same turnover rate of 30%, our logic above indicates that she may as well, after the investment, declare the property to have a value of $200,000. However, this increases her tax bill by $30,000 (30% tax on the increased value of $100,000). The investment is not worth it. Although the value she gains from the asset regardless of whether the buyer acquires it has now increased by $100,000, she is forced to pay $30,000 of this amount to the government, which comes on top of the $75,000 investment. She loses $5,000 rather than making a profit.

But the investment can be improved by adjusting the tax. If a lower tax rate were charged, say 10%, then the possessor would still be able to capture $90,000 of the benefit from the investment ($100,000 minus the 10% tax payment). Now the possessor will profit from a $75,000 investment, or even a larger investment.

But if we lower the tax to improve incentive efficiency, then won't we also harm allocative efficiency? At a 10% tax rate, by increasing the price beginning at her reservation value, the possessor could still capture $.3\Delta P$ of value from a potential buyer, but she would now be forced to pay only $.1\Delta P$ to the tax authority. She would thus have an incentive to raise the price, which would block transactions with buyers who value the property only a little more than the possessor does.

One might assume that the loss in allocative efficiency would offset the gain in investment efficiency. However—and this is a key point—the opposite happens. When the tax is reduced incrementally to improve investment efficiency, the loss in allocative efficiency is less than the gain in investment efficiency. The reason is that the most valuable sales are ones where the buyer is willing to pay significantly more than the seller is willing to accept. These transactions are the first ones enabled by a reduction in the price as even a small price reduction will avoid blocking these most valuable transactions. In fact, it can be shown that the size of the social loss from monopoly power grows quadratically to the extent of this power. Thus, reducing the markup by a third eliminates close to $5/9 = (3^2-2^2)/(3^2)$ of the allocative harm from private ownership. Furthermore, in this example the distortion to investment is eliminated.

More generally, if we considered all scenarios in which an investment could raise the value of the asset to $100,000, the only investments that would be deterred by a 10% tax are those that cost more than $90,000 to make. These investments are both rare and not terribly valuable, as the net value they create is small. By the same reasoning as above, it can be shown that only roughly one-ninth of the total distortion to investment from the 30% tax is caused by a 10% tax. Such a policy achieves five-ninths of the allocative benefit of the 30% tax at only one-ninth of its cost to investment.[44] Furthermore, because different possessors often differ in their willingness and ability to invest to improve land (like the feudal lord and peasant farmer), allowing land to flow into the hands of the person best able to use it may also encourage investment.

Because of this quadratic structure, it is always optimal to have at least a very small tax. For example, a 1% tax will hardly distort investment at all but can still significantly improve allocative incentives. The owner will self-assess with reasonable accuracy to minimize her tax bill, but she will not be deterred from making valuable investments in the property. It is typically optimal to set a moderate tax rate, below turnover rate, that balances these two forces.

We refer to this tax as a "common ownership self-assessed tax" (COST) on wealth. The COST on wealth is also the cost of (holding) wealth. "Common ownership" refers to the way in which the tax modifies traditional private property. The two most important "sticks" in the bundle of rights that compose private property are the "right to use" and the "right to exclude."[45] With a COST, both rights are partly transferred from the possessor to the public at large.

First, take the right to use. In the popular image of private property, all benefits from use accrue to the owner. Under a COST, on the other hand, a fraction of this use value is revealed and transferred to the public through the tax; the higher the tax, the greater the fraction of use value transferred.[46] Second, and of far greater significance, consider the right to exclude. In the private property system, the owner keeps her property—which means keeping other people *off* her property—until she voluntarily sells it or gives it away (with some marginal exceptions). With a COST, the "owner" does not enjoy this right to exclude vis-à-vis anyone who offers to buy at the self-assessed price. In fact, any member of the public may exclude the current owner in exchange for this price. The lower the price, therefore, the greater is the extent to which the exclusion right is held by the public at large rather than the "owner." The price falls as the tax rises, so raising the COST also gradually shifts the exclusion right to the public at large, any member of whom can pay a price to claim the property.

We can conceptualize a COST as sharing ownership between society and the possessor. Possessors become lessees from society. Their lease terminates when a higher-value user appears, whereupon the lease is automatically transferred to that user. Yet this is not central planning. The government does not set prices, allocate resources, or assign people jobs. Indeed, as we will argue below, the government's role would be more limited than it is today because there would be no need for discretionary interventions, like eminent domain or public ownership of property in the conventional sense, to solve holdout and other monopoly-related problems. There would also be much less need for distortionary and discretionary government taxes to raise revenue for the state. Furthermore, control of everything would be radically decentralized; a COST thus combines extreme decentralization of power with partial socialization of ownership, showing that they are, perhaps surprisingly, two sides of the same coin. Far from creating a form of centralized planning, the COST creates a new kind of market—a flexible market in uses, to replace the old market based on permanent ownership.

## Brass Tacks

Imagine that you want to develop gas resources through hydraulic fracturing. A large swath of land deep in the Canadian Rockies looks promising. You open an app on your cell phone and enter your requirements: the desired size of the territory, the spots within it that research has indicated will be most productive, their proximity to roads, and their topographic characteristics. In an instant, the app displays a map of the area you are interested in with spots numbered in order of how well they meet your criteria—a process like searching for restaurants on Yelp. On the app you can see detailed satellite images of each piece of land and its topographic characteristics. When you circle around a group of tracts of land on the map with your finger, the app displays the total price you would have to pay to the people who currently possess this area. You find your ideal stretch of land, composed of four tracts currently possessed by four different people. You click a button on your app and funds are transferred from your bank account to the accounts of the current possessors. The following week you send a team to begin prospecting.

Along with our opening vignette, this scenario gives you a sense of how a COST would work in practice.[47] Every individual and business would have to list each of their possessions in a public register hosted on an online application and enter valuations for each item—or accept default valuations based on the original purchase price or on a database of prices of used goods (like today's Blue Book for used cars)—and would pay an annual tax based on the time-average price they listed over the course of the year. These lessees could change their valuations at any time, a process that could be automated by using general preferences or past behavior.

Anyone interested in acquiring ("possessing") a specific good would search the database to find local items of interest. Barcode scanning or photographic recognition software would display the price of something in front of you. By clicking on the item, you transfer funds from your bank account into escrow, and the funds would then be deposited to the current possessor's account on delivery of the asset. Nondelivery would be penalized as theft.

Actual implementation of the system would require working out countless details. Here we summarize some important features.[48]

1. Possessors would be allowed to group their assets into clusters and to pull them apart, as they choose. That way, they would not be at risk of having their right shoe taken and being left with a useless left shoe.
2. Depending on the asset type, the possessor would have a reasonable period of time to surrender it to the purchaser and the purchaser would bear the cost of picking up and transporting it. In the case of assets like a house that are costly to surrender, the possessor could, at some cost, extend the surrender period.
3. For assets that require some inspection prior to purchase, such as a house, the purchaser could freeze the listed price and pay the possessor a small percentage of the listed value to be able to inspect the property before deciding whether to proceed with the purchase.
4. Because tax rates would, ideally, be adapted to assets based on turnover rates, some assets unlikely to turn over often (family heirlooms and photographs, diaries) would be taxed at very low rates, while others (such as trendy gadgets) would be taxed at high rates. When tax

rates are very low, the possessor can prevent others from taking an item by paying a small tax. For typical assets, we estimate that turnover once every fourteen years is reasonable and thus (combined with other factors below) a 7% tax annually is a good target.

5. To avoid double taxation, the possessor could deduct the cost of any mortgages or other liabilities from her tax bill. However, she would have to stand ready to pay the amount against which this deduction is granted to anyone willing to relieve her of her mortgage. Thus, the tax would be calculated based on the net worth of the asset to its possessor, not on the value of the asset itself. For example, a person who possesses a $200,000 house with a $180,000 mortgage would be taxed on his $20,000 equity, not on the $200,000 house. The possessor would have to stand ready to sell the house for $200,000, but also to pay $180,000 to anyone who comes along and offers to take on the burden of the mortgage payments (effectively refinancing the house).[49] Possessors who cannot raise such cash (who do not have the credit to refinance) could tie their mortgage obligations to the house as a cluster so that anyone offering to discharge the mortgage would also have to purchase the house so no possessor could be forced to refinance (without selling the house) unless she chose to separate the asset from the liability.

6. For some assets, where maintenance is clearly required and easily monitored, possessors would have to take care of them, in the same way that a renter cannot trash an apartment, lessees of public lands must not pollute them, and homeowners are required to clear snow from their walkways. Maintenance could be monitored either

by inspections or by embedded technology. If possessors make improvements that can be verified technologically using, for example, image analysis, they could receive a subsidy for this investment to offset the COST's tendency to discourage investment.[50]

7. A number of technologies and institutions would have to be built to make the system easily navigable. Digital pricing systems could enable people to determine an appropriate valuation for items that they would feel they had to replace if they were taken by another citizen. In case people are temporarily short of money to pay for an item they really need, a financial institution could arrange a mortgage-like scheme to pay part of the cost in exchange for part of the value if a sale occurs.

### Killing a Flock of Birds with One Tax

We have loosely referred to every problem that inhibits privately owned assets from flowing to their best use as the "monopoly problem." This is how George, Jevons, and Walras used the term, but contemporary usage in economics breaks the problem into many components. We highlighted one emphasized by Myerson and Satterthwaite, but other economists have given other reasons why assets are not passed on to their best use. As we will see, a COST alleviates all these problems simultaneously.

One such problem is what economists call "signaling" or "adverse selection," concepts for which economists George Akerlof and A. Michael Spence were awarded the Nobel Prize.[51] The possessor of an asset, such as a used car, often knows the quality of the asset better than a potential purchaser. The possessor may thus demand a high price for the car not only because she guesses the buyer may be willing to pay it, but also because a high price signals she is reluctant to part with it, a ploy to convince the buyer the car must be valuable. Such signaling is one of the oldest tricks in the bargaining book. Anyone who has haggled in a marketplace is familiar with the elaborate stories a seller tells to illustrate an item's supposed value. By taxing signaling, a COST minimizes its harms.

Another barrier to trade, highlighted by another Nobel Laureate, Richard Thaler, is the "endowment effect."[52] Thaler found that people's minimum willingness to pay to buy an object is usually lower than their minimum willingness to accept to part with it, even if they have never actually touched or used it. Even just owning an object in the abstract seems to make a person value it more. Some recent evidence shows that the endowment effect is less a fundamental psychological attachment and more a heuristic used to jockey for position in bargaining. If it appears you really love a possession, people are likely to think it is valuable and thus offer you a lot for it. The endowment effect does not appear with experienced traders, and it does not appear in societies where bargaining and strategic trade are uncommon.[53] The endowment effect seems to be a characteristic of people who lack the time and ability to navigate the complex pricing decisions required in a market society. If high prices are discouraged, and property becomes more like renting, the costly barrier to trade created by the endowment effect would dissipate.

Barriers to borrowing are another obstacle to trade and efficient use of resources. Many assets, from houses to factories, can be fully used only if owned (at least partially) rather than rented because a renter cannot undertake the customization and investment required. An example would be a disused factory that could be transformed into lofts. Yet in the current system of private property, buying assets outright is very expensive and thus often requires large reserves of cash or the capacity to borrow. Barriers to borrowing include lack of trust, bad incentives created by loans, and the risk created in the lending relationship. Enormous resources have been spent by governments to help low-income people borrow to buy homes, in many cases saddling them with debt that they cannot pay.[54]

A COST would mitigate this problem. Because possessors anticipate the taxes they will pay in the future, the price they will set on an asset will fall dramatically, as it would be discounted by the amount of the future COST payments. Furthermore, people will lower prices they charge to minimize their COST payment on those assets. At the tax rate we advocate, asset prices would fall by between a third and two-thirds from their current level. In popular and congested areas like San Francisco and Boston, where very modest houses sell for $600,000 or more, their price could fall to as low as $200,000. This would reduce the need for borrowing and allow many more people without the necessary cash on hand to start businesses or (partially) own a house without taking on massive debt. This benefit of the COST would be especially important for low-income people.

Economists tend to neglect three other impediments to trade: laziness, incompetence, and malice. Private property allows lazy or misanthropic owners to hoard assets and to do so not for gain, but out of sloth. This problem seems to have been particularly prevalent under feudalism, when landowners were not accustomed to prudence, thrift, or hard work. Nobel Laureate John Hicks once wrote, "The best of all monopoly profits is a quiet life."[55] A COST disrupts the quiet life of a lazy monopolist by forcing her to generate the income to sustain a high valuation or turn her assets over to someone who can better use them.

Beyond alleviating all these barriers to trade, a COST would render unnecessary all the hassles and work-arounds presently used to deal with the problem of bargaining. Gone would be long bargaining sessions with an auto dealer to negotiate the price of a new car, followed by the realization that we will be gouged for the automobile financing and paid a pittance for our trade-in. The buying and selling of houses is so stressful that most people hire real estate agents and lawyers, who often overcharge them. These and many other hassles would be avoided with a COST, a transparent, liquid, low-capital system of asset exchange.

This would add up to a very large total benefit. One of us along with Zhang estimated that alleviating only the problem identified by Myerson and Satterthwaite using COST would increase the value of assets in the economy by 4% or output by roughly 1%.[56] However, with all the other benefits we highlight here and the reduction in other inefficient taxes a COST could fund (see below), we estimate a 5% increase in output. Given that the total loss from misallocation of assets in the economy has been estimated at 25%, we think our estimate is reasonable.[57]

## Optimizing Public Leases

It would be imprudent to leap head first into a system that would change the texture of markets and the economy in such basic ways. People might not know how to assess their possessions accurately. How would they feel if they lost something important to them because they underpriced it out of ignorance? Would people be willing to attach prices to items they don't really want to sell, or rely on technology to do that for them? Wouldn't a COST disrupt daily life if items you own are suddenly taken from you, even if you receive a bundle of money at the same time?

Certain aspects of a COST are familiar. Most people already take the risk of forced sales without even realizing it. That's what could happen to your house or car if you miss your mortgage or car loan payments. You might wake up to find your car has been repossessed and is gone. Renting carries with it the risk that you will be evicted if you miss a number of rental payments or cannot afford your rent after it has been increased by the landlord. People "self-assess" valuations in difficult circumstances whenever they buy insurance and are required, even if only implicitly, to decide how much money they would need if their house or car is destroyed. The sharing economy—exemplified by Zipcar, Uber, and Airbnb—is helping to accustom us to temporary "possessing" rather than "owning," and simultaneously consuming and selling (and hence setting a price on) the same product. However, a COST would change life radically, which is why it should be tested in limited public and commercial markets before being applied more broadly.

The most promising near-term application of a COST is to assets currently owned by governments and that have been or may soon be either sold off or leased to private citizens or businesses. Rather than sell off these assets permanently or lease them for fixed terms, governments could partially sell them under a license that included a COST-based license fee. The government would start by auctioning off the asset. The winning bidder would self-assess a price and pay a tax on that price. Anyone else could subsequently force a sale of the asset at the stated price.

Consider the radio spectrum. Since the early 1990s, long-term spectrum licenses have been auctioned off by governments around the world.[58] But the monopoly problem has emerged in secondary markets: the companies that acquired the licenses at auction have been reluctant to sell them to higher-valued users. New uses often require a repackaging of the licenses, creating holdout problems like those that inhibit the building of railroads or shopping malls. Huge swaths of spectrum now held by broadcast television stations with low viewership could be put to better use for wireless Internet.

In response, the US Congress passed legislation authorizing the FCC to buy back and repackage large parts of the spectrum, a process that has taken eight years. During that time the United States has fallen behind technological leaders like Israel, Korea, and Taiwan. In joint work with Milgrom and Zhang, one of us has recently argued that redesigning spectrum licenses to include a COST-based license fee would solve this problem and could be implemented in a variety of ways consistent with existing FCC rules.[59] This approach, which they call "depreciating licenses," would address many recent complaints about license design for the newly available 3.5 GHz bands of the spectrum; their small geographic scope and short durations under current plans were intended to maximize flexibility but may undermine investment incentives. A COST-based design would further enhance flexibility but provide greater stability for investment, helping to satisfy both the demands of high-tech companies who prize innovation and flexibility and those of telecommunications companies who need to make large investments to deploy 5G wireless technologies.

Assigning Internet domain names and addresses is another natural application for such licenses. At present, a person who purchases a domain name has a right to hang on to it indefinitely, as long as he pays an annual fee and is not blatantly violating someone else's trademark. This creates dramatic distortions to allocations during their terms, with cybersquatters sitting on domain names in a sort of ransom scheme. They are betting that someone who has a pressing reason for using the name will someday offer a lot of money for it.[60] For example, during the 2016 presidential cycle in the United States, clicking on the domain address http://www.clintonkaine.com led to an empty page; a cybersquatter had held out for a price the Clinton-Kaine campaign was unwilling to pay. The owner ended up selling instead to a group affiliated with the rival campaign.[61] A COST could help address holdout in this and other forms of intellectual property, such as those created by patent trolls who buy up patents and refuse to sell them to technology companies except at exorbitant prices that many companies refuse to pay.[62]

A COST would be useful for handling many other public assets. For example, ranchers lease grazing rights from the government, which often doesn't know how to price those rights. A COST, in which ranchers would effectively "buy" grazing rights from each other at self-assessed prices, would work more smoothly. A COST could also be used for leases on mineral, fishery, farming, and other natural resource leases, which are frequently sold off at arbitrary prices.

### A True Market Economy

These experiments will provide increased economic value, but if eventually a COST is applied broadly throughout the economy, improvements will be much more dramatic. As we noted above, the economy underperforms by as much as 25% annually because of the misallocation of resources to low-productivity firms. A fully implemented COST could increase social wealth by trillions of dollars every year.

Moreover, a COST would raise substantial revenue. At the rate of roughly 7% annually that we imagine being near-optimal, a COST would raise roughly 20% of national income. About half of that money would suffice to eliminate all existing taxes on capital, corporations, property, and inheritance, which economists agree are highly inefficient; to encourage investment in the way we described above; and to wipe out the budget deficit and significantly reduce debt, further stimulating investment.

The other half of COST revenue would be roughly $5,300 per person in the United States under present capital valuations and almost certainly would skyrocket under our proposal because of the more efficient allocation of assets, the revelation of capital income hidden at present, and the growth of the economy our proposal would ignite. These funds could be used to finance government services, public goods (such as investment in basic research), or social welfare programs for the poor. One could also imagine a system in which the revenue generated by the COST is simply sent back to the population on a per capita basis as a social dividend— akin to the universal basic income, which is currently being touted by leading commentators.[63] In this form, a COST would also serve as a much more effective way to collect a tax on wealth, which some economists have recently advocated for other reasons, because it has a built-in self-enforcement mechanism in the form of a buyer's right to force a sale. This would avoid establishing an elaborate and ineffectual government monitoring apparatus as exists for other attempts to collect taxes on capital income and wealth.[64]

To envision the egalitarian potential of a COST, consider how it would affect a typical American family. Let's assume that half the revenue the COST generates is used to reduce other taxes on capital and thus has no effect on asset values, while the other half is sent back to the population on a per capita basis. According to the US Census, the median household of four headed by someone between the ages 45 and 54 has about $60,000 of home equity and $25,000 of other assets. With a 7% COST, the value of these assets would fall by roughly a third, to $40,000 and $14,000, respectively. At these reduced values, a 3% COST net of reductions in other (existing) capital taxes would be roughly $1,400 a year, and the family would receive a social dividend of more than $20,000 annually. Thus, even if family members were so deeply attached to their property to the extent that they valued it at twice the market price, they would still benefit on net by $17,000 annually from the COST. A median household in the top 20% of the income distribution in the same age range has $650,000 of net worth. A similar calculation yields that such a family would pay roughly $14,000 in COST and thus would still benefit by $6,000 a year because of the $20,000 social dividend. The rich would be hardest hit. The average wealth of the top 1% of households is $14 million. Each household in this group would pay a COST of about $280,000 annually.

For families in weak financial situations, such as those with negative equity in their homes or who are burdened with credit card or student debt, a COST would actually be a subsidy. Because the liability would be worth more than the asset, the individual would receive a net tax refund on her private assets, even before the social dividend. Effectively, a third of their net debt would be immediately forgiven.

Consider a family that owns a house worth $300,000 and with a mortgage of $420,000. As noted above, the capitalized value of a 7% COST payment would reduce the value of assets, as well as liabilities, by about a third, accounting for future tax payments for the assets and future subsidies associated with liabilities. Thus, the value of the home would fall to $200,000 and the mortgage to $280,000.[65] The family would then receive a subsidy of 3% (again, relative to existing taxes) of its negative net worth of $80,000 ($2,400) annually to defray the cost of servicing the mortgage in addition to the $20,000 annual social dividend they receive.

Adding these benefits implies a significant redistribution of income from a COST. Estimates based on current measured returns on capital imply that capital's share of income in the United States is 30%, and that 40% of this wealth is held by the top 1%.[66] As previously noted, our proposal would redistribute roughly one-third of the return on capital and thus would reduce the income share of the top 1% by 4 percentage points, or roughly half the difference between recent levels and the low points in the 1970s.

The most persistent distributive conflict in capitalist economies arises from the concentration of wealth. Because most of the returns to capital flow to the very wealthy, a broad distinction exists between those who live primarily off the returns to capital and those who live off their labor. A COST would make most of the return to capital flow to the public, making it more equally distributed than wages. The COST would thus end the conflict between capital and labor, making differences in labor income the leading source of inequality.

## Optimal Buddhism and a Just Commonwealth

A COST might change our relationship to property. You may treasure a certain pen because it reminds you of the person who gave it to you, or you might love your car because you have gone on adventures in it. You know there is always a chance that you will lose a pen, or your car will be destroyed in an accident. We tolerate these risks all the time, and we manage them by taking precautions. With a COST, if you want to minimize the risk of loss through a forced sale, you can easily do so—by setting a high price. This means that people must pay a tax on things in proportion to how much they value them. And while we doubt that the tax is in practice going to be very high—how much will a stranger pay for a used pen, or an old car?—the notion of taxing things that we invest with personal value can strike people as offensive.

Our design of the COST deals with items that have such great personal meaning that it never makes sense to sell them. When the natural turnover rate of an item is low, the tax rate is also low, so that the "price" (in the form of tax payment) to protect it from potential sales is also low. Family heirlooms are almost always valued more by their possessors than by strangers, so in practice it would not cost much to protect them. Or it may well make sense to exclude family heirlooms and other personal items, within reason (to avoid creating a tax haven), from the COST system altogether. The aggregate value of these things is just not very large, so the economic impact of incorporating them into the COST system would also not be large. In the United States, all states have laws known as exemption statutes that identify personal items that cannot be taken by creditors when a person files for bankruptcy (clothes, Bibles, a limited amount of furniture, even guns). The "heirloom" problem is as much a problem in the regular system of private property as in the COST system, and our legal system makes accommodations to handle it. The items listed in these statutes might be excluded from the COST as well.

The COST could also make us think about property in a different and healthier way. A COST taxes objects, not personal relationships. Wouldn't it be better if people invested less of their emotional energy in objects and more in their personal relationships? The tradition of car-loving in countries like the United States and Germany has been eroding as fewer people develop mechanical skills and car companies now manufacture automobiles so that they can be repaired only by professionals. Thus, the process by which an owner develops an attachment to an object by incorporating her labor into it has been undermined. People have also quickly made the transition to services like Zipcar and Uber. Now, rather than own a car, one either rents it (Zipcar) or rents a ride (Uber). RelayRides enables the owner of a car to rent it while he is not using it, almost as if the COST were already in place. One cannot develop an attachment to a car that one uses for a few hours, and no one seems the worse for this. Fetishistic attachment to a privately owned automobile—an extremely expensive durable asset, which even enthusiasts seldom drive for more than an hour or two per day—is, thankfully, becoming a thing of the past. Increasing economic evidence suggests that excessive attachment to homes is inhibiting employment and dynamism in the US economy, a problem a COST would greatly reduce.[67]

Young people in wealthy countries increasingly invest their time and energy in having experiences (taking a special trip, eating out) rather than in amassing possessions. Because a COST both penalizes excessive attachment to objects and lowers their prices, it would give people, especially lower-income people, greater access to diverse goods than they enjoy today— just as a public museum makes fine art available to the masses by buying it up (albeit at considerable expense) from private collections where it sat unobserved, and accessible to only a handful of wealthy people, most of the time. Opportunity and dynamism would flourish, while obsessions with material possessions would diminish.

It is hardly a new notion that people invest unhealthy amounts of time and resources collecting things that they hardly ever use and don't really need. Every major religion (Buddhism especially, in popular imagination) and quite a few secular philosophies encourage people to put their energies elsewhere. Common intuition and psychological research tell us that the accumulation of goods beyond a basic threshold does not lead to a happier life and that experiences are more fulfilling than possessions.[68] Even economists have gotten into the act. And not just Karl Marx, who railed against "commodity fetishism." Since Thorstein Veblen's 1899 *Theory of the Leisure Class*—which argued that people often buy goods for "conspicuous consumption" (to show that they are wealthier than other people), and not because these goods directly contribute to their well-being—a dissident strain of economics has emphasized the pathologies of private property in the market system.[69]

A COST would also encourage attachment to communities and civic engagement, which have sometimes been damaged by capitalism. A COST would not just broadly distribute present wealth, but also the increases in wealth that economic progress creates. As the economy grows, the revenues generated by the COST would be redistributed back to citizens, just as employees who own stock in their employers benefit when the employer's profits increase. From Friedrich Engels to George W. Bush, commentators and politicians have argued that owning a share in the national capital stock, usually through the stock market or a home, could help stabilize politics and enhance support for policies that raise the value of the capital stock, a position supported by some research.[70]

A world in which everyone benefits from the prosperity of others would likely foster higher social trust, a factor essential to the smooth operation of the market economy and political cooperation.[71] The sharing of wealth would be in accord with many commonsense notions of justice. Wealth is rarely created solely by the actions of the people who are paid for it under capitalism. They normally benefit from the help of friends, colleagues, neighbors, teachers, and many other people who are not fully compensated for their contributions. A COST would better proportion the distribution of wealth to the labor that created it.

A social policy based on a COST would strengthen support among workers for our political system, help ease the flow of commerce among strangers, and provide citizens with a sense of having been justly rewarded for their social contributions. The COST would create a Radical Market in property, one that emphasized use over ownership. It would be a Radical Market because the root market principles of exchange and competition would be extended far beyond their current institutional embodiment; because the new system would transform economic relations; and because human well-being would be greatly advanced through the reduction of inequality and the advance of prosperity.

# 2

# Radical Democracy

## A MARKET FOR COMPROMISE
## IN OUR SHARED LIVES

Kentaro Adachi started saving voice credits as soon as he reached voting age. He resented the liberal governments that held power for decades. He was angry when the Yasukuni Shrine to Japan's war dead was converted into a memorial for foreign victims of imperialism. Despite his frustration, for years he never spent more than a few voice credits on a parliamentary election or referendum. He was saving up to spend on the cause of his life.

Kentaro spotted his first bear rustling in the forest behind his family's lakeside cottage in Hokkaido prefecture. Bears were a regular sight during his childhood, and as their population grew, thanks to environmental conservation efforts, they went from a novelty to a menace. His father assiduously trained him in how to avoid attracting them and how to scare them away by a controlled burn of forest brush and loud shouts, and how to retreat undetected. Until, that is, the day one carried his father deep into the forest.

What possessed his father to go into the forest so soon after cooking, with the sun so low, Kentaro would never learn. When he found him, all his battered father talked about in his last minutes was Kentaro's responsibility to his mother, the care he must take of his sister, and the importance of the Buddhist incantations that had comforted him throughout his life. His father was a kind and devoted man, but Kentaro could not help seeing him as a weak and effeminate pacifist, the kind of man Japan was filled with after eighty years of postwar peace. Kentaro vowed to never allow himself to become like that.

Kentaro trained his body and worked every day to support his family. Although he seldom articulated it, his defining aspiration since the day he found his father dying in the woods had been simple: to master marksmanship and single-handedly control the bear population in his rural neighborhood.

Kentaro was not a rule-breaker. To win some of the gun rights enjoyed by Americans, Norwegians, and Swiss, he patiently campaigned and gathered vote commitments for years. At last, a national referendum to allow personal ownership of hunting rifles in rural areas was on the ballot thanks to the commitments of voice credits he had collected. He now could take the ⓠ400 (400 voice credits) of the ⓠ800 he had accumulated over the past forty years to cast 20 votes in favor of this issue so dear to his heart.

After the votes were tallied, the country was shocked to find that despite 75% of voters opposing the initiative, it won an overwhelming victory with 60% of votes cast.

The average opponent had cast 1.5 votes against it, but the average supporter of personal hunting rifle ownership cast a stunning 6.75 votes. A poor use of votes, perhaps, with many other referenda squeaking by 52–48 and a hung parliament. Yet Kentaro felt vindicated. His voice had finally been heard. The fight of his life was won. And it was time to finally cull those bears, so no other child in Hokkaido prefecture would be left fatherless as he had been.

The idea of saving up for an important vote, in the same way we save up money to buy a car or a house, seems farfetched. We are used to a political system in which each person casts one vote and the majority prevails. Yet Kentaro may cast more than one vote, allowing him to exert more influence on an issue that he cares about than he could under the one-person-one-vote system (which we will henceforth call *1p1v*), if he is willing to give up influence on issues he cares less about. He possesses the same right to participate as everyone else, and accumulates credits to spend on votes at the same rate as everyone else, but he chooses to focus his votes on the issue most important to him. This freedom came with an important proviso: the voice credits are used to cast votes according to a quadratic or square root function. One voice credit ($Q1$) buys one vote on a given issue; $Q4$ buy two votes; $Q400$ buy only 20 votes; and so on.

In this chapter, we will show that these two elements—the capacity to save up voting power, and the square root function—would be a much-needed cure to the pathologies of the traditional voting systems used in democracies. We call this system Quadratic Voting, and in this chapter, we show how it creates a Radical Market for politics.

## Origins of Democracy

In Ancient Greece, the strength of a phalanx, the most common military formation of the time, was largely a matter of numbers: a larger phalanx beat a smaller phalanx. By identifying the host with greater numbers, one could thus predict the outcome of a battle. Majority prevailed without sword ever meeting shield.[1] By some accounts this was the origin of majority rule in Athens's governing body, the Assembly, which consisted of all those adult male citizens, regardless of their social status or property holdings. The Assembly had the power to pass laws, issue decrees, grant special privileges, and punish political leaders with ostracism and other sanctions, including death. Every member of the Assembly had one vote.

Yet the Athenians were aware of the dangers of majority rule. In one famous incident that occurred during the Peloponnesian War, the Assembly condemned to death a group of generals for failing to rescue survivors and recover the bodies of the dead after a naval victory off the Arginoussai Islands. Later, the Assembly was persuaded that a storm had prevented the generals from acting, and condemned to death the generals' accusers.[2] Events like these made many Greek thinkers deeply skeptical of democracy. They were concerned about the shifting passions of the mob and its susceptibility to demagogic leadership, as well as the disruptive power of the poor, who were in the majority, to redistribute wealth from the rich to themselves.

After the defeat of Athens in the Peloponnesian War, a loss blamed in part on the bad decisions made by the majority, Athenians introduced a more moderate form of democracy. It gave more power to independent bodies, including a commission that proposed legislation, and a People's Court, which had the power to strike down decrees that had been passed by the Assembly but that violated the laws. The members of all these bodies were selected by lot. This new system required multiple majority votes involving different groups of people, which amounted to needing a supermajority to get anything done. Thus began a long tradition of attempts by democratic governments to limit majority rule.

Perhaps the most successful such effort in the classical world was the "mixed constitution," under which different social classes—typically, the masses, the aristocracy, and a hereditary ruler—were assigned ways to influence government and veto outcomes they disapproved of. In the Roman Republic, for example, the Senate was dominated by aristocrats but certain important offices were reserved for plebeians. The constitution gave ordinary people a voice, but advantages to ancient families and wealthier citizens.[3] The idea was to prevent the masses from expropriating the wealth of the rich through the sheer power of numbers that would otherwise prevail under straight majority rule, while also giving the masses the power to block the rich from exploiting them. This system, which lasted centuries, was the greatest governance success of its time. But eventually the large number of veto points led to gridlock, which powerful leaders such as Julius Caesar resolved with extraconstitutional acts, leading eventually to civil war, dictatorship, and then empire.

Over the next millennium democratic institutions retreated, but then slowly reappeared during the Middle Ages. Anglo-Saxon kings sought advice from lords about the state of their realm and convened the king's advisory council, called the witan, to receive reports, a practice that eventually evolved into a parliament. These early British institutions did not employ simple majority rule based on 1p1v. The British House of

Commons began to use majority rule in the fifteenth century, but Great Britain had a classic mixed constitution, with the aristocracy able to exert power through the House of Lords and the monarch able to act on his own on some issues. In practice, political outcomes were decided by implicit supermajority rule.[4] In the Roman Catholic Church, canon law provided that many decisions would be made by majority rule, but a complicated set of laws permitted outvoted minorities to appeal to higher officials and to prevail if they could persuade those officials that the majority vote had been contaminated in some way—by the personal interests or motives of voters in the majority, or simply because it was wrong.[5] Under the doctrine of *maior et sanior pars*, a minority comprising people with superior judgment, such as those with greater experience and wisdom, could overrule a majority—a form of weighted voting, which we will discuss in greater detail below.[6]

Democracy made limited progress in these early years for many reasons. Rulers did not want to cede power to the public; religious and political traditions favored monarchy or aristocracy; and the constant threat of civil and foreign war required that strong leaders be in place. But the inherent limits of democratic institutions also played a role, as would become clear in the modern era.

### The Rise and the Limits of Democracy

It took a long time for democracy to shake its reputation as mob rule. In the mid-seventeenth century, Thomas Hobbes argued that absolute monarchy was the only secular remedy for the "war of each against all" that would prevail in the "state of nature."[7] Even though Hobbes defended monarchy, his secular and instrumental justification for it contrasted with previous arguments based on the Divine Right of Kings, and could be turned against them. This paved the way for Britons to demand restraints on royal power, as they did in the Glorious Revolution at the end of that century. This revolution overthrew King James II, who was viewed as overstepping the bounds of monarchical power and thereby confirmed the ideal of the limited or constitutional monarchy.

John Locke's defense of the revolution helped establish the modern conception of liberal democracy. The king now had to share power with a Parliament that represented, however imperfectly, the interests of the people. Locke and other Enlightenment figures, including Voltaire and Jean-Jacques Rousseau, developed the secular theory of sovereignty and located it collectively in the people. The works of these thinkers influenced Thomas Jefferson, who wrote in the American Declaration of Independence that "governments are instituted among men, deriving their just power from the consent of the governed."[8] The ideas of the Enlightenment also lay behind the French Revolution and a dramatic expansion of the franchise in Britain.

Such liberal thinkers were united in rejecting monarchical privilege in favor of placing authority in the hands of the people, but they struggled to explain how the people should wield their power. Democracy, yes, but what does democracy mean? And how to avoid the self-destructive and chaotic effects of mob rule they knew from classical history?

## THE UNITED STATES

The framers and early interpreters of the American Constitution had to confront the hazards of majority rule as they engaged in the first large scale experiment in democracy. They wanted to allow the majority to govern, but they worried that majorities would violate the rights of minorities. "If a majority be united by a common interest, the rights of the minority will be insecure," noted James Madison.[9]

The framers thus divided the national government into three branches to "check and balance" each other, and limited the majority's voting power by placing the final decisions on the presidency with intermediary electors and on senators with state legislatures. They also created numerous supermajority rules. To ratify a treaty, a president must obtain a two-thirds supermajority of the Senate.[10] To overcome a presidential veto, two-thirds of each house must vote for a bill.[11] A supermajority is needed to amend the Constitution.[12]

These arrangements helped protect minorities, like religious dissenters, the planter aristocracy in the South, the merchants of the North, and the wealthy everywhere.[13] Yet the founders did not simply want to protect any minority at any time: they sought to protect people with interests they considered legitimate, and who could not depend on being able to join a majority coalition to protect their interests.

The founders worried that if legitimate minority interests were not protected, the survival of the union would be at stake. Most citizens find themselves, at one time or another, in a minority group of like-minded people: those with very important interests or preferences that are not shared by the rest of the population. Those with the most intense preferences who are repeatedly victimized in the political process have strong incentives to rebel or secede. Threats of such rebellions became a central theme of US history, and the fear of disunion animated many of the framers' choices. Supermajority rule institutionalized the power of minorities with intense preferences so that it flowed through peaceful political channels.

Yet the framers were also aware of the opposite problem: gridlock. Before the Constitution, the states operated under a document called the Articles of Confederation. The national government could act only with the support of the states, and most actions required a supermajority or unanimous vote. Rule by unanimity and other high voting thresholds in politics is vulnerable to the same problem that property rights create in economic relations (see chapter 1): the ability of a person to hold out for unreasonable concessions, with the result that either gridlock or unfairness results. The holdout problem led to paralysis, decline in international stature, and a near collapse of cooperation among the states. Even in the middle of the Revolutionary War, the national government could not raise sufficient revenue. After the war, it was unable to put down rebellions and could not raise the revenue necessary to protect commercial shipping from pirates. There was always some state that either objected to the initiatives or, more commonly, simply wanted to pay less to support them. So the American framers settled on a compromise between the extreme of tyranny of the majority and paralysis.

History has shown this balance to have endured passably well, despite a bloody Civil War. But Americans continue to struggle with the limits of the supermajority and check-and-balance system. The United States avoided the instability of many European democracies, but the tyranny of the majority at the hands of a conservative majority, or political paralysis induced by conservative interests, became the central theme of American political history. Racial, ethnic, and religious minorities who suffered various types of abuse could not obtain legislative relief because they were outvoted.

In the second half of the twentieth century, federal courts stepped in to rectify the problem of conservative tyrannies by recognizing the rights of minorities to effective political representation, equal education, and other benefits and resources. In one formula, members of "discrete and insular minorities"—minority groups who had historically been excluded from politics—could not be burdened by legislation that targeted them or that did not have a strong public justification. As courts expanded the range of judicially protected minority rights, Congress stepped in with civil rights laws. This would turn out to be the greatest contribution of American legal and political thought to the problems of majority rule.

But, like the central planning we saw in the previous chapter, judicially enforced rights rely heavily on the benevolence, wisdom, and legitimacy of a respected elite. Federal judges are unelected and unaccountable to the public: this is what enabled them to advance minority rights in the first place, but it also put them in a precarious position in a country with strong democratic norms. Moreover, after the courts struck down a first generation of obviously discriminatory laws that deprived African Americans of the franchise, education, and the like, they faced significantly more complex laws that seemed to have a strong public-interest justification but also burdened minorities in a way that often seemed unfair. Consider some familiar examples:

- A stop-and-frisk law that reduces crime but disrupts the lives of mostly minority men.[14]
- Eminent domain projects where a city forces the sale of several private properties, possibly at below value to the owners, to build a park or revitalize the downtown.
- An anti–same-sex marriage law like California's Proposition 8, which reinforces traditional notions of marriage supported (at the time) by most Americans but that deprives gays and lesbians of advantages enjoyed by opposite-sex couples.

- Controls, aimed at reducing violence, on weapons that are typically used in military contexts but that may also be used for hunting and militia training.
- Sanitation and antidrug laws that interfere with religious rituals of minority religious groups.

People hold different and strong opinions about these laws, but the laws all pose the same dilemma. Each one helps (or plausibly helps) the majority and possibly the public at large, including even some members of the affected minority. But the law also puts a burden on the minority, one that may seem unfair and in some cases sufficiently egregious to cast into doubt the desirability of the law in question. Yet the tradeoffs are so complex that judicial intervention often seems arbitrary. In many cases, judges appear to substitute their policy preferences for those of the legislature that enacted the law—a practice that has no justification in democratic or constitutional theory, and that is a thinly disguised form of rule by an elite.

## FRANCE AND THE EUROPEAN CONTINENT

While the United States pioneered the practice of liberal democracy, much of the theory emerged in Europe, especially during the French Revolution. One French revolutionary in particular, the Marquis de Condorcet, pioneered the mathematical study of voting.[15] Condorcet's 1785 classic, "Essay on the Application of Analysis to the Probability of Decisions Rendered by a Plurality of Voices," not only highlighted the virtues of democracy, but also revealed its paradoxes.

Addressing the ancient Greeks' worries about the ignorance of the masses, Condorcet's "Jury Theorem" considered a situation in which all members of a community share a common interest but may have different information. He argued that, merely as a matter of statistics, if people are more likely right than wrong about what is in their collective interest, make up their minds independently, and can vote, large populations will outperform small governing elites as their large numbers will overwhelm mistakes. The Jury Theorem goes some way toward quieting the ancient worry that the public cannot govern itself because it lacks the wisdom of the elites.

But while Condorcet saw the potential of democracy, he also realized it lacked the capacity of markets to produce outcomes (political rather than economic) that coherently reflect the conflicting preferences of citizens. To see why, imagine that three people (Antoine, Belle, and Charles) are asked to vote among three possible outcomes: Louis XVI's head will be chopped off; he will be restored to the throne; or he is given his freedom as a private citizen. Suppose that each voter ranks the outcomes differently. For Antoine, who fears most that Louis will lead a counterrevolution: chop off head, restore, go free. For Belle, a royalist: restore, go free, chop. For Charles, who hates the monarchy but also dislikes violence: go free, chop, restore. We first ask them to cast a vote in a contest between chop and restore. Chop prevails by a 2–1 vote because both Antoine and Charles prefer chop to the alternatives, and only Belle does not. Next, we ask them to vote for restore versus go free. Restore prevails by a 2–1 vote, because Antoine and Belle prefer restore to the alternatives, while only Charles does not. Finally, the voters consider chop versus go free. Go free prevails over chop by 2–1. But this means in aggregate there is no determinate outcome: execution beats restoration, restoration beats freedom, but freedom beats execution.

It would appear hopelessly ambiguous who should win. The problem is that Antoine, Belle, and Charles cannot vote based on how intensely they care about the different proposals. The voting system is a straitjacket that throws out information. A vote can tell you only whether a person prefers one outcome to another, but not how much that person prefers the outcome. If we could directly measure how much the three outcomes affect the well-being of each person in our trio, then we could select the outcome that makes them jointly better off. For example, if restoration of Louis XVI would cost Antoine *his* head, while execution of the king would cause a revolution that greatly harmed all three of our voters albeit at different levels, then letting Louis XVI go free is the best outcome from the standpoint of the three voters. Regular voting can't pick this outcome.

Kenneth Arrow, a student of Vickrey's, Nobel Laureate, and perhaps the most eminent economist of the twentieth century, would later formalize and generalize this argument in his famous "impossibility theorem," showing that no voting rule in which individuals rank candidates could overcome problems of this sort.[16] Note, in contrast, that in market transactions it is possible for people to signal the intensity of their preferences for goods and services—by offering to pay more or less. This is an important reason why many economists believe that the price system allows efficient outcomes while voting does not.[17]

Anticipating Arrow's insights, Condorcet eventually concluded there was no solution. When asked in the early 1790s to draft a constitution for the revolutionary government, he advocated a variety of checks, balances, and supermajority rules to restrain popular democracy and protect the liberties of individuals in much the same way that his American predecessors had.[18] Condorcet's worries about voting paradoxes evidently trumped his confidence in the Jury Theorem. Condorcet's thought and related ideas spread throughout continental Europe and helped lay the foundations for European democratization during the nineteenth century. Yet the European democracies suffered paradoxes even more troubling than those Condorcet discovered.

One is strategic voting, the idea that in standard democratic systems, especially those like the US system based on plurality rule, voters tend to cast votes based partly on their desire to "make their vote count."[19] For example, in the United States, two parties prevail and voters are usually forced to support the winner of one or the other major party primary, even if they detest both candidates.[20] As we discuss further below, this problem appears to have been particularly severe in the 2016 US election.

The most alarming example, however, was the rise of the Nazis. In his book *The Coming of the Third Reich*, historian Richard Evans observes that no more than 10% of the German public ever were strong supporters of the extreme right.[21] Yet in the 1930 election, Hitler won an additional 10% from people who cast protest votes against a political system that they saw as corrupt and unresponsive to their needs, catapulting the Nazi party to a leading position as the major right-of-center party in the German parliament. In the following election, in 1932, many middle-class Germans voted for the Nazis as their only chance to prevent Stalinist Red Terror from spreading to Germany, doubling the Nazis' share and allowing Hitler to become Chancellor. At the same time, fear of Hitler led many Jews, minorities, workers, and leftists to vote for the Communists, further reinforcing the middle-class fear that if Hitler lost, Communists would prevail. This downward spiral of mutual fear, violence, and mistrust ushered in Nazi dictatorship the next year.

Even before Hitler eliminated all democratic institutions, he was able to crack down on dissenters while actually increasing his popular backing. How? Many of Hitler's initial moves to curtail dissent and the rights of leftists and minority groups were popular in this atmosphere and so helped Hitler to draw into a coalition with him the two major parties of the German mainstream right. After all, these groups were *minorities*, and unpopular—even dangerous—ones at that. Yet what the more traditional German right failed to anticipate is that once the Communists and Socialists were eliminated from the political stage, the centrist Catholics with whom the traditional right had long aligned became the next target.[22] After that, Hitler suppressed his traditional-right allies and then even dissenting groups within the Nazi party.

At each stage, Hitler enjoyed effective majority support from those remaining within the polity, so in some sense each purge was "democratic" even as it undermined the universalistic basis of democracy. This is the logic of political scientist Richard McKelvey's theory of "majoritarian cycling": majority rule with no check on the ability of majorities to exploit and repress minorities can easily degenerate into the rule of a narrow clique or even the dictatorship of a single person.[23] As German Protestant theologian Martin Niemöller famously put it,

> First they came for the Socialists, and I did not speak out— Because I was not a Socialist. Then they came for the Trade Unionists, and I did not speak out—Because I was not a Trade Unionist. Then they came for the Jews, and I did not speak out—Because I was not a Jew. Then they came for me—and there was no one left to speak for me.[24]

The continental European experience with democracy left strong cautions against majority rule and 1p1v without strong protections for minorities or those whose interests were disproportionately affected by given policies. Yet, as in the United States, Europeans found no simple way to build these protections into democratic systems.

## BRITAIN

Unlike Continental Europe and the United States, Britain democratized through gradual reforms rather than sudden convulsions. The Glorious Revolution and further political developments established the supremacy of Parliament over the monarch in the UK by the Age of Enlightenment. Yet the franchise was restricted to adult males who possessed land yielding an income of forty shillings—fewer than one in every thirty Britons.[25]

Beginning around the time of American Independence, the British Philosophical Radicals began to press for extension of the franchise. The group, founded by politician William Beckford and philosopher Jeremy Bentham, favored public policy based on the "utilitarian" principle of achieving "the greatest happiness for the greatest number." Their work led to the Reform Act of 1832, which doubled the franchise to include all males with wealth equal to the previous standard, eliminating the requirement that the wealth take the form of land, and it also reapportioned parliamentary seats to make them more representative. Yet, while the Radicals fought for broader representation, they were confused and divided about exactly how far this push should proceed.

Bentham reasoned that broader representation should bring policy closer to his utilitarian principle, but in his definitive 1829 defense of his doctrines, he anticipated the majoritarian cycling problem we mentioned above and worried that a majority would find it advantageous to dispossess or even enslave a minority.[26] Such an outcome would not promote the greatest happiness for the greatest number, Bentham argued, because those enslaved would lose more than the enslaving majority would gain.

Bentham's legacy was carried on by his closest colleague James Mill and Mill's son, John Stuart Mill. Both Mills favored expanding the franchise but harbored serious reservations about universal suffrage in the near term. James believed that some property qualification was needed to avoid excessive influence of those parts of society that have no stake in the nation's prosperity, but favored allowing the majority of men to vote.

John Stuart went further, becoming the first member of Parliament to advocate women's and eventual universal suffrage. Yet he too worried about tyranny of the majority, based in part on his fear that the masses of uneducated people would exercise political influence unwisely. He briefly advocated giving more votes to those with extensive education or strong interests in an issue, only to abandon this proposal as impractical because of the impossibility of determining who had this superior knowledge or interest.[27] He considered a variety of other devices to allow those with special knowledge and interest to have greater influence, such as making voting inconvenient and burdensome in terms of time and travel so that only those with a strong interest would exercise the right to do so. He also advocated long legislative terms to give greater independence to an elected and partly representative elite. Yet, ultimately, Mill was frustrated by his inability to find an appropriate solution to avoid the "collective mediocrity" that seemed to spread as democracy advanced in the UK.

## Radicalizing Democracy

The creators of modern democracies thus built a new political order, but they were uneasy with their handiwork. Failures to protect minority rights, the tyranny of the majority, paradoxical victories for bad candidates, repeated use of majority rule to establish dictatorship, and the tendency of democracy to ignore the views of the very knowledgeable: all reflected the inability of democracy to give consideration to the intensity of people's needs and interests, and to the superior wisdom or expertise of certain voters. There is a better way to allocate resources to people with stronger needs and interests, and reward those who demonstrate special talents or insight—markets.

### MARKETS FOR COLLECTIVE DECISIONS

Politics is concerned with creating "goods" (which economists call "public" or "collective" goods) that affect the entire population or large groups of people—in contrast to the "private goods" exchanged on traditional markets that individuals consume by themselves. Examples of public goods include clean air, military defense, and public sanitation. Private goods are currently allocated through markets. Public goods can't be using standard markets, or at least not with good results. As the legendary economist and Nobel Laureate Paul Samuelson explained in his 1954 article, "The Pure Theory of Public Expenditure," standard markets are designed to allocate private goods to those who value them the most.[28] This is clearest in an auction—where the highest bidder is assumed to be the person who values the good most—but the price system as a whole works as a kind of decentralized auction.

Yet the logic of public goods is fundamentally different: rather than being allocated to the single individual who values them most, the overall level of public goods must be determined to maximize the total good of all members of society. In order for collective decisions about such public goods to bring "the greatest happiness to the greatest number," as Bentham suggested, every citizen's voice must be heard *in proportion* to how important that good is to that citizen. Standard markets will not accomplish this because those who care most will always be willing to pay more than anyone else.

In standard markets, the cost of more of any good, such as food, is proportional to the amount of that good you want. If you want twice as many burgers you usually pay twice as much. Suppose we tried to decide on public goods in the same manner. Suppose every citizen could increase or decrease the amount of pollution by paying a price proportional to the amount of this change. Unless this price was reasonably high, many citizens would submit conflicting demands to change the policy; this "excess demand" would, in a normal market, bid up the price of influence. Eventually only the few citizens who care most about the issue (in either direction) will end up with any say. Such a market would replace the tyranny of the majority with the tyranny of the most motivated, or richest, citizen willing to pay more than anyone else.

This argument has been enormously influential in explaining many maladies of modern politics. Building on Samuelson's ideas, economist and political scientist Mancur Olson argued that small groups of well-organized special interests can use expenditures, lobbying, and other forms of political action to persuade the government to act in their interest rather than for the public good.[29] Much of the public ignores complex issues, like bank regulation, while the banks who can profit from government fund lobbying organizations that control the agenda. Many economists are cynical about collective decision-making because it seems so easy to manipulate.

But not all of them view it this way. Again, enter our hero, William Vickrey. He realized that the problem with applying the principle of an auction to politics lay not in the auction itself but in the way that principle had been misinterpreted. As we saw, selling political decisions to the single highest bidder leads to terrible outcomes, because it treats a public good like a private good. The idea behind an auction, Vickrey realized, *is not* allocating the good to the highest bidder. Instead it is that *each individual must pay an amount equal to the cost that her actions impose on others.*[30] In a standard auction of private property, this "externality" of my winning is denying the good to another bidder, so the highest bidder should win at the price equal to the losing bid of the second-place bidder. But, as Edward Clarke and Theodore Groves realized independently in the 1970s, a decade after Vickrey's work, this principle also suggests a way to organize *collective* decisions that produce public goods, and not just economic markets involving private goods.

In the case of collective decisions, people affected by the possible public good should have the right to vote as much as they wish, but everyone should have to pay the cost that her votes impose on others. When you buy corn from a store, the price represents the value of the corn in its next-best social use. To buy it you must therefore compensate society for what it gives up by allocating the corn to you. When you hit someone with your car, the law requires you to compensate her for the injury, the pain and suffering you inflict on her. Similarly, in voting, you should have to pay for the harm you impose on people by outvoting them in referenda (or other types of elections) in which a collective decision is made. The amount you pay equals the amount by which your vote denies your fellow citizens the value they would obtain from the different outcome they would prefer.[31]

So just how was this scheme supposed to work? How do we calculate how much harm one person causes to others by swaying an election with his vote(s)? A hint was provided a few years later by Groves in his work with economist John Ledyard and in related, unpublished work by Aanund Hylland and Richard Zeckhauser.[32] They realized that the price individuals should pay for influencing public goods should not be proportional to the degree of influence an individual has, but *to its square.*

To see why, consider an example. A power plant benefits all residents in a town by supplying them with low-cost electricity, but it also emits pollution. While the benefits of the power plant are well-reflected by the price residents pay for power, the harms caused by the pollution are uncertain: they include possible negative health effects, which will depend on the preexisting health conditions of residents, and foul odors that might bother some people more than others. The government can issue regulations that force the power plant to install machinery that reduces the amount of pollution, but it's not sure whether to do so. The government can issue regulations of increasing strictness; the stricter the regulations are, the greater the reduction in pollution but also the higher the electricity bills. The question, then, is how much people care about pollution. To answer this, the government could hold a referendum that asks people to vote on a tolerable level of pollution.

Yet this idea suffers from the tyranny of the majority. The problem is that most people might not care much about pollution, and their vote will carry the day, but there will be others, probably in a minority, who care a great deal. This group might include asthmatics, elderly people, and others with health conditions; nature-lovers and outdoorspeople who are sensitive to natural conditions; and owners of certain businesses, for example, laundries or perfumeries, which may need to install insulation to protect their operations from the bad air. If we care about the overall or aggregate well-being of everyone in the town, then we need a way of determining whether the intense preferences of the minority outweigh the weak preferences of the majority. A referendum that operates based on majority rule cannot serve that function.

Let's imagine that instead of holding a referendum, the town undertakes an ambitious experiment. It asks each citizen to report how much each extra unit of pollution will cost in terms of dollars. (In other words: how much would she be willing to pay to avoid that extra unit?) Most citizens may be willing to put up with a bit of pollution that is hardly noticeable, but the more pollution there is, the more dangerous each additional unit becomes. Citizens fill out a form indicating how much it would be worth to them to stop pollution from increasing 1 to 2 parts per million, 2 to 3, 3 to 4, and so forth. Economists call these numbers a "marginal cost schedule." The city knows the value of pollution to weigh against this: it is just the market price (less cost) for the power that could be produced by creating this pollution. To determine the best standard, the government will compare this schedule of benefits of pollution to the total cost borne by all citizens. The optimal standard is at the point where the benefit of the next unit of pollution is exactly offset by the total cost to all citizens of the next unit.

Figure 2.1 shows these relationships as a function of the amount of pollution in parts per million.[33] The declining line shows the value of economic activity that generates pollution, which decreases as the power plant has limited capacity and the town only needs so much electricity, so the more power is produced, the less valuable on net it is. The bottom upward-sloping line represents the marginal cost to a particular citizen, Nils, who owns a laundry and thus suffers a disproportionate share of the harm from pollution. The intermediate upward-sloping line is the total marginal cost to people other than Nils. The top upward-sloping line is the total marginal cost to all citizens of pollution, which is the vertical sum of the other two upward-sloping lines.

If Nils were not living in the town, the optimal amount of pollution would be the point shown by the base of the right dotted line (point A), the intersection of the cost to those other than Nils, and the benefits of pollution. However, once Nils is added, pollution becomes a bit costlier because of the harm imposed on Nils and thus its optimal level drops to the base of the left dotted line (point B).

So how much should Nils have to pay in order to strengthen the clean-air standard to take into account his well-being? According to Vickrey, Clarke, and Groves, he should have to pay the amount by which the reduction in pollution that he seeks costs others living in the town (who are thereby denied the net benefits of those last units of electricity). This additional cost is how much value others would have received on net had pollution occurred at A rather than B, meaning at a level where (for others) the additional pollution was worth it to produce extra electricity. In other words, because Nils owns a laundry that is harmed by too much pollution, the price of electricity must be raised. This discourages some use of electricity from which others would benefit more than pollution harms people *other than* Nils. Nils's entry tips these uses to being not worth

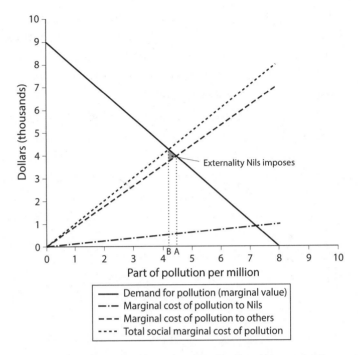

**FIGURE 2.1:** Determining the optimal level of pollution and how much Nils should pay for his request.

*Source:* Adapted from N. Tideman & F. Plassmann, *Public Choice* (2017). https://doi.org/10.1007/s11127-017-0466-4.

it and thus eliminates the net benefit of this electricity production before he arrived. Nils should have to pay the value beyond the cost of production these others would have gained from the electricity had he not demanded less pollution. This quantity is given by the shaded triangle in the figure.

Because it is a triangle, its overall area grows as the *square* of the distance between B and A. This is what we call "quadratic" growth—based, yes, on the same quadratic function that we saw in chapter 1. To better understand this quadratic growth, let's imagine that in addition to owning a laundry, Nils had bad asthma, and his cost schedule was twice as high. The gap between the cost schedules with and without Nils would be twice what it was. Clearly this would cause the gap between A and B to grow (to double, to be precise). However, it would also cause the vertical gap at B between the lines to double. Because the area of a triangle is half the product of its base and height, this means that reporting twice as much harm, and causing twice as large a reduction in pollution, would cost Nils four times as much. More generally, the proportionate effect on both the height and width of the triangle implies a general quadratic growth of payments in the amount of influence an individual has. Nils should thus pay *quadratically* in the gap between B and A; that is, the payment should be proportionate to the *area* of the triangle with two sides of length (proportional to) the distance from B to A, rather than proportional to just the *length* from B to A.

Another way to look at this is that, as Nils seeks larger reductions in pollution, his demands become costlier to others in two different ways. First, he is seeking a larger reduction in pollution, which straightforwardly harms others by preventing them from consuming electricity for which they would be willing to pay the cost (to everyone other than Nils). But, second, he is requesting the elimination of *increasingly beneficial* pollution-generating economic activity. While the costs and benefits of a slight reduction below A are perfectly balanced for those other than Nils, once pollution has been reduced by a bit, we start to approach more productive uses of electricity where the benefits significantly outweigh the costs. Thus, by seeking more reduction in pollution Nils is not just asking for more mitigation of pollution, but also costlier mitigation (at the margin). His cost should thus grow not linearly but quadratically in his request. If you imagine a triangle like this (◄), it almost perfectly provides a representation of the effect of his decision. With each incremental reduction in pollution (horizontally), the harm to others becomes "wider" (vertically).

We have described a highly idealized way in which the town could make a collective decision that aggregates the well-being of all rather than allowing a majority to dictate outcomes that benefit it at the expense of others. But can people actually provide such complex cost schedules? One would be right to be skeptical—the insights of Vickrey, Clarke, and Groves did not lead to practical reform. It took another three decades before economists would see how these ideas could be used to design a voting system.

## Quadratic Voting

After returning from his trip to Rio in 2007, chronicled in our preface, one of us became fascinated with the problem of assembling land. While thinking about how landowners might vote on whether to accept a developer's offer without disadvantaging the few owners who really want to stay in their homes, he stumbled on a solution in 2009 that allows the Vickrey-Clarke-Groves idea to apply to practical voting.[34]

To see how it works, let us return to the example with which we began this chapter. Suppose that Japan holds periodic referenda on important issues, like gun control or immigration reform. Every citizen is given a budget of "voice credits" every year, which he may spend on referenda that year or save for the future, as Kentaro did. To convert voice credits to votes, a voter can dip into his budget and spend as much of the balance as he wants to buy votes—but the cost of a number of votes is its square in voice credits. Thus, we call this system Quadratic Voting (QV). One vote costs one voice credit, which from now on we'll denote as ℚ1. ℚ4 buys you 2 votes (the square root of four), ℚ9 buys you 3, and so on. The square root is also known as the "radical" (another word for root), hence "radical democracy"—which is a kind of Radical Market, except it is one in which the goods are public rather than private. A referendum is approved if the votes in favor exceed the votes against.

Consider the gun control referendum Kentaro voted in. Every Japanese has the right to vote for or against the proposal. Rural voters like Kentaro strongly favor the proposal. In the story, he spends ℚ400 for 20 votes; other rural voters spend ℚ81 for 9 votes, ℚ121 for 11 votes, etc. Most Japanese people live in cities and disapprove of guns. However, most of them have other priorities than gun control, given how low crime is in Japan and how the proposed reform exempts urban areas; they buy one vote against for ℚ1 or two votes for ℚ4. The government counts the votes: if the number of votes in favor of gun rights exceeds the number of votes against, the reform is adopted. In the story, the intensity of the support of Kentaro and other rural voters is enough to win the day and outweigh the mild opposition of city-dwellers.

This system enables people to cast votes that reflect the strength of their preferences. The key defect of the current system—that one can effectively register only three preferences: yes, no, indifferent—is eliminated. This makes two important things possible. First, a passionate minority can outvote an indifferent majority, solving the problem of the tyranny of the majority. Second, the outcome of the vote should maximize the well-being of the entire group, not the well-being of one subset at the expense of that of another.

Yet recall that for this to be true, by Samuelson's rule, every citizen must vote *proportionally* to how much she cares about the issue. How exactly does QV achieve this, avoiding the free-rider problem?

Recall that the problem with a standard pricing model of public goods, where influence is based on a one-to-one relationship with how much you pay, is that those who care most about an issue want to buy all the votes, while those who care only a little buy none. The problem is that votes are too cheap for those who care a lot, but too expensive for those who care little. The way to solve this is to make *the next vote* more expensive to those who have already bought many votes than it is to those buying their first vote. This can induce those who care little to at least buy a few votes and restrain those who care a lot from buying too many. This is precisely what QV does, as we illustrate in table 2.1, which shows the total cost of votes and the marginal cost (the cost of the next vote).

What's important is not so much the total cost of each number of votes, but that the *marginal* cost of casting *the next* vote grows proportionally to the number of votes cast. The table shows the marginal cost of casting a vote as a function of the number of votes cast. It shows that this is always (within ℚ1)[35] proportionate to the number of votes cast. It costs twice as much at the margin to cast four votes as to cast two votes (ℚ7 rather than ℚ3); twice as much to cast eight votes as to cast four votes (ℚ15 rather than ℚ7) and so on. For this reason, this quadratic rule is the only one that induces rational individuals to buy votes in proportion to how much they know and care about the issue, as we now explain.

If, all else equal, Kentaro values being able to change the outcome in his favor twice as much as his neighbor Meiko would value changing it in her favor (against gun rights), Kentaro will pay twice as much at the margin as Meiko does. For example, Kentaro buys sixteen votes while Meiko buys eight

TABLE 2.1: Votes and their cost under QV

| Votes | Total cost | Marginal cost |
|-------|-----------|---------------|
| 1 | Q1 | Q1 |
| 2 | Q4 | Q3 |
| 3 | Q9 | Q5 |
| 4 | Q16 | Q7 |
| 5 | Q25 | Q9 |
| 6 | Q36 | Q11 |
| 7 | Q49 | Q13 |
| 8 | Q64 | Q15 |
| 16 | Q256 | Q31 |
| 32 | Q1024 | Q63 |

votes. The exact number of votes that Kentaro and Meiko buy depends on their estimates of how likely it is that they will be pivotal voters, or other reasons that Kentaro and Meiko are motivated to vote. So, if Kentaro buys sixteen votes for Q256 ($16^2$), this does not mean that the value he places on the project is equal to the value of Q31. But assuming that Kentaro and Meiko have similar degrees of motivation to vote as a proportion to how much they care about the issue, it does mean that Kentaro will always vote twice as much as Meiko will.

QV achieves a perfect balance between the free-rider and the tyranny of the majority problems. If the cost of voting increased more steeply, say, as the fourth power of votes cast, those with strong preferences would vote too little and we would revert to a partial tyranny of the majority. If the cost of voting increased more slowly, those with intense preferences would have too much say, as a partial free-rider problem would prevail.

Thus, under QV, the communities can determine which group of people—the supporters or opponents—is willing to give up more total voice for the project even though it does not know how much any individual (or the group) values the project. Crucially, QV gives weight both to numbers and to the intensity of interests. A large group of people with weak preferences might outvote a very small group of people with intense preferences but not a somewhat larger group of people with intense preferences.

QV does not perfectly achieve the greatest happiness for the greatest number, which we will call "optimality," but rather only approximately so. The quality of this approximation depends on how closely different individuals share the same degree of motivation to vote in proportion to the value they place on changing the outcome. For perfectly rational and selfish individuals who only care about the outcome of the vote, the only motivation to vote is the chance that their vote changes the outcome. For such individuals, the conditions under which QV achieves optimality are closely related to the conditions for perfect competition in a market economy.[36]

But when citizens are not perfectly rational and selfish, QV may run into greater problems. If citizens vote for reasons other than their narrow desire to influence the outcome they most want, QV will perform well to the extent that these other motivations are largely uncorrelated (in proportion to individual values) with how individuals are affected by the issue at hand. If, for example, the supporters of gun control do not really care about the issue but are induced by social motives to cast many votes in favor of it, it may pass despite it being appropriate for it to fail, unless similar social motives propel the proponents to vote more as well.[37] A similar problem may arise from collusion, vote-buying, or fraud, just as in 1p1v systems.[38] As with 1p1v, guarding against such possibilities will require strict legal enforcement against fraud and abuse; social norms against pressure, vote-buying, and collusion; and a sense of a civic duty to participate in proportion to one's knowledge.

A more fundamental issue QV raises is what notion of value or "happiness" it maximizes or should maximize. This brings us to a fundamental problem: how can we measure "the greatest happiness for the greatest number"? How is it possible to compare the happiness of one individual to that of another? Many economists have argued that this task is impractical. They suggest that all we can hope to do is ensure that no one's happiness can be increased without decreasing anyone else's, a condition called *Pareto efficiency*, and that the total happiness is distributed fairly.

Just like markets, QV (approximately) ensures Pareto efficiency. A natural notion of fairness is to divide influence over public goods equally: give every individual an equal endowment of influence or voice measured in units of that voice.[39] If markets with equal incomes are a natural model of a just distribution of private goods, we hold that QV with equal voice is a natural model of just choices about collective decisions.[40]

QV addresses the problem of varying intensities of preferences by allowing those with stronger preferences a way to influence the outcome in proportion to the strength of their preferences. They may still lose to the majority, but they will not lose to a majority with weak preferences (unless the majority is extremely large). Majorities will prevail over minorities— as they should—when the intensities of everyone's preferences are similar. But when minorities have sufficiently intense interests, they can protect their interests from majority domination. Furthermore, as we will revisit below, QV provides a satisfying resolution to the paradoxes of democracy we discussed at the beginning of this chapter.

## QV in the Wild

Political systems are slow to change. Why would anyone want to adopt QV without evidence that it works? To address this problem, we created a company, ⱭDecide (pronounced Q-Decide, and formerly Collective Decision Engines), to commercialize QV for practical everyday purposes. The venture has given us a chance to test, learn about, and improve QV. We hope that these explorations will lay the foundation for QV in the political realm. Below are some of the ways we've used QV so far.

### POLLING AND MARKET RESEARCH

Political polling began as a way to predict election outcomes, and such "horse-race" polls remain the bread and butter of the industry. But more useful to political leaders in shaping their policy priorities are the battery of issue opinion surveys that try to measure public views and their intensity. The most common method is the "Technique for the Measurement of Attitudes" proposed by psychologist Rensis Likert in 1932.[41] In a Likert survey, participants are asked to rate a variety of issues on a scale from "strongly disagree" to "strongly agree" or something similar. Participants can choose any point on this scale they wish.

Unsurprisingly, in practice most participants in Likert surveys cluster to the extremes. Figure 2.2 shows an example. "Very strongly against" is −3 and "very strongly in favor" is 3, with more moderate opinions arrayed in between. The distribution of responses displays a characteristic "W" shape, with most participants clustering toward the extremes, some expressing indifference, and few in between. Most researchers agree that the W shape does not display the true distribution

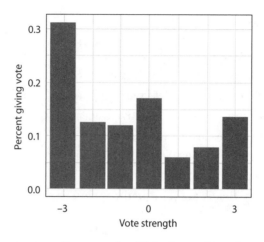

FIGURE 2.2: Frequency of participants' expression positions ranging from strong disagreement to strong agreement with a national ban on abortion in the United States. *Source:* Adapted from David Quarfoot, Douglas von Kohorn, Kevin Slavin, Rory Sutherland, David Goldstein, & Ellen Konar, Quadratic Voting in the Wild: Real People, Real Votes, 172 Pub. Choice 283 (2017), p. 6.

of preferences, which in reality is most likely a bell-shaped or normal curve. In the case of abortion rights, for example, most people are in the middle, with a small number who are extremely pro or con. But since the Likert test does not force respondents to truthfully display the intensity of their preferences, respondents tend to exaggerate—to "shout" their views, saying "very strongly" in favor or against rather than "just a little." We see the same pattern in Amazon reviews: nearly everyone claims to love (five stars) or hate (one star) a product, when most people are likely in the middle. And even when people try to respond accurately, the Likert test reveals very little. Does a person who "very strongly" opposes abortion rights mean that she will vote against any candidate who supports those rights, or just that it is one among many factors that she will take into account?

QV offers a solution to this problem. Rather than allowing respondents to freely express any position they wish, a poll based on QV endows each participant with a budget of voice credits and allows her to spend the credits on the range of issues available as she wishes. We have patented the use of QV and related methods to solicit opinions digitally. Figure 2.3 displays the software interface, called "weDesign," developed by our colleague Kevin Slavin and others at QDecide to enable this implementation.

FIGURE 2.3: A user interacting with QDecide's weDesign software on an iPhone. Photo: CDE.

Participants start with a pool of credits and may use them to "buy" as many votes as they wish in favor of or against each issue. The cost in credits of votes is, of course, quadratic. While this relationship sounds abstract and complex when described mathematically, it is simple and intuitive for most users when engaged in this visual and tactile manner: participants see their credits dwindle at an increasing rate as they express opinions. Even math-phobes are able to navigate the system smoothly.

Respondents are asked to use their fixed budgets to buy votes across a range of issues: abortion rights, healthcare, minimum wage, and so on. If a respondent truly cares about only one issue (which is very unlikely), she will spend her entire budget to buy relatively few votes to take a position on one issue. If she cares about many issues, she must decide how to allocate her votes across them. She may discover, for example, that while she cares a lot about abortion rights, she doesn't want to use up so many credits to vote in favor of them that she can't even buy one vote in order to take a position on Obamacare or the minimum wage.

Typically, respondents (especially those with less formal training in mathematics) quickly run into a constraint, running out of credits, and then returning to correct course. Economist Sendhil Mullainathan and psychologist Eldar Shafir have shown in their 2013 book that running into this type of "scarcity" quickly focuses the minds of participants so that they complete the survey carefully.[42] In practice, it also seems to deeply engage users: they typically spend a third longer working on QV surveys than a standard Likert survey, even though the same fraction in both cases completed the survey. Respondents in QV surveys also participate more actively, revising their answers to reflect their preferences much more frequently and often providing feedback that taking the QV survey had helped them learn their own preferences more accurately by forcing them to make difficult, even frustrating tradeoffs.

To test whether QV manages to solve the problems with Likert, in 2016 QDecide's chief data scientist and now professor of mathematics education David Quarfoot, along with several co-authors, ran a nationally representative survey with thousands of participants that took versions of the same poll using Likert, QV, or both depending on which group they were assigned to.[43] Figure 2.4 pictures a representative set of responses, on the question of repealing Obamacare, with the Likert survey on the left (with its signature W-shape) and the results from QV on the right.

Two things are noteworthy. First, QV produces a roughly bell-shaped distribution, the sort of distribution of responses that characterizes most individual preferences. The QV results are thus much more plausible as a representation of population preferences than is the artificial W shape from Likert.[44] Second, while Likert conceals the range of intensity of preferences

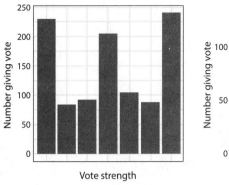 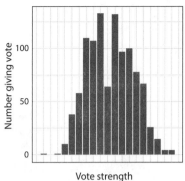

FIGURE 2.4: Participant opinions on Obamacare under a standard Likert (left) and QV (right) survey. "Vote strength" in both graphs represents degree of support (on left) or opposition (on right) for Obamacare.
*Source:* Adapted from David Quarfoot, Douglas von Kohorn, Kevin Slavin, Rory Sutherland, David Goldstein, & Ellen Konar, Quadratic Voting in the Wild: Real People, Real Votes, 172 Pub. Choice 283 (2017), p. 6.

by grouping all, or nearly all, of the responses at the extremes, QV reveals these gradations. QV shows, for example, the greater intensity of preferences for repealing Obamacare, compared to those for retaining it, which helped fuel the success of Republicans in the 2016 election.

A nice illustration of this second point is figure 2.5, which shows the voting patterns for two different voters who expressed the most extreme preference on almost every issue under Likert. The survey involved ten public policy questions, and the respondents in both cases gave in to the temptation, possible under Likert, to say that they cared maximally (either pro or con) about nearly all of them. This is not possible under QV. Under QV the participant on the left showed herself to actually have a reasonably strong interest in a range of issues, though to varying degrees. However, the voter on the right cared about only three issues, and to varying extents. All this richness of individual preference is hidden under Likert, but revealed by QV. Quarfoot and his co-authors show that these

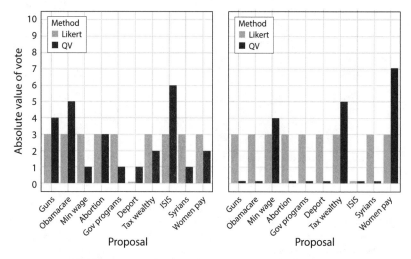

FIGURE 2.5: The differing QV preferences of two participants who both voted at the extremes on almost all issues on Likert.
*Source:* CDE.

additional details predicted the willingness of participants to take actions that were potentially costly to them, indicating that their findings were meaningful rather than spurious. They asked participants if they wanted to receive emails about various issues, and found the likelihood that a participant signed up for emails was predicted by the variation in preference intensity that was revealed in the QV results and lacking in the Likert results. Other research on QV has shown a tight correlation between QV votes and voting turnout intentions on referenda.[45]

Leaders, political campaigns, and political scientists have begun to explore whether using QV to elicit public opinions allows them to more accurately answer the questions so crucial to their jobs: how can we form a platform and reach compromises that will respect the strongly held views of a range of citizens? In the coming years, experiments with QV will offer a proving ground for the practical utility of QV.

## RATING AND SOCIAL AGGREGATION

Rating and social aggregation systems fuel today's digital economy. Reputation systems are the crucial trust mechanisms that allow "sharing economy" services like Airbnb, VRBO, Uber, and Lyft to win consumer acceptance and give providers the confidence to adopt the system.[46] They play a core role in the popular search services offered by Amazon, Google, Apple's app store, and Yelp. Yet a growing body of evidence suggests these systems are badly broken. As noted above, almost all reviews cluster toward five stars, and a few at one star, making the resulting feedback biased and what statisticians call "noisy," that is, not very accurate.[47] Other online platforms, such as Facebook, Reddit, Twitter, and Instagram, gather limited information because they only allow "likes," and other limited forms of response, rather than allowing participants to exhibit exceptional enthusiasm, or distaste, for particular content.

With QV, users could have voice credits that they receive for participation (say, a certain number for every stay, ride, or post) that they then could use to evaluate the performance of others on the system. The cost of votes pro and con would grow quadratically and participants could save their credits for future interactions or use saved credits for those about which they feel more strongly at present. Such a system combines the best of both tipping and rating, creating a real cost to expressing enthusiasm, but also discouraging free-riding and allowing other participants to benefit from the feedback.

A version of this system is being implemented by a social network called Akasha, based on the increasingly prominent Ethereum cryptocurrency.[48] QV fits with the framework of cryptocurrencies, which require formal governance rules to allow for the decentralized management they rely on, so using it also for social aggregation in such a context is natural. However, the exact implementation is unclear at the time of this writing, and not available to the public; much in the world of cryptocurrencies is secretive. However, we hope that broader use of QV in these contexts will provide a more powerful test than political polling of how QV would work if adopted in social settings where norms and values would adapt to its use.

## BROADER APPLICATIONS

The commercial applications of QV do not end there, however. Collective decisions pervade our society and economy. Corporations are governed by groups of shareholders and must respond to the demands of groups of employees.[49] Residential and commercial real estate is frequently governed by cooperatives, in which co-owners vote on issues of common interest. Book groups, warrior guilds in massive multiplayer online video games, unions, clubs, friends choosing a restaurant, start-ups hiring new workers, academic funders allocating grants, crowds funding new products, citizens funding campaigns, and colleagues scheduling a meeting: all must frequently make collective decisions that bind all members.

Most people share their lives in these and other ways. But because no good mechanisms exist for making collective decisions, these aspects of life are often extremely frustrating, leading many people to avoid them when possible. An inconvenient but all too common solution to the agony of arguing with one's fellow co-op members over whether to repair the building's roof this year or next year, is to own one's own house. If a better mechanism could be invented, and be used as a default method of helping people make group decisions across many areas of life, then the shared portions of life would expand and the private portions would contract. QV, based on a platform that allows people to vote in collective choices across many areas of life, would be a step in that direction.

But the real goal is to extend QV to political decision-making. What would such a system look like?

## Democracy Squared

### MULTI-CANDIDATE, SINGLE-WINNER ELECTIONS

Recall that in many 1p1v systems, voters can find themselves in the position of having to vote for the lesser of two evils, leading to the possibility of a candidate everyone dislikes winning based on a cycle of fear of other leading candidates.[50] A recent example of this was the 2016 US presidential election, in which both eventual nominees of major parties were widely loathed, while other members of their parties had broad public support. QV, when properly applied to multi-candidate elections, avoids this possibility.[51] In such a system, voters could cast as many votes as they wish in favor of or against any candidate. The total cost in voice credits would be the sum of the squares of all votes on individual candidates: the quadratic cost kicks in at the candidate, not the election, level.

Why would such a QV system avoid the pitfalls created by strategic voting? Recall that the driving force behind it is that voters feel compelled to vote for one of the two leading candidates to avoid "wasting" their votes. We propose a system in which votes could be cast either in favor of or *against* candidates, and one could vote for (or against) as many candidates as one wishes. As a result of the quadratic pricing, it is cheaper to divide one's credits between votes for a favored candidate and votes against his or her opponent(s), than to spend credits only on the favored candidate. This means that any voter inclined to favor awful candidate A just to spite appalling candidate B would also wish to register her opposition to B in even greater measure. These strategic votes would thus cancel out and sink any two candidates who are widely despised, allowing less hated candidates to rise up. In fact, for any candidate to get positive votes she would have to be more highly regarded than most of the other candidates.[52]

In the 2016 US example, we can guess at what might happen under QV based on Likert surveys on preference intensity for candidates taken during the campaign. A consensus moderate Republican candidate would have been most likely to win under QV among the major candidates considered by the survey.[53] The eventual winner of the election, Donald Trump, would have come in last of all candidates.

Yet beyond this specific result, this logic suggests that QV is not limited to binary referenda, or continuous public goods decisions. For almost any collective decision problem, there is some form of QV that achieves the socially optimal outcome. As such, QV offers a coherent basis for a complete democratic system.

## REPRESENTATIVE DEMOCRACY

Designing a representative system is not within the scope of this book, but we offer a few thoughts here. Voting for representatives under a system of QV could take different forms. Consider, as one of many possible approaches, a system as similar as possible to the US political system, but where elections were conducted using QV. The QV system would operate at the level of the office—at the district level for representatives, at the state level for senators, and at the national level for the president. At every election, a voter could spend as much or as little of her budget on as many votes as she can afford, spread among all of the candidates at all levels—for, against, or zero. This allows voters to focus on the level of government they care about most—perhaps more local in case of people who are rooted to their community, perhaps more national for young, mobile types. The theory behind QV applies to representatives in the same way that it applies to referenda. Under the QV system, the representative will be chosen whose expected performance maximizes the aggregate well-being of voters. Knowing this, candidates will select positions that maximize the welfare of their constituents, just as they choose positions accommodating the preferences of swing voters under majority rule.

In turn, QV could be applied to a representative body itself. Every legislator would receive a certain number of voice credits upon election and could allocate them across the issues most important to her constituents. Representative institutions face the same problem of preference aggregation that exists in the referendum-style votes. Each representative serves a different group of constituents who have different interests. A particular bill will affect those groups in different ways—some greatly, others hardly at all. This means that representatives who seek reelection will also vary in their interests in passage of the bill.

Under the current system, party leaders must bribe, cajole, and threaten legislators. The Emergency Economic Stabilization Act of 2008, which was needed to address the financial crisis, was initially blocked in the US House of Representatives. Leaders were able to pass the bill only after arranging for a range of payoffs, including a reduction in the depreciation schedule for improvements to restaurant buildings; extension of tax credits for solar energy installations; and tax exemptions or subsidies for a number of entities such as film and television producers, rum producers in Puerto Rico and the Virgin Islands, racetrack facilities, manufacturers of wool products and toy wooden arrows. Yet for each ugly "success story" such as this, there is a corrupt bargain that harms the country and causes years of gridlock. Under QV, legislators whose constituents care little about some legislation would save their credits for a future vote, while those whose constituents care a lot would be decisive pro or con.

While a better basis for collective decisions, QV, like 1p1v, is more a foundational paradigm for collective decision-making than a literal rule. Many institutions would be built around and incorporate QV in a variety of ways that are hard to imagine. But we hope the potential of QV is visible.

## NATURE OF CURRENCY AND SCOPE OF TRADE

The survey application of QV does not allow a full expression of preference intensity because there is no way for participants who care about *all* the issues more than other people to reveal this fact. Some people don't care much about politics, others care a lot. The latter group might be willing to give up something else they care about—money, for example—in order to have greater influence than the first group. But the survey doesn't allow this.

Consider an economic, private goods analogy. If trade is only possible among, say, fruit, every individual will get her favorite fruits but there will be no way for people who produce fruit to sell it to get other necessaries. The division of labor and the benefits of trade depend on broadening the scope of trade. The same is true in QV: the more uses that can be made of voice credits, the more benefits QV brings by allowing individuals more freedom to choose how and where to use their influence.

Of course, such freedom carries risks. Just as some people foolishly squander their savings on goods and services, allowing saving and spending of saved (or perhaps even borrowed) voting credits could leave some individuals vulnerable. But in general, we believe that, with appropriate regulations, the broader the scope of use of voice credits, the better.

## A Radical Market for Reasoned Compromise

How much value would QV generate? In general it is much harder to estimate the effect of political than economic institutions on inequality and growth. The only serious attempt to do so that we know of estimates the effect of democracy on growth, and finds that the introduction of democracy to a country on average causes a 20% increase in national income.[54] While there is no reason to expect QV to bring precisely the gains over 1p1v that democracy brought over pre-democratic forms of government, this seems a reasonable benchmark. As we have highlighted, democracy as currently practiced is highly imperfect. It seems plausible that QV will improve, at least in terms of its effects on economic productivity, over existing democracy as much as democracy did over the average system it replaced.

But that understates the economic benefits. Despite centuries of progress, markets for public goods are hopelessly deficient. If we are right about QV, then it should bring markets for public goods in line with markets for private goods, with incalculable benefits for all citizens.

Yet, as with the COST, some of the most powerful ways QV could reshape our society are the hardest to quantify: its effect on social institutions and cultural imagination. While perverse election outcomes, gridlocked legislative votes, and protests over "judicial activism" are the most visible manifestations of our dysfunctional politics, they may not be the most important ones. Even more insidious for our political system are polarization, a political discourse plagued by sound bites and platitudes (or worse, hate speech), a sense of helplessness among much of the public, rigid political boundaries that poorly align with the actual views of the public, resentment of political elites, and decay in public trust.[55]

The influence of QV on such problems would be indirect and hard to predict. Yet there are reasons to be hopeful. QV empowers citizens to express their views in a fundamentally richer and deeper way than 1p1v allows. It encourages citizens and politicians not just to try to win over poorly informed swing voters or to motivate disaffected members of their own base, but to engage with people who have different views. It would allow citizens to focus their voting on topics of their true passion and knowledge, rather than force them to vote on issues on which they feel ill-informed and thus liable to conform to stereotypes and party identification.

Because QV penalizes extreme views by making them costlier to express, it encourages moderation and compromise. By offering broader freedom, subject to a budget constraint, it gives citizens greater responsibility and control over collective decisions. In the same way that participation in public protests often gives citizens a sense of ownership over policy choices, QV would offer citizens the chance to feel their voice had been more fully heard, both helping them win on the issue most important to them and reconciling them to the losses they suffer. These features are much like the social effects of market economies for private goods. Because citizens tend to resent and feel coerced by rationing in planned economies, they experience the abandonment of planning as a blossoming of freedom, as was so clear with the collapse of communism in the 1980s and 1990s. When people have the freedom to choose what to spend their money on, they are afforded a sense of dignity and responsibility for the things they have and choose to forgo. A political culture based on such a market mentality could give people a stronger sense of dignity and responsibility in politics.

As with the COST, the most enthralling potential benefits of QV are the most speculative and concern the way that it would change our relationship with our fellow citizens. Most people live in urban settings and interact with others over telecommunications networks, implying their well-being is closely tied to and influenced by others around them. In such large-scale, connected societies, it is usually easier to provide benefits to many people as a group than to individuals separately. Information is easily shared by many; applications for social interaction have little value if used only by a few; public transport shared by many is often more economical than individual vehicles. Yet such large-scale services at present are either provided by monopolistic corporations or by dysfunctional public authorities. Fear of the failures of these providers often leads us to wastefully retreat from public life behind the walls of our homes, our gated communities, our private servers, and our individual cars.

As early as the 1950s, economist John Kenneth Galbraith called this the paradox of "public poverty" among "private affluence": while children are "admirably equipped with television sets," "schools were often severely overcrowded and . . . underprovided."[56] He complained that a "family which takes its air-conditioned . . . automobile out for a tour passes through cities that are badly paved, made hideous by litter, blighted buildings and posts for wires that long since should have been put underground."

QV offers a different path, toward a balance of affluence between private and public at all levels. It shows that the public goods that we all share can be provided as efficiently and smoothly as the market provides us smartphones and mattresses. It gives us a path toward truly shared and cooperative lives in our local communities, our online social networks, and our national governments. It allows a world where our choices between the private and richly varying levels of public life are determined by the natural development of social relationships rather than by our fear of the incompetence or corruption of collective institutions.

# 3

# Uniting the World's Workers

## REBALANCING THE INTERNATIONAL ORDER TOWARD LABOR

The town of Amiens was not Delphine's image of France. Television access was intermittent during her childhood in Haiti. She would crowd into her neighbors' creaking shack every few evenings to watch TV. The images of Parisian cafes or of chic life along the Côte d'Azur brightened her bleak life. Then the terrible earthquake came and her family, like many others, was forced to head to Port-au-Prince. There, a television was more a spectacle for a crowd than a daily escape.

Delphine's childhood ended when she was twelve. Work was hard, responsibilities exhausting, and fear of starvation never far away in that harsh and overcrowded city. But those TV images of beautiful women smoking cigarettes, of men more likely to carry flowers than guns, of fresh-baked croissants—they never left her.

On the way home from the trash pile she picked through each day, she met Fabiola. Fabiola was something of a queen in the camp. She spoke perfect French, worked in the French-speaking hotel downtown, and was feared but respected by others in the camp. But Delphine wasn't afraid of her. All she wanted was to sit every evening for fifteen minutes at Fabiola's feet and practice her French. She knew she would one day be able to match the tones of those actresses on TV. One day she would greet a stranger with a perfect "bonjour" and they would think she was from Africa, not Haiti.

So when French recruiting agents began combing through her camp for the few whose French they could understand, Delphine pushed her way to the front of the line. The agents warned her of the difficulties and dangers that awaited her, but they all seemed nothing in comparison to what she had already gone through. They explained that she would be able to take home only a few thousand euros a year after her basic rations and tiny room were paid for. A few thousand euros? This was more than Delphine had earned in the last decade.

Amiens was not Paris, though. Rustic charm it had aplenty, but few people resembled the glamorous characters in *Plus belle la vie*, her favorite soap opera. Delphine tried to avoid the temptations of downtown in any case: in one night there, she could easily lose money she knew would buy her mother and brother back home a toilet, a house, a business. The reborn factory on the town's edge was most of her life. Her taciturn host Fabian would drive her and the three other Haitians his family hosted out to the factory each morning.

The arrival of the Haitians meant almost as much to Fabian as it meant to them. He was a manager in the factory now, almost twenty years after he had been laid off from his job when the factory closed. Labor costs had been too high to employ workers like him at prevailing French wages, and the work had moved to Vietnam. Fabian had always hated migrants and voted for the *Front National*. When the reformist government of Emmanuel Macron adopted what he was sure would be a disastrous new migration policy, he had no way to make ends meet other than giving a go to sponsoring migrants. The €15,000 his family made from hosting the Haitians, after paying to put up the small and cramped house on the edge of their family's lot and give them a meal every night, finally made up for the income he had lost when he switched to waiting tables. The migrants had even given him advice to help the restaurant where he waited tables improve its cuisine. Plantains added a smooth sweetness to the restaurant's signature duck pâté and helped distinguish the restaurant from the standard regional cuisine.

But what really changed his life was his new job at the factory. The fresh supply of Haitian labor had persuaded the entrepreneurs who had bought up his old workplace to reopen it, and Fabian's familiarity with the Haitians made him a perfect manager. It was also a safer job, a cleaner job, a job with more dignity, power, and respect. He had hated so many Muslim immigrants who he had felt were changing the culture of the country, but he came to have a paternalistic and condescending love for the Haitians he managed and hosted. Their love of France, their gratitude, their struggles to adapt and learn . . . they all melted Fabian's jaded heart.

Fabian was therefore much sadder than he let on when Delphine decided, after ten years, to return home. Having earned enough in those years to finally open the hotel that Fabiola had always dreamed about, she was resolved to build a piece of France in the Caribbean. She had learned so much and was glad for the trips she had been able to take, but France was not her home and the opportunities opening in Haiti these days made it the right place for her.

Globalization has transformed many aspects of society and yet left other parts virtually untouched. Foreign products surround us. Consider the goods and services most Americans use: our clothes are made in Vietnam, our mortgages owned by Chinese companies, our luxuries imported from Europe, and our cars made in Latin America. Foreign tourists swarm our cities, and talented foreign workers and immigrants populate our start-ups, banks, and universities. Globalization has increased foreign trade, capital flows, tourism, and the migration of highly skilled workers.

Yet, for all the controversies about refugees and (in the United States) illegal immigration, migration of people with ordinary skills proceeds at a trickle. From the standpoint of economic theory, this "migration imbalance," as we will call it, is puzzling. Economists believe that global wealth increases when *all* factors of production—goods, services, capital, labor—are allowed to flow across borders to the locations where they can be most efficiently employed. What is special about migration (a term that we will henceforth use to refer to migration of ordinary workers rather than highly skilled workers and tourists)?

## The Origins of Free Trade

Long-distance movements of goods and tools have been a feature of human civilization since the beginning of agriculture. The Mediterranean trade was central to Athenian, Carthaginian, and Roman development. Mohammad was a trader and the trading routes of the Muslim world and on to Asia via the Silk Road helped maintain the light of civilization through the Middle Ages in the West.[1]

Mass migrations were also a feature of early history. Many of the great empires were established and later destroyed by nomadic tribes that flooded from the North Asian steppe southward, westward, and eastward. The Germans, the Huns, the Mongols, the Turks, and other groups moved, often violently, through established civilizations to find, conquer, and eventually settle more fertile and civilized lands, only to be attacked by the next wave of nomads.

The advent of long-range sea power in Europe in the fifteenth century brought this era to an end. By this time, most of the planet was occupied by sedentary agricultural societies. Europeans discovered sea and land routes to most of the world and colonized regions viewed as having weak or "inferior" civilizations. Trade across settled homelands, and plunder of colonies, expanded as the skill of navigators improved. Trade became a leading question of state.

During the sixteenth and seventeenth centuries, the dominant philosophy uniting colonialism and trade was *mercantilism*. Mercantilists believed that sovereigns should try to sell goods abroad while importing as little as possible, allowing them to accumulate capital, ideally in the form of hard currency. To stimulate wealth accumulation, mercantilists advocated state control of the economy, including subsidies for exports and taxes on imports. Some mercantilists, such as *Robinson Crusoe* author Daniel Defoe, advocated unrestricted immigration, hoping that migrants would compete with native workers to drive down wages.[2] For the same reason, they were wary of emigration, which reduced the size of the national labor force and hence its ability to produce exports.[3]

Mercantilism reflected the interests of the ruling classes of the time.[4] Mercantilist policies burdened ordinary people but generated savings for the state that rulers could use to achieve military supremacy and maintain public order. Those rulers saw their populations as resources to be exploited rather than citizens whom they served.

During the late eighteenth century, many of the Radical thinkers we discussed in earlier chapters developed a new theory of trade. Bentham, Smith, and David Hume shifted the focus of economic analysis away from the interest of sovereigns in accumulating wealth and toward the desire of ordinary people to enjoy prosperity. They believed that economic freedom of many kinds (to exchange across borders, to borrow and lend, to repurpose and sell land and other capital, etc.) was critical to maximizing the total welfare that a nation's economy could deliver to its citizens. With their focus on the benefits of markets, they embraced free international trade and opposed monopolies and state-imposed restrictions of domestic markets like price controls. The Radical Market of the time was one that extended beyond the borders of nations.

## Before Migration Mattered

While the early Radicals passionately advocated free trade, they said little about migration.[5] This might seem odd: the logic of free migration and free trade is the same, namely, that the expansion of economic openness generates wealth for nearly everyone. Some of these thinkers also mentioned, in passing, that they supported the free movement of people, not just goods. For example, both Smith and David Ricardo argued for free mobility of workers from the countryside to the city and across occupations, and in an offhand way remarked that the same should apply across borders. They also emphasized the importance of the free movement of ideas. Yet free trade overwhelmingly dominated free migration in their thought.

One reason for the emphasis of trade over migration was that in the eighteenth and nineteenth centuries, the gains from trade were far more important than the gains from migration. The reason is that while different nations went through periods of relative prosperity and decline, persistent differences in mass living standards across countries were unknown until the late nineteenth century. Even the most extreme gaps, such as between China and the United Kingdom, were only a factor of 3. This contrasts with the 10 to 1 gap that opened up by the 1950s.[6]

A natural way to measure inequality is to determine the percentage by which an average individual's income could be increased if income were equally distributed.[7] For example, suppose there are two individuals, one with income of $1 million and one with income of $1,000. If we equalized income, the first person's income would fall to $500,500, or nearly 50%. The second person's income would rise to $500,500, an increase of 500 times, or 50,000%. Thus, equalizing incomes would cause a large average percentage increase in income of slightly less than 24,975%.[8] By contrast, this measure of inequality would be 0 for a society in which everyone has equal income. The higher the number, the more unequal the society.

Figure 3.1 shows the evolution of inequality, both in total, and across and within countries, from 1820 to 2011. Inequality across countries increased from about 7% in 1820 to about 70% in 1980. This cross-country inequality has retreated to about

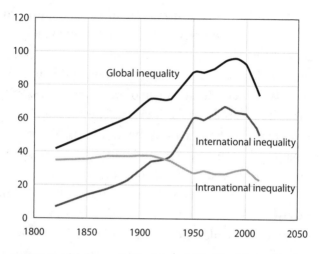

**FIGURE 3.1:** Global inequality, both in total (black) and decomposed into between (dark gray) and within (light gray) country components from 1820 to 2011.

*Source:* This series is based on a merger of the data of François Bourguignon and Christian Morrisson, Inequality Among World Citizens: 1820–1992, 92 *American Economic Review* 4 (2002), and Branko Milanovic, Global Inequality of Opportunity: How Much of Our Income Is Determined by Where We Live?, 97 *Review of Econonomics & Statistics* 2 (2015), performed by Branko Milanovic as a favor to us.

50% since that year, thanks to the rapid development of China and India. On the other hand, average inequality within countries has changed gradually over this period. It increased from about 35% in 1820 to about 38% at its peak just before World War I and then declined to a low of 27% in the 1970s. Since then it has fallen a bit more, to 24%. The average of within-country inequality declined because the increase in inequality within wealthy countries, which we highlighted in the introduction, was offset by the reduction of inequality within many poor countries.

Together these patterns imply that inequality across countries has gone from a relatively insignificant phenomenon in the grand scheme of global inequality, accounting for only a little more than 10% of global inequality in the 1820s, to being the dominant source of global inequality, accounting for two-thirds or more in the second half of the twentieth century and still today accounting for 60–70% depending on whose measurements you rely upon.[9]

This puts into quantitative perspective the very different world we confront today, compared to the one nineteenth-century political economists faced. Theirs was a world where a farmer or factory worker in one country enjoyed a standard of living similar to that of a farmer or factory worker in any other country, and all were much worse off than aristocrats. Ours is a world where a child born to an average family in India or Brazil faces a much more impoverished life than a child born to a family in the United States or Germany. Moreover, in modern developed economies, a family of average income enjoys a standard of living similar to that of the very wealthiest families in poor countries. Theirs was a world in which migration did most people little good; ours is one in which migration can be a primary route to well-being and prosperity for most people in the world.

This is not to say that migration, even on large scales, was unknown in the earlier period. Merchants and aristocrats traveled, but rarely to migrate permanently to another country. They did, however, meet with foreigners, learn foreign languages, and intermarry with foreigners. A cosmopolitan outlook emerged that distinguishes the upper from the lower classes to this very day. Leading families also married across national boundaries in order to create alliances, to the extent that kings and queens of countries often were not even nationals, and sometimes did not even speak the national language very well.

On the lower end of the scale of fortune, slaves were abducted from Africa and transported to countries in the Middle East and the American colonies. Poorer Europeans, oppressed by governments or by a lack of property, would migrate to rough-hewn colonies for the opportunity to eventually enter the propertied class. In exchange, they would often sell themselves into indenture arrangements where they would owe service to a master for several years in exchange for the cost of the passage. The hard life of labor available on colonial plantations was hardly much of a lure, one reason that planters resorted to the slave trade.

In such a world, it was natural for the Radicals to focus on the freeing of markets for goods and capital from aristocratic privilege, such as the ending of the British Corn Laws, or ending unfree migration in the form of the slave trade rather than emphasizing free migration.

First, putting aside the important but limited exception of migration to colonial possessions (starting with the New World centuries earlier), free migration would not have significantly increased the well-being of ordinary people. No one benefited from moving from one country to another if he or she was a proletarian or landless peasant in both. Second, migration was relatively unrestricted across countries, and controls upon it were scarcely enforced since there was little demand to migrate and because the primitive, risky, and uncomfortable nature of transportation at the time deterred all but the most desperate or ambitious.[10] Third, free trade across countries could break the monopolistic control of landlords over crucial national resources, greatly enhancing national wealth and shifting its distribution from the feudal aristocracy to capitalists and laborers.

Major intellectual debate about migration began only in the late nineteenth and early twentieth centuries. In the United States, debate was stimulated by the enormous waves of immigration provoked by strife and famine in Europe, and the lure of newly discovered gold, as well as rapid economic development, which attracted millions from Asia as well as Europe. By this time, attitudes among economists toward migration had become more complicated, partly in response to public sentiment.

Karl Marx, for example, worried that strategic use of Irish migration by British capitalists divided the international working class and undermined socialism.[11] Radicals and progressives in many countries, including John Stuart Mill and Henry George, who sometimes dabbled with ugly racist and eugenic arguments, shared these sentiments.[12] In the early twentieth century, a decisive shift in attitudes toward migration took place. With the growing affordability of travel across continents and oceans, and the increasing differentials of wages across countries, the economic advantages of migration greatly improved, not least for displaced populations following World War I. The United States slammed its doors in the late teens and 1920s. In Europe, with the rise of ethno-nationalistic sentiments, countries tried to keep out those who were thought to pollute their cultural heritage or racial gene pool.

## Globalization

These ethno-nationalist sentiments peaked at the outbreak of World War II, which in turn transformed the global order. After the war, Western leaders tried to build an international system that would generate prosperity and prevent economic chaos and nationalist conflict from igniting another war. Among wealthy countries, there was a renewed commitment to open trade and international and regional governance institutions. Starting in the 1980s and 1990s, these international commitments spread, encompassing China and other parts of Asia, Latin America, and Africa. But, while significant intellectual and political resources were used for the building of trade and investment institutions, migration received little consideration.

The postwar economic system stood on three pillars: international trade, monetary and macroeconomic stabilization, and development finance. Each pillar was represented by an institution: the General Agreements on Tariffs and Trade or GATT, the International Monetary Fund or IMF, and the World Bank. The GATT tried to establish an equitable baseline for trade among all participants that would supplement the web of bilateral trade agreements and unilateral tariff policies of the antebellum period. It was gradually strengthened in successive rounds of negotiation, culminating in the Uruguay Round, which created the World Trade Organization, or WTO, in the early 1990s.

This patchwork of international cooperation was mirrored at the regional level, and in the case of Europe these regional institutions became especially strong. Trade agreements spread throughout the continent and gradually strengthened into a web of economic regulation that culminated in the creation of the European Union (EU), followed by the establishment of the Eurozone monetary union involving most of the EU member states. While it never cohered into a federal government structure, European integration moved substantially beyond the purely commercial institutions of the global order to establish substantive governance in many areas of European economic and social policy.

Throughout this period, gaping and growing inequalities between rich and poor countries, together with dramatic advances in transportation and information technology, stirred citizens of poor countries to migrate to wealthier ones. These aspirations were particularly palpable where poor and rich countries met in close quarters: the Rio Grande, which separates the United States and Mexico; between Western and Eastern Europe; and across the two sides of the Mediterranean. In Europe, governments encouraged migration for postwar reconstruction; in the United States, the government permitted Mexicans to cross the border to engage in seasonal agricultural labor. But political opposition to these policies ensured that they were temporary and often involved workarounds and winking at illegal immigration. In Germany, for example, the government allowed Turkish workers to settle in the country but did not grant them citizenship; in the United States, legal immigration programs were replaced by illegal immigration since the border was not controlled. But whether legal or illegal, migration never reached the level that would satisfy demand in the host countries and the supply of people willing and able to migrate.[13]

In Europe, migration between EU member states was institutionalized. Citizens were permitted to move to any member state for a job. But the law did not produce as much migration as was hoped. Linguistic and cultural barriers kept most people at home, and income differences between European countries were modest by global standards, reducing the incentive for migration. Where migration did take place, it typically involved movement from lower-wage Eastern European countries like Poland to higher-wage Western countries, including France and the UK, which generated a political backlash in the host states. Additional tensions were created in 2015 and 2016 when Europe grudgingly accepted a massive influx of refugees from war-torn Syria and other countries in the Middle East and southwest Asia. Guest worker systems in other parts of the world, including the states of the Persian Gulf, have been much more successful, as we discuss below, but overall the amount of migration throughout the world has remained limited relative to the potential gains.

Together these institutional developments have created an imbalanced global order. Capital, goods, and highly educated labor flows rapidly across borders, generating significant wealth, while less educated workers tend to stay at home. These weaknesses in globalization have long been recognized by "antiglobalization" activists, though not always expressed in precise economic terms.[14] As leftist Latin American journalist Eduardo Galeano put it, "We must not confuse globalization with 'internationalism' . . . One thing is the free movement of peoples, the other of money. This can be seen . . . (at) the border between Mexico and the United States which hardly exists as far as the flow of money and goods is concerned. Yet it stands as a kind of Berlin Wall . . . when it comes to stopping people from getting across."[15] Those promoting globalization, with their focus on capital rather than on ordinary people, failed to ensure that welfare gains would be widely shared.

## The Migration Imperative

There is a consensus that the economic gain from further opening international trade in goods is minimal. Studies by the World Bank and prominent trade economists find that eliminating all remaining barriers to international trade in goods would increase global output by only a small amount, 0.3–4.1%. For global investment, the most optimistic estimate in the literature finds a 1.7% increase in global income from the elimination of barriers to capital mobility.[16] Many believe that liberalization of international capital markets has gone too far. Three top IMF economists recently argued that even liberalization that has already taken place has brought limited gains to economies while generating inequality and instability.[17]

At the same time, the benefits of liberalizing migration have dramatically expanded. Sharp reductions in transportation costs have made the natural barriers to migration *de minimus* compared to the potential gains. On the other hand, the potential economic benefits of migration have exploded. A typical Mexican migrant moving to the United States increases her annual earnings from roughly $4,000 to roughly $14,000, and Mexico is a quite wealthy country by global standards. Potential gains from migration from poor countries to Europe and the United States, especially if language barriers are low (as in the case of Haiti and France, for example), would involve gains of as much as ten times, involving tens of thousands of dollars per migrant.

To take an extreme but illuminating example, imagine that the countries of the Organisation for Economic Co-operation and Development (OECD), the club of wealthy countries, were to accept enough migrants to double their population, presently at 1.3 billion. This would move roughly 20% of the global population to the OECD. Suppose too that each migrant on average created income gains of $11,000. This would constitute an increase on average of roughly $2,200 for every person on the planet. Given that global income per capita is approximately $11,000, this is roughly a 20% increase in global income. If historical experience is any guide, gains to those who stay in poor countries would be equally dramatic, as most migrants remit a large fraction of their income to the countries they came from.[18] In sharp contrast to trade, these gains have transformative potential for global well-being, if they can be harnessed and shared.[19]

## Why Not Just Expand Existing Migration?

Some scholars who are aware of these numbers have declared that opening borders is the only morally acceptable response. If countries allowed unlimited immigration, then the poor workers in capital-starved countries would migrate to wealthy countries like the United States, where their wages would be much higher. While the huge surge of migration would reduce the wages of workers in wealthy countries, global well-being would increase enormously.

The idea is not as farfetched as it might seem. The borders of the United States were open for more than half of its history, and the effects were as theory predicts. Migrants benefited from higher wages and Americans benefited from the migrants, who helped build railroads and canals, who worked in mines and on farms and in factories. The social problems brought on by migration were often severe—including a considerable amount of civil strife—but manageable, and over the long term the country prospered. But today, open borders are impractical both economically and politically.

In their famous 1941 treatise, "Protection and Real Wages," Wolfgang Stolper and Paul Samuelson (who we met in the previous chapter) investigated the effect of international trade in goods or labor on the incomes of various people within different countries.[20] While trade between a pair of countries always increases the aggregate wealth of both countries, it can have important redistributive effects. Trade tends to benefit the factors of production that a nation has in relative abundance and to hurt those it has in relatively scarce supply. Wealthy countries, by definition, have a greater relative abundance of capital as compared to labor than do poor countries. It is thus natural that trade and migration should both benefit capitalists in wealthy countries and laborers in poor countries at the expense of laborers in wealthy countries and capitalists in poor countries.

While the logic of the Stolper-Samuelson Theorem is widely accepted among economists, the exact extent to which various categories of workers are harmed or benefited by immigration is more complex. There is significant evidence that immigration reduces the wages of native workers whose backgrounds are similar to those of migrants. For example, illegal immigration to the United States from Mexico and Central America tends to hurt native workers with low education and weak language skills.[21] However, the effects of migration on the broader labor markets are murkier. Some scholars believe that the native workers are in aggregate harmed, albeit only to a limited extent.[22] Others argue that effects are negligible or even that most workers may benefit because migrants buy more goods, which native workers produce, or take the lowest rungs on the employment ladder, pushing some native workers up into better-paying supervisory roles.[23]

These small and mixed effects are dwarfed by the large benefits migration brings to the migrants themselves and their employers.[24] Moreover, the fiscal structure of migration prevents significant sharing of these benefits through government and may even impose costs on domestic workers. The nature of and reasons for this arrangement differ between the United States and Europe.

In the United States, the tax system is limited in its progressivity and effectively excludes a huge number of immigrants, those who are undocumented. While high-skilled, well-educated legal migrants are net contributors to the tax system in the United States, because of the low tax rates on labor and capital income in the United States, such migrants do not make significant contributions that directly benefit native workers through the fiscal system. Many start businesses that generate employment opportunities,[25] but these opportunities are in high-growth, entrepreneurial sectors of the economy that are geographically concentrated in prosperous metropolitan regions, away from where most workers live in the United States. Together these considerations mean that few native workers see large, direct benefits from high-skilled migration.

Most low-skilled migrants work outside formal channels of employment. They tend to pay few taxes. Furthermore, because most of these migrants come from poor countries and have indigent families in their homelands, they send much of their earnings back to the poor countries from which they come, recycling less of their earnings into local economies than native workers at similar income levels. Thus, migrants make at most a very modest contribution to public coffers relative to the benefits they and their employers gain from their migration, and some studies even suggest migrants may be a modest net fiscal drain on the state.[26] Patterns in the UK resemble those in the United States, with low-skilled migrants from Eastern Europe taking the place of those from south of the border in the United States, though in smaller numbers and with a smaller gain.[27]

In contrast to the United States, European countries other than the UK have highly progressive systems of capital and labor taxation that allow the broad public to benefit from the successes of migrants. However, because of these tax systems, because the Continent no longer hosts the world's greatest universities, and because the Continent has been less successful in fostering entrepreneurship than the United States, fewer high-skilled migrants relocate to Europe than to the United States.

On the low end of the skill distribution, illegal migration to Europe in large numbers is a relatively recent phenomenon dating back only a few years to the migrant crisis triggered by the Syrian Civil War. Much of legal low-skilled migration comes from Eastern Europe. Most low-skilled non-Europeans in Europe either hail from distant former colonies or are refugees taken in for primarily humanitarian rather than economic reasons. These migrants tend to be significantly poorer than those coming to the United States. Furthermore, continental European countries have a more generous set of social benefits, transfers, and public services than the United States. Because migrants are generally entitled to equal access to these benefits, low-skilled migrants are a significant drain on public finances in Europe in a way that they are not in the United States.

Underfunding of public services in Europe has contributed to these tensions. Many Europeans are not just abstractly aware of the possibility that migrants strain social services, but also see with their own eyes migrants competing for access to these services. Because of the historical homogeneity of many continental European countries, this competition is visually striking because migrants are easily recognizable by skin color or religious practice. In short, both the impression and to some extent the reality European workers' experience is of migrants acting as an added burden on public services and a weak economy.

While one might assume that natives living in areas with the highest migrant populations object to migration more than other people do, social science evidence is mixed. Often it is in the rural and economically depressed regions where few migrants reside that opposition to migration is strongest.[28] Workers in such areas see migration adding to economic vibrancy in other communities, but not in their own. They gain none of the ancillary social and cultural benefits that dynamic city-dwellers gain from migration, of increased variety in food, color in urban life, or exposure to other cultures that can expand career opportunities. Instead, they see the rest of their country moving in directions that distance it from their experience in ways that increase their isolation and consignment to the cultural periphery.

Let us sum up. While migration offers enormous advantages to the migrants themselves and their families back home, to employers and owners of capital, and to the high-skilled workers who they complement and live among, migration offers few benefits to and imposes some costs on most workers in wealthy countries, who are already left behind by the forces of trade, automation, and the rising power of concentrated finance. Coupled with natural human instincts toward tribalism, which have been stirred up by nativist politicians, broad and growing political opposition to migration has set in. Majorities are unlikely to support migration policies that do not benefit most citizens. In the United States, the elites who controlled government and supported migration managed to evade political opposition by refraining from enforcement of immigration laws, but in doing so they set the stage for a populist backlash.[29] In this sense, slogans such as "America First" and "*on est chez nous*" (this is our home), while offensive to many, capture an inescapable aspect of political reality.

## Auctioning Visas?

Most migration to OECD countries is controlled by government bureaucrats or private employers, who can apply for visas for high-skilled workers whom they want to hire. Another portion of the immigration system allows for immigration of close family members of citizens (especially in the United States) and for people of the national ethnic stock (especially in European countries). These systems are to a large extent top-down and statist or controlled by concentrated economic interests like employers. It is thus hardly surprising that they benefit employers and migrants the most. In short, the system of migration suffers from the same problems as our economy and democracy: a combination of inequity and often arbitrary government discretion.

In the previous two chapters, we have seen that auctions offer a simple framework for replacing such systems, though they often need to be adapted to practical considerations. The same is true of immigration. In an insightful 2010 lecture, the late Nobel Laureate Gary Becker proposed a simple auction-based system for migration: set a quota for migration and auction off the rights to enter the country to the highest bidder.[30] The revenue raised by this Radical Market could be used to fund public goods or a universal social dividend, as we saw with common ownership of property in chapter 1.

As with the simplest auction-based ideas of the previous chapters, this scheme has a number of limitations that we will address. However, notice that it immediately addresses a number of weaknesses in the present migration system.

First, it ensures that a large share of the gains from migration accrue to ordinary people rather than businesses. Hence, it would advance equality. Second, and as a consequence, it would soften political opposition to migration. Third, the program would greatly reduce the role of government bureaucrats and instead harness the knowledge of the migrants who best understand the economic prospects open to them. A stream of recent economic research has shown that migration systems that rely most heavily on bureaucratic judgments of migrants' merits (so-called points-based systems, where migrants with educational credentials and the like receive priority) tend to fail.[31] Systems that put employers in charge seem to work better than points-based systems but, as we have noted, allocate gains mostly to employers. An auction-based system avoids both of these pitfalls.

An auction-based system could raise a remarkable amount of revenue to improve the living standards of ordinary citizens in wealthy countries while still delivering enormous benefits to migrants. Suppose that OECD countries accepted enough migration to increase their populations by a third. Suppose too that migrants on average bid $6,000 per year for a visa. This sum seems plausible given that even illegal Mexican migrants to the United States gain more than $11,000 annually under the current highly inefficient system. Average GDP per capita in OECD countries is $35,000, so this proposal would boost the national income of a typical OECD country by almost 6%, comparable to their growth in real income per person in the last five years.

Imagine that the gains from this growth are equally distributed among all citizens. This would effectively reduce the share of the top 1% of income earners by 6% as only a small part of this gain would accrue to the top 1%. This equals a reduction by about 1 percentage point, going an eighth of the way toward restoring the trough of inequality midcentury in the United States. Median household income for a family of four in the United States is about $50,000. Such a family would earn roughly $8,000 under such a system and thus would see their income rise by about 15%, roughly equal to all inflation-adjusted gains for such families since the 1970s.

Gains to migrants would be even more dramatic. Depending on who migrated, an increase of $5,000 (the $11,000 gain minus the $6,000 bid) of income could increase migrant income by many times, given that most migrants would come from countries with typical annual incomes of a few thousand dollars or less. Under this scenario, about half the dollar gains would accrue to OECD countries and about half to migrants and those they remit funds to. Because the OECD represents half of global income, the global economy would grow roughly 6–7% as well.

Nonetheless, the auction system in its purest form has several weaknesses. Clearly, money is not the only thing that matters in migration. Cultural fit to local communities, likelihood of committing crimes or disobeying the terms of a visa, and the willingness of employers and host country citizens to welcome a migrant are all crucial components of the social value of the migrant. A pure auction ignores these factors. Nor is money the only factor that is important to sustaining political support for migration. Positive cultural, social, and economic interactions at a personal level between migrants and natives is critical. A simple auction would do little to ensure this occurred. But, drawing inspiration from the auction and important features of existing migration law, we can formulate a solution.

## Democratizing Visas

In the United States, under the H1-B program employers "sponsor" migrant workers. Google can hire a software engineer from another country (say, India) by obtaining a visa for the worker, which allows the worker to reside in the United

States for three years, renewable for a second three-year period, subject to various restrictions (including the limited number of available visas). Family members can also sponsor visas under the Family Reunification policy. Our proposal, which we call the Visas Between Individuals Program (VIP), would extend this system so that any ordinary person could sponsor a migrant worker, albeit with some adjustments to reflect the difference in circumstances, and for an indefinite period rather than a renewable three-year period. We would allow people to sponsor one migrant worker at any moment in time. This could either bring a rotating cast of temporary guest workers (one at any time) as in our opening vignette or one permanent migrant over a lifetime.

The major difference, of course, is that sponsors are no longer necessarily employers or family. When Google sponsors a migrant worker, it gives her an office and (probably) helps her find a home and settle in the community. The worker contributes to Google's bottom line by writing code, and Google compensates the worker out of that surplus. Google also employs an experienced bureaucracy to fill out a lot of the paperwork and deal with immigration authorities, and also search for and evaluate foreign workers who possess the desired skills. The worker flourishes in Google's multicultural workforce where people are evaluated according to their merit, not their race, ethnicity, or national origin.

By contrast, Anthony is a recently laid-off construction worker who lives in Akron, Ohio. He has a high school education, a small amount of savings, and limited prospects. He has not met many foreigners, and feels a bit of resentment toward a group of Middle Easterners who recently moved into his neighborhood and opened restaurants that serve food that Anthony does not like much. (He does acknowledge, however, that they have brought new life to his neighborhood and many of them have taken jobs that he wouldn't touch.) Anthony learns of a new program offered by the State Department that allows him to sponsor a migrant worker and earn money in the process. Anthony is interested, but what's in it for him? Unlike Google, he can't simply place the worker in an office and expect the worker to generate revenue for him.

Using a website operated by a company that contracts with the State Department, Anthony describes the sort of worker he is willing to sponsor. English is a necessity. Anthony asks for someone in his twenties, who has worked in the construction industry, and has no criminal record or health problems. Anthony knows from job contacts that several new construction projects are being planned on the outskirts of Akron, and hopes to place a foreign worker at one of them. And if this falls through, Anthony also wants to start a handyman business and can use the worker as an employee. The website puts Anthony into contact with a Nepalese man named Bishal. Bishal has worked as a guest worker in the United Arab Emirates, where he improved his patchy English. Anthony interviews Bishal over the web, where he spells out his plan, and the two agree that Bishal will work for Anthony for one year in the United States for $12,000 (likely to be as much as five times what Bishal can earn in Nepal if he is lucky enough to get a job). Anthony will need to use his savings to buy Bishal a plane ticket. They agree that Bishal will reside in Anthony's spare room.

We can, of course, tell an optimistic story about what would happen next, and our opening vignette offers one such story, but we are under no illusions that every story must end happily. In the happy story, Bishal arrives in the United States with the clothes on his back but little else. But Bishal, who has experienced hardships that few Americans can even imagine, flourishes. For the first month, he works as a handyman in the neighborhood. Anthony charges customers just $10 per hour for Bishal, and so after paying Bishal $1,000 for the month, Anthony barely breaks even. But then Bishal obtains the construction job. The construction company realizes that Bishal has some significant skills that he obtained in the construction industry in the UAE, and ultimately pays him $20,000 for the remaining eleven months. Anthony collects the $8,000 balance. Meanwhile, Anthony and Bishal get to know each other. Perhaps they become friends. Bishal helps around the house, and Anthony acquires a taste for Nepalese food.

Of course, it need not turn out this way. What if Bishal cannot find work? Or he becomes ill and needs to be hospitalized? Or what if he commits crimes, or simply disappears? (He travels to another part of the country and works illegally.) It is necessary to make Anthony responsible in such a case so that sponsors have good incentives to screen out migrants who will not contribute. Rules of this sort exist elsewhere in our current immigration system. For example, sponsors under family reunification programs must provide financial support for migrants who cannot support themselves.

In our case, Anthony will be required to obtain basic health insurance for Bishal before he arrives (though this would come out of Bishal's earnings). If Bishal is unable to find work, Anthony must support him for as long as he remains in the country. Bishal is not entitled to welfare payments. If Bishal commits a crime, he will be deported after serving his sentence; Anthony will be required to pay a fine. If Bishal disappears, Anthony will also be fined. We do not think that the fine needs to be large, but it should sting. Also, Anthony and Bishal might not be able to stand each other. Perhaps Anthony can find Bishal a place to stay and pay the rent. Or they can mutually agree that Bishal will return to Nepal after being paid for his time in the United States. It may also be possible, through mutual agreement, for Anthony to place Bishal with another sponsor (such as a Nepalese family that lives down the street).

For this system to work, the law must make two further adjustments. First, migrant workers must be permitted to work for below the minimum wage. Under current law, a worker paid the federal minimum wage would receive almost $15,000 in one year. By way of comparison, the average annual income in Nepal is less than $1,000 and typical Nepalese make closer to $500; Haiti has similar living standards. Application of the federal minimum wage to migrant workers would block the enormous welfare gains that the VIP would otherwise produce. However, all other worker protection rules—for example, those relating to workplace safety—would apply to them.

Second, immigration enforcement would need to be strengthened. If Bishal disappears into the underground economy, there must be a reasonable likelihood that he will be caught and deported. Existing illegal migrants would have to be fit into the system through a combination of a one-time amnesty with a path to citizenship, finding sponsors, or being deported. Enforcement against future illegal migrants would have to be more stringent to avoid undermining the rights of both the large new class of legal migrants and their hosts. No legal reform can be effective unless it is enforced. However, enforcement of the VIP system would be easier than the current system because migrants desperate to enter the country can more easily find sponsors and thus avoid the risks of illegal entry.

Many people may object to this system. Perhaps to some readers it is uncomfortably similar to indentured servitude, even though migrants would be free to leave at any time. Or perhaps it just seems exploitative. But our proposal is continuous with existing programs that are broadly accepted.

Consider the H1-B visa program, which provides the major avenue for migration by skilled workers to the United States. Under this program, an employer sponsors a worker by certifying that the worker satisfies various criteria and that he will be paid the prevailing wage. After the worker arrives, he must work for that employer. If the employer fires the worker, then (subject to a few exceptions) the worker must return to his home country. The major difference between the H1-B program and the program that we propose is that we would allow ordinary people to be sponsors. The H1-B program is not controversial. The risk of exploitation is minimal because foreign workers are protected by the same health, safety, labor, and employment laws that Americans benefit from, and foreign workers can return to their home country if the employer mistreats them.

One might believe that employers—or, at least, large corporate employers like Google—will treat foreign workers in a more benevolent way than ordinary people would, or at least in a bureaucratic rather than exploitative way. Can ordinary people be expected to "manage" a foreign employee? Indeed, they can. There is another program that is even closer to the one we propose. Under the J-1 visa program, Americans can sponsor people, typically young women, who work as au pairs for a year or two and live in their homes. While the J-1 visa program was initially designed for cultural exchange, Congress has permitted people to use it for what is essentially low-wage nanny work. The program is very popular. Note that ordinary Americans serve as employers and sponsors, relying on intermediary institutions—private companies—which help match American sponsors to the foreign workers, provide training to the au pairs, and monitor working and home conditions after they arrive, all subject to regulations and supervision by the State Department.

The au pair program, while nominally a cultural exchange program, is virtually the same thing as the guest work program that we propose, except that it is limited and more highly regulated than we believe necessary. While some people argue that the au pairs are exploited, we have not found any studies that document abuses.[32]

The au pair program also provides clues as to how our program might work in practice. The intermediary institutions have developed easy-to-use websites that allow families and au pairs to match up with each other. The host family is allowed to register its preferences about such things as whether the au pair is licensed to drive, how well she (usually) speaks English, what part of the world she hails from, her experience, her interests, and so on. The au pair applicant also registers her preferences. The institution then sends a small number of profiles of matching applicants to the families. The profile includes detailed information about the applicant's background, interests, skills, and so on. The host family can interview some or all of the applicants, or reject them, whereupon the agency will send the family another group of profiles. The interview takes place over Skype.

Once an applicant is selected, she goes through a week of training—in which she learns about American ways of doing things—and then is sent to the host family. The agency periodically sends people to check on the au pair and family. Among other things, it interviews the parties privately. If one or both sides are unhappy, then the agency will try to match the au pair with another family, so that she will not have to return to her home country.

While the VIP would grant the primary right to sponsor migrants to individuals, communities could also be granted the right to regulate migrant entry. Localities should be allowed to put limited constraints on their residents' use of the VIP program, akin to zoning regulations. We might predict that some communities will prefer a higher level of openness and impose no or few restrictions, while offering amenities that attract foreign migrant workers. These communities might hope for a vibrant, culturally mixed public life. Other communities will prefer homogeneity and use tax and zoning restrictions to limit the influx of migrants. Natives might move across communities, to the opportunity offered by more open cities. In this spirit, it might be natural to pilot VIP in a community that would act as a "special economic zone," using the program as a way to revive a currently depressed area and to investigate its potential advantages and drawbacks without disrupting a whole community.

While the VIP would achieve nearly all the benefits of Becker's visa auction, it would also address its primary weaknesses. Becker's auction is run by the government, not by individuals or communities. It will attract migrants who are willing to pay the most regardless of whether certain types of migrants may cause social or cultural harms to the communities in which they settle. The VIP places the discretion with natives, subject to community regulation. Individuals and communities care about money and thus VIP would likely lead to prevailing prices migrants would have to pay to hosts to be fairly similar to those prevailing in the auction. But as anyone who has worked or has offered a job to someone knows, money is rarely the sole factor in determining the success of such relationships. By placing individuals and communities in charge, VIP allows these individuals and communities to include other factors in decisions about which migrants to allow.

Also unlike Becker's auction, the VIP would involve personal contact between natives and migrants, and responsibility on the part of natives for the success of a migrant. Such mutually beneficial contact is likely on average, though surely not in every single case, to build the sort of positive relationship between hosts and migrants necessary to soften political opposition to migration. By empowering communities to decide the texture of their cultural life, the VIP would avoid the negative reactions that are possible when people feel rapid changes are being imposed from above.

## INSTITUTIONAL SUPPORTS

With the powerful advantages that it has over the existing system of migration and over the auction, the VIP system comes with some drawbacks. Anthony may be too busy and lack the personal or managerial skills or the knowledge of the local economy needed to navigate the VIP system. Call this the "competence problem."

Anthony might also mistreat or exploit Bishal. While Bishal has the formal right to leave at any time, he may be unwilling to exercise that right, even in extreme circumstances. Imagine that his family depends on his remittances, or that he left Nepal in the first place to escape crime and corruption. He will put up with a great deal in the United States before returning to Nepal, and this means he is vulnerable to abuse. Knowing this, Anthony might illegally withhold wages from Bishal, deprive him of adequate food and housing, and even compel him to engage in criminal activity. Call this the "exploitation problem."

Issues such as the competence problem show up in virtually every aspect of market economies. People must manage their pensions, mortgages, credit cards, job searches, and other complex economic relationships. Dozens of institutions have emerged to help individuals navigate these obstacles. Some individuals educate themselves to become experts; others draw on markets for personal services or assistants; others use online platforms that spring up to help with screening. In the worst case, some people will abstain from participating as sponsors. But we suspect most will use institutions to help them navigate the VIP system.

Exploitation is a more serious problem. Labor and human trafficking laws exist to prevent employers from trapping workers in coercive relationships. Excepting the minimum wages we discussed above, the full force of such laws should be applied to the VIP.

It is important to recognize the powerful ways in which the structure of the VIP would reduce the risk of exploitation relative to the current system of migration. Workers are most vulnerable to exploitation when their employment options are limited or they operate as illegal immigrants, outside the protection of the law. When potential employers are forced to compete, workers tend to prosper. This competition is precisely what the VIP promotes: at present, only a few powerful corporations can sponsor visas. Under VIP, every citizen will be able to. The more countries that adopt a VIP system and the more citizens that decide to host, the more options will be available to migrants.

### Could VIP Work?

The restructuring of migration we propose is radical—another Radical Market, this time in labor. Could it ever attract the necessary popular support or be sustained? Some recent experience is encouraging.

The migration systems in the UAE, Qatar, Kuwait, Bahrain, Oman, and Saudi Arabia (countries of the Gulf Cooperation

Council, or GCC) are often criticized, but they tell an interesting tale. Where the United States has roughly nine natives for every foreign-born resident, the ratio in the UAE is reversed.[33] Bahrain and Oman host roughly one migrant for every native. In Saudi Arabia, the GCC country with the fewest migrants per native, there is one migrant for every two citizens.

Nor are the GCC countries the only successful countries with such large noncitizen populations. Singapore hosts two migrants for every three natives. Australia and New Zealand have roughly one foreign-born resident for every two natives. Some prosperous and successful cities, such as Toronto, have levels of foreign-born residents (50%) similar to the GCC.

Yet despite these large migrant populations—in all cases, involving mostly low-skilled migrant workers—none of these countries (with the possible exception of Australia) has experienced as large a popular backlash against migration as OECD countries with far fewer migrants.

All of these countries have migration systems *designed* for the benefits of migration to be broadly shared among natives rather than exclusively accruing to a small group of geographically concentrated capitalists, entrepreneurs, and high-skilled workers. Despite this sharing, the total benefits per native created by migration in these countries to migrants and the countries that send them is far greater than in the more closed OECD countries, because the volume of migration is so much greater. Beyond these features, the migration systems of these countries differ widely.

In the GCC, migrant workers enjoy few civil rights, are tightly controlled by the government and, except for the large domestic servant population, live in segregation from natives. However, in these countries most natives have benefited from publicly owned wealth distributed in a reasonably egalitarian manner, and the state has firm control over the social organization of migrants to prevent crime and uprisings. Furthermore, as in VIP, natives can sponsor migrants for tasks that benefit them. Thus, political support for this massive scale of migration has been strong and sustained for years.

Of course, an important cost of these systems is their neglect of the rights of their migrant labor force. After all, the GCC countries are monarchies and many conform to traditional Islamic law in harsh ways. In some cases, some GCCs have allowed natives to exploit migrants who are unable to leave because their passports have been confiscated by their employers. For all these reasons, the GCC countries are not a model for OECD countries. Yet Singapore has sustained near-GCC level migration with many fewer concerns about violations of migrants' rights.

While we do not want to imitate the systems in these countries, we describe them because they hold an important lesson. A political backlash against massive migration is not inevitable. Even in closed societies, migration receives political support as long as its benefits are widely distributed in a visible way.

## An Internationalism of People

There are about 250 million adults in the United States. In principle, they could sponsor 250 million migrants every year under the VIP program. In practice, we suspect that many people—especially the elderly, those busy with their jobs, and students—will forgo the opportunity. Imagine, then, that 100 million people sponsor migrant workers. Currently, there are about 45 million foreign-born people in the United States. Of those, about 13 million are legal noncitizens, and 11 million are illegal aliens. If our program replaced existing migrant worker visas, the number of migrant workers would increase dramatically, from 24 million to 100 million, but not in a way that would disrupt society and overwhelm public services. It would leave the ratio of foreign-born to natives in the United States below the numbers in even the most restrictive GCC countries.

We expect that the people who use the program would be a cross-section of society. We already know that upper-middle-class people use the J-1 program to sponsor au pairs. Our aim is to involve working-class people who would be attracted by the financial benefits of sponsorship. A low-income person who can earn $6,000 on net from sponsoring a low-skilled migrant worker will significantly increase her well-being; in contrast, a middle-class or wealthy person is not likely to find such an opportunity attractive.

This is the key reason for the program. If ordinary people like Anthony both gain financially from migration and learn something about the humanity and needs of foreigners, their opposition to immigration will decline. Eventually the number of migrants could be expanded if no serious social problems were encountered and the program was popular.

To be sure, the increase in the number of migrants will likely suppress wages for some jobs. In this sense, our proposal is no different from proposals to open borders or increase the number of visas. The key difference is that in our proposal, many of the people who might be hurt by wage suppression will also gain by participating as sponsors in the program. The benefits of migration will be distributed more fairly, reducing political opposition to it.

Furthermore, the large increases in migration would likely make activities that are currently uneconomic in OECD countries viable again, as the example of the GCC countries and our opening vignette illustrate. Factories that have moved abroad could return, offering new jobs for natives, if abundant migrant labor were available, as a political party in Australia led by Nick Xenophon has argued in recent years. Many of the fears of the effects of migrants on wages are actually more justified at our current, low levels of migration. In GCC countries, where migration is much higher, migrant wages are so low and migrant labor so plentiful that migrants engage in activities (domestic service, low-skilled manufacturing, etc.) that are clearly uneconomic for employing natives. Such activities are usually large enough in scale that they require native employers and supervisors, offering direct benefits and often even employment to natives, as illustrated in our opening vignette.

In some ways, the effects of large-scale migration as we envision it would be similar to those of women's entry into the labor force over the mid-twentieth century, as economist Michael Clemens argues in a forthcoming book, *The Walls of Nations*.[34] Yes, women competed with men in the workplace, causing some dislocation and resentment. But because most men had close relationships with women, as fathers, husbands, brothers, and sons, they benefited from greater opportunities for women more than they were harmed at work and thus were reconciled to the additional competition. At the same time, while sexism persisted, a growing professional presence for women began to break down stereotypes and patriarchy.

Similarly, our proposal to tie the economic fate of hosts and migrants would gradually reduce conflict between the workers of the developing and developed worlds and benefit both. VIP would be less disruptive to the identity of host country workers than women's entry into the workforce because it would not directly affect existing hierarchies in the highly intimate sphere of the home.

The greater fairness of VIP can be seen by comparing it to the present arrangement. Under the H1-B program, as a practical matter, only large and sophisticated employers—the Googles—can sponsor migrant workers. Why should they alone enjoy this benefit? Why shouldn't ordinary people? It's as if wealthy women were allowed by the government to enter the workplace, while poor women were prevented from doing so "for their own good."

One might worry that Google will try to take advantage of our program by encouraging its employees and others to sponsor programmers and contract them to Google. But now, serving as middlemen, sponsors would obtain a cut of the profits. If Anthony hears that Google's Akron office needs programmers, he can look for programmers. Anthony will still gain from the sponsorship, as will the migrant worker and the local economy.

Who would come? Most likely a mix of unskilled workers like Bishal and skilled ones as in our Google example. The illegal economy is currently dominated by low-skilled workers—strawberry pickers, nannies, gardeners, slaughterhouse workers. VIP would put this work on a legal footing, while channeling some of the surplus away from the employers and into the pockets of native workers. Skilled migrants would be treated like any other migrants under our system. They would earn far greater income than unskilled migrants and thus there would be substantial competition among hosts to gain a share of their income. The program might also be designed to allow a host to sponsor permanent citizenship in exchange for that host relinquishing her right to host again during her lifetime. Skilled migrants would thus also likely be able to negotiate permanent citizenship or sharing a smaller fraction of their income with hosts.

Probably the most important concern is that VIP would increase inequality in host countries. Host country middle and working classes would benefit, while a new class of very poor (by American standards) migrant workers will form a new subordinate class, which might seem intolerable under liberal norms.

However, there are three reasons for resisting this conclusion. First and most important, it is crucial to recognize that such migration would not *create* inequality (in fact it would reduce it). It would merely make more visible the inequality that is currently obscured by national borders. To the extent this occurs, we believe it would largely be a salutary effect as it would begin to expose and soften a global system that keeps extreme poverty out of sight and mind for the people of wealthy countries.

Second, this process of disruption through greater awareness and proximity of inequality will be greatly mitigated by the likely temporary nature of migration in the VIP. The new class will consist of a constantly changing flow of foreigners who come here voluntarily to obtain wealth and skills, and then return to their home countries where they will be able to make a better life. Evidence from sociological and economic studies of migration indicates that when migrants have the option, most prefer temporary migration for work in circular patterns over permanent migration.[35] The experience in the GCC countries is strongly consistent with this pattern, with waves of migrant workers rotating in and out. Only when this option is foreclosed do most attempt to move permanently. This kind of circular migration does not create the pathologies normally associated with class divisions, where the lower class consists of people who are born into an involuntary status they can never leave.

Third, while inequality *within* the United States might rise (reflecting the lower wealth levels of the foreign workers), both inequality among US natives and *global* inequality will decline. That is of course the lesson of the GCCs. Bishal will see his annual income increase by five times, or more. He will send home remittances to his family, and when he returns home, may have accumulated enough capital—as well as skills, including improved English language skills—to start a business or get training for a higher-paying job. In the era of open borders in the United States, many migrant workers who came from Europe to the United States returned home to do just this. By reducing global inequality, this process will also gradually reduce the demand for migration and raise the wages of workers all over the world.

Fourth, we need to acknowledge that we in the United States already have a subordinate class of low-wage workers— they are illegal aliens. Americans have exploited this class for decades, and it has for those decades been tolerated by the US government because of its importance for many industries. By bringing this underground economy into the open, our approach would allow it to be regulated and monitored. It would be put on a more rational basis so that better matches are made between the needs of the US economy and the interests of foreign workers. And rather than its benefits flowing to capitalists, it would be shared by all citizens.

The nature and extent of these concerns will depend on the volume of migrants. If most citizens, rather than just a third (as we envisioned), chose to participate, migration could nearly double the population of the host country. However, VIP would be self-regulating. As more migrants arrived, the gains to natives would fall, and fewer natives would choose to sponsor migrants.

The VIP program, if adopted in multiple countries, would create a vast and fluid international market in migrant labor.

Immense benefits would flow both to the poorest of the poor in the developing countries, and to the left-behind, alienated, angry working classes of developed countries, who have been the locus of so much political conflict. It is not unreasonable to hope that as foreigners cycle through developed countries, the local populations not only gain monetary benefits but also develop some sympathy and understanding for different cultures. Such a decline in xenophobic sentiment could pay dividends for international cooperation.

This is not to deny that there is something disquieting about the subordinate position in which VIP would naturally place migrant workers. The attitude toward these workers that it would engender, at least in the short term, is unlikely to be enlightened and egalitarian respect. Instead, we would expect some hosts to develop a sense of paternalism and condescension toward the migrants they host, as illustrated in our vignette.

While such an outcome is far from true equality, it is the best that can be hoped for in the near term. Many of the sophisticated cultural elites most likely to object to this sort of unequal relationship should contemplate their own relationships to migrants. In our experience, most people living in wealthy cities who consider themselves sympathetic to the plight of migrants know little or nothing of the language, cultures, aspirations, and values of those they claim to sympathize with. They benefit greatly from the cheap services these migrants offer and rarely concern themselves with the poverty in which they live. The solidarity of such cosmopolitan elites is thus skin deep. But it is better than the open hostility many ordinary citizens of wealthy countries feel toward migrants.

The VIP program would thus move the desperation of the world's poorest out of the shadows, offer a real path to opportunity, and turn the indifference and hatred of the rich world into benevolent condescension (at worst) and, in many quarters we suspect, real sympathy. This is a moral gain relative to the hypocrisy of our current system and perhaps the only plausible way toward a more just international order.

# 4

# Dismembering the Octopus

## TOWARD A RADICAL MARKET
## IN CORPORATE CONTROL

"Sir, sorry, it's your 3 pm."

Oblomov sat up on his couch and unsteadily looked around. His office came into focus as he pulled the electrode cap off his scalp. Surfacing still needs work, he thought. He sighed at the memory of the quiet meadow and the gurgling brook. The sound was a bit off but the art department had surpassed itself.

"It's Hajjar," the voice crackled urgently through the speakerphone. "He seems a bit annoyed. You've kept him waiting."

Hajjar? For a moment Oblomov's mind was blank, then his heart raced. *That Hajjar?*

He hadn't seen Hajjar in ten years. Oblomov owed everything to Hajjar. He had dropped out of grad school at 19 and had taken a routine coding job, surprising everyone. He was a genius, yes, but not a Jobs or

Zuckerberg. He was more a dreamer than a doer. And so, while he had been one of the first of the somniocoders, no one thought his work would amount to anything.

Except Hajjar. It was also Hajjar who first realized that video gamers would prefer realistic dreams. Everyone else thought that customers would not want to give up on agency, but wasn't agency an illusion in any event? It was Hajjar who persuaded Oblomov to quit Google, and it was Hajjar who staked his life savings on Sleepscapes and forced him to become its whiz kid CEO for PR purposes if no other. Hajjar understood things he did not. Why he had to meet with venture capitalists, again and again. Why he had to meet personally with division heads even if it meant traveling 300 days a year. Why he had to give a TEDz talk. The black turtleneck thing. Amazingly, it all worked. Sleepscapes went from nothing to a Fortune 100 firm in five years. He was named Billionaire of the Year by the president at a gala at the Trump Center. And the firm got the attention of the Institutionals.

But, Oblomov groggily recalled, it was not pleasant. Hajjar once threw a rock through his window when he was late for a meeting with the angels. He still has the scar on his arm. For years, Hajjar would greet him with the same phrase—"*My* money made you." Snarling, screaming, profanity, over and over. His ears ached at the memory. But he had to admit it kept him going. Two near-bankruptcies. Angry investors. Lawsuits. A broken marriage. Some legal hanky-panky that Hajjar took the heat for. Hajjar protected him but drove him on.

And then one day it was over. He had been complaining for years about Hajjar, and finally his general counsel asked him why he bothered returning Hajjar's calls. In an instant, Oblomov understood. Of course, Hajjar was not the owner of the company anymore. Hajjar hadn't been "the owner" in quite a long time. Hajjar's share, though worth billions, had been diluted to less than 1%. Then who was the owner of the company? Oblomov knew that the Institutionals were the five largest shareholders, and yet he never heard from them. They occasionally talked to the GC about obscure legal issues, or so he understood, but other than that—nothing.

Hajjar had hammered home that the two other competitors—Dreamland and Somniak—were the "enemy." Every one of their new products had to be matched; every price cut as well. This is what had kept Oblomov awake at night. He had argued with Hajjar. He admired Somniak's pornsoms, and thought there was room enough for three companies in a vast market that had replaced video games, TV, and film. Give Somniak porn, education, and new age; let Dreamland do what they do best—adventure and romance—and the rest for us. "No, no, no," Hajjar screamed, the vein on his forehead bulging as it always did when he became furious, which he so often did. "You just don't understand. It's kill or be killed."

But it was Hajjar who didn't understand. Oblomov stopped answering Hajjar's phone calls, and Hajjar was pushed off the board. Oblomov assigned himself the title of "Chief Neuromancer" and handed over day-to-day operations to a flunky whose name he could not remember. That meant—sleep. Every afternoon; mornings sometimes. Prices didn't need to be cut. Development could be more leisurely. The tech media didn't get it; things were good enough, better than they ever had been. The firm was more, not less profitable, even after it ceded education and romance.

Wait a sec. Oblomov, fully awake now, felt a chill draft against his cheek. Oblomov never followed finance much, but had heard something about the Justice Department forcing the Institutionals to break up. Now only Fidelity had a stake. They put Hajjar back in charge. "It's a new dawn," Hajjar told the press. "Sleepscapes is going to win again."

"Tell him I'm out," he said.

BlackRock, Vanguard, Fidelity, State Street. Most people might recognize the names of these companies, but hardly anyone knows what they do. Something about retirement accounts? They are unhelpfully known as *asset managers* or *institutional investors*. They keep a low profile, and are rarely discussed outside the specialized financial press, yet they are the most powerful companies in the world. Each manages several trillion dollars of assets. Together, they control more than a fifth of the value of the US stock market, and this means that they control the familiar brand names that we tend to think of as autonomous companies—JP Morgan, United Airlines, Verizon, Google. According to the OECD, all institutional investors collectively own about a quarter of the US stock market. The same institutional investors dominate the stock markets of other major countries.

How can these asset managers fly so securely under the radar while wielding financial power unparalleled in the history of the world, with the possible exception of Roman emperors? The key features of these investors, which keep them "boring," is that they are *diversified* and many of their investments are held somewhat *passively*. Diversification means that they own stock in a wide range of companies rather than in any one company or group of similar companies. Passivity means that they do not frequently buy and sell stocks, but instead mostly hold onto them. They also often *manage* the assets that are technically owned by workers and other ordinary people. Vanguard has been rightly praised for pioneering low-cost index funds, which enable workers to diversify their retirement savings and avoid the hazards of stock-picking. These features give the impression that these institutions play no active role in guiding the economy.

Yet economic research suggests that diversified institutional investors have harmed a wide range of industries, raising prices for consumers, reducing investment and innovation, and potentially lowering wages.

This outcome is not, as far as we know, the result of any deliberate conspiracy among the managers of the institutional investors. In fact, the intentions behind the creation of the institutional investment industry were admirable. We will also see that the solution to restore competition is surprising: it actually involves giving institutional investors more control over companies—but over individual companies rather than over industries.

## The Monopolist with a Thousand Faces

The word "monopoly" was coined by Aristotle in a discussion of the mathematician and philosopher Thales of Miletus, who showed the value of philosophy in practical affairs by cornering the market on olive presses ahead of a harvest.[1] Yet during the early modern era, the major source of monopoly was not this type of individual initiative, but the state, which authorized well-connected individuals or groups to dominate various lines of business. Adam Smith and his contemporaries saw these legal arrangements as the primary source of monopoly. The movement for American Independence was partly a struggle against the monopolistic control of the British East India Company over the trade in tea.

In Smith's era, most businesses were small and relied on local banks or on family for capital. Large enterprises or projects, like the construction of canals, which required greater capital, were usually undertaken or coordinated by governments. Yet, as we saw in chapter 1, advances in technology and developments in the law eventually allowed entrepreneurs to form business enterprises large enough to undertake vast industrial projects. To obtain capital for these enterprises, entrepreneurs sold stocks and bonds on a huge scale, to anonymous investors whom they would repay over many years.

As these large pools of capital developed, economists became concerned about the possibility that the businesses could restrict competition, becoming monopolies without any aid from the state beyond the protection of the corporate form and property rights. In the nineteenth century, Antoine Augustin Cournot developed some of the first mathematical work in economics to study monopolies' incentives to impede trade and reduce production in order to raise the price they could charge. Engineer and economist Jules Dupuit developed the idea of the quadratic triangle that featured so prominently in chapters 1 and 2 to illustrate the social cost or "deadweight loss" associated with monopoly control: when monopolists charge high prices, people who value goods less than the price but more than the cost of production are unable to buy them. These thinkers would influence the great economist Léon Walras, who we met in chapter 1.[2] Walras saw private monopolies (along with private landownership) as both the primary impediment to the operation of free markets and the central cause of inequality, writing in the 1890s, "Look in America for the sources of the enormous fortunes of multimillionaires . . . and you will find . . . the operation of businesses without competition."[3]

Americans did not need French economists to explain to them the dangers of monopoly. During the nineteenth century, vast enterprises appeared in a very short period of time—about the last thirty years of the nineteenth century. They dominated every major industry—transportation, energy, manufacturing, finance. They typically resulted from acquisition: one company would buy up others. Rockefeller's Standard Oil Company started as a partnership involving Rockefeller and a few business associates. The company then bought up its competitors. To avoid limits created by state law, Rockefeller arranged for separate firms to be owned by a single national trust, which determined policy across all the different firms, causing them to act as one. Other prominent trusts were U. S. Steel and the American Tobacco Company. Many firms became so large that competition was all but eliminated.

The trusts worried the public, commentators, and politicians because of their financial and political power. They contributed to the economic and political inequality of the Gilded Age immortalized in the novels of F. Scott Fitzgerald. Standard Oil was depicted in cartoons of the era as an octopus whose tentacles entwined markets and state legislatures (see figure 4.1). In 1890, Congress passed the Sherman Act to forbid (among other behavior) "combinations in restraint of trade."[4]

While enforcement was initially slow, the new law became a powerful tool in the hands of the Progressive movement that was just blossoming. Henry George led the way,[5] using arguments similar to those of Walras.[6] The first great Progressive

FIGURE 4.1: The financially obscured accumulation of political and economic power by "robber barons" was the impetus behind the first American antitrust laws.
*Source:* Udo J. Keppler, Next! (1904), http://www.loc.gov/pictures/item/2001695241/.

president, Theodore Roosevelt, promised to bust the trusts. Though legend has exaggerated what he achieved, his administration did bring numerous antitrust lawsuits. The basic dilemma was that while the trusts damaged market competition, enabling them to overcharge for their goods and services, they also could spread the fixed costs of production over many more consumers because of their vast scale, resulting in lower prices, and eliminate local monopolies by buying up land and local business monopolies in what economists call "vertical integration." It would thus never have made sense simply to abolish big business. Yet antitrust law could do some good by outlawing "horizontal" concentration among competitors when it did not generate scale economies. The William Taft administration brought even more antitrust suits than Roosevelt's did. In 1911, it dismembered Rockefeller's octopus.[7]

Under Woodrow Wilson, two more anti-monopoly laws passed. The Clayton Act of 1914 strengthened antitrust law by blocking certain types of behavior thought to be inherently anticompetitive and directly prohibiting mergers and other asset purchases that could reduce competition. The Federal Trade Commission (FTC) Act of the same year created a new administrative agency that was given the power to regulate competition, sharing enforcement responsibilities with the Department of Justice (DOJ)'s Antitrust Division.[8]

Yet these new interventions did not halt the growing power of concentrated businesses. As legal scholar Einer Elhauge documents, business concentration, and the income inequality many blamed on it, continued to rise during this period.[9] It took a Great Depression and the rise of Franklin Roosevelt's New Deal to establish an activist antitrust and regulatory policy toward private monopolies. Regulators and courts became more aggressive about searching out and blocking methods businesses use to expand their economic power. Congress got involved as well. The original Clayton Act tried to stop concentration by prohibiting firms from buying the stock of other firms. Businesses figured out that they could get around this rule by buying the underlying assets of firms rather than the stock in them.

This problem has many names, but our favorite is from biology. There it is called the "Red Queen" phenomenon, named after the Red Queen in Lewis Carroll's *Through the Looking-Glass* who tells Alice, "Now, here, you see, it takes all the running you can do, to keep in the same place."[10] Just like Alice in the fable, regulators must play "catch-up"—recognizing the work-around used by business, ascertaining its harm, and then getting new laws or regulations in place to stop it—just to avoid the recreation of monopoly. In 1950, Congress amended the Clayton Act so that it also would cover the purchase of assets.[11]

Because of this activism, American antitrust law became a model internationally: it spread first to Britain and then to the European continent and farther around the world.[12] Yet just as American authorities gained the admiration of the world, they stepped off the Red Queen's treadmill. Beginning in the 1970s and accelerating from the 1980s onward, antitrust authorities lost track of the ways in which capital markets reconfigured themselves to maintain monopoly power. In order to understand the reasons why, we must examine the evolution of the corporate form and its governance in the United States during the twentieth century.

## Acephalous Cephalopods

During the twentieth century, the public stock corporation had become the standard legal form for operating a large business. The key advantage of a corporation is that its stock and debt typically trade on an exchange. If you thought that a firm would be the next Standard Oil or Google, you could buy some shares on the exchange. If you later realized that it was being mismanaged, you could sell those shares just as easily. Ownership became *liquid*: it became easier to sell an ownership interest once it was embodied in shares of stock, which traded on a public exchange. It was exactly this liquidity that, in chapter 1, we wanted to create for the uses of all assets.

Yet liquid public ownership also created a paradox identified by Adolf Berle and Gardiner Means in their path-breaking 1933 book, *The Modern Corporation and Private Property*. Corporations enabled entrepreneurs to raise vast pools of capital to fund huge projects like railroads and steel mills by attracting millions of shareholders from around the country and world. These owners enjoyed the right to the corporation's profits— either in the form of dividends or the proceeds of liquidation of the corporation after its creditors were paid off. However, they also, at least in principle, were supposed to "control" the corporation by hiring the corporation's directors, who in turn appointed and monitored the CEO and other managers of the firm, the people with day-to-day operational responsibility. Shareholders also exercised the vote on major corporate decisions like mergers.

Yet, as Berle and Means pointed out, "ownership" of a corporation was very different from ownership of ordinary property. If you own your car, you both control it (by driving and parking it) and enjoy the right to profit if it is used by others (if you rent it or sell it). In the case of a large corporation, millions of owners exist. Who, in fact, controls it? The problem goes back to voting, the topic of chapter 2. If you own three shares of Google, you can vote them all you want, but your vote is unlikely to make a difference. And because of that, you are unlikely to pay much attention to how Google is operated in the first place, so you are in no position to exercise your vote in an informed way. Nowadays, most people realize that stock ownership is beneficial only because it gives you the ability to enjoy gains in the market without paying attention to it.

So, who does control corporations? Usually the managers. The directors are supposed to ensure that the CEO and other managers act in the interests of shareholders, but are usually beholden to the CEO, who may have appointed them in the first place. Directors are also typically outsiders who lack the time, incentives, and information necessary to ensure that the CEO acts in the interests of shareholders.

The separation of ownership and control gives rise to what economists call "agency costs." The agent—here, the CEO—does not necessarily act in the interests of the principal—the collection of shareholders. She might instead use the corporation to enrich herself (for example, by overpaying herself, causing the corporation to purchase a jet so that she can have access to it, and so on), or she might just be lazy. The development of stock markets gave investors the power to obtain liquidity, but the price to be paid was loss of control—agency costs.

How can we ensure that managers act in the interest of shareholders? While economists believe that a market for takeovers—where another firm or group of investors buys an underperforming firm and fires the CEO—is important to frighten CEOs into maximizing profits, most current thinking focuses on corporate compensation and the structure of corporate management. CEOs should be paid with stock, so that they are rewarded when the stock price rises and penalized when it falls. The board should be relatively independent. Shareholders should be given ample opportunities to vote. And so on. Governments have tried to encourage firms to adopt "best practices" like these, yet none really resolves the basic problem identified by Berle and Means.

Taking a broad view, we can see three major things that happened as the economy moved from a type of personal ownership—where a single person owns a mill or farm—to the modern system of capital markets, in which equity is dispersed throughout the population. It became much easier to raise capital for businesses and other projects. But it also became much easier for industry to concentrate through acquisitions, resulting in monopoly prices, depressed wages, and political corruption. And it also becomes possible for managers to operate firms for their private benefit rather than for the benefit of shareholders. The government has responded episodically with antitrust and corporate governance enforcement, but there is reason to think that these two styles of regulation are in tension. This contradiction lay under the surface for many years, but has come to the fore with the rise of institutional investment.

### Effortless Capitalism

The logic of shareholder capitalism suggests that investors wish to do as little work as possible while gaining a maximal stable return. Starting in the 1950s, economists developed financial ideas that came to be known as "portfolio theory" based on these principles.[13] The major insight was that for the average investor, it makes more sense to buy shares in a diverse group of corporations mimicking the whole economy than to pick stocks based on conjectures about which companies are best managed. When an investor buys and holds just one stock, she bears the risk that the stock price will fall for reasons specific to that stock, such as its management being incompetent or deceitful. Investors can avoid these stock-specific risks by diversifying widely across the economy.

Further theoretical development reinforced these conclusions. The so-called efficient capital markets hypothesis emphasized that anyone trying to pick an "undervalued" stock is deluding herself. She is instead likely to be beaten to the punch by skilled professionals, who will raise the price of the stock before an ordinary investor can get there. This means that there is little point in stock-picking in the first place, certainly for amateur investors.[14] "Behavioral finance" holds that ordinary investors often act irrationally.[15] All this theory exhorted investors to simply diversify while paying as little as possible to dishonest money managers who claim to be able to "beat the market."

The cheapest way to do this is via low-cost mutual funds (especially index funds) that track broad market indices. A mutual fund is a portfolio of stocks that may have an industry focus (e.g., energy) or a strategy (e.g., growth). An index fund (which is a type of mutual fund) holds a portfolio of stocks designed to exactly mimic the index of interest (e.g., S&P 500). Beginning in the 1970s, a huge demand developed for such funds, in part because of the shift of pension savings into the stock market spurred by various government reforms and in part because governments, persuaded by financial theory, encouraged investors to park their savings in such low-cost, diversified funds. The overall effect was that institutional investors, which controlled these funds, became the largest owners, and thus the largest controllers (at least in principle), of the major corporations.

Who are the institutional investors, anyway? They include companies that manage mutual funds and index funds, asset managers, and other firms that buy and hold equities on behalf of their customers. The largest names are those we mentioned above: Vanguard, BlackRock, State Street, and Fidelity. Index fund operations are relatively mechanical, so their costs are low; today they comprise probably less than a quarter of the offerings of institutional investors.[16]

Figure 4.2 displays the growth of the fraction of the US public stock market controlled by institutional investors. The control of institutional investors has risen dramatically, starting roughly in 1980 at about 4% control and leveling out around the Great Recession at 26%. While 26% is still a minority of the entire market, most of the equity in the largest public corpora-

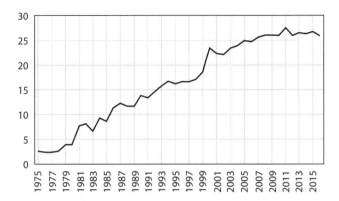

**FIGURE 4.2**: Asset holdings of mutual funds and index funds over time since 1975.

This series was created using data from the 2016 edition of the Investment Company Institute's *Institutional Investor Fact Book* and the World Bank's 2017 World Development Indicators. From 2000 onward, we calculate institutional investors' stake in US equities as the sum of all non-World equity fund assets plus half of hybrid fund assets. In total these are roughly 40% of total institutional assets during the 2000–2015 period. Prior to 2000, the *Fact Book* reports only aggregate assets; to extrapolate our analysis backwards, we assume that 40% of these assets are US equity holdings. We then divide these numbers by the World Development Indicators' total size of US public equities.

tions is held diffusely by individual households who have no capacity to play a role in governing these corporations.[17]

This contrasts sharply with the heft of institutional investors. Since the late 1980s, BlackRock, Fidelity, Vanguard, and State Street have not just grown large in absolute terms. They have also become the largest shareholders of major US corporations.[18] Table 4.1 shows a typical example from the US banking industry. Nor is this trend limited to the United States: figures are similarly high in Canada, Denmark, France, and Sweden, among other countries.[19]

As these institutions grew, they became the largest owners of the firms in which they invested. In the 1990s, scholars began

**TABLE 4.1:** The top five shareholders of the six largest US banks

| JP MORGAN CHASE | % | BANK OF AMERICA | % | CITIGROUP | % |
|---|---|---|---|---|---|
| BlackRock | 6.4 | Berkshire Hathaway* | 6.9 | BlackRock | 6.1 |
| Vanguard | 4.7 | BlackRock | 5.3 | Vanguard | 4.5 |
| State Street | 4.5 | Vanguard | 4.5 | State Street | 4.2 |
| Fidelity | 2.7 | State Street | 4.3 | Fidelity | 3.6 |
| Wellington | 2.5 | Fidelity | 2.1 | Capital World Investors | 2.4 |

| WELLS FARGO | % | U.S. BANK | % | PNC BANK | % |
|---|---|---|---|---|---|
| Berkshire Hathaway | 8.8 | BlackRock | 7.4 | Wellington | 8.0 |
| BlackRock | 5.4 | Vanguard | 4.5 | BlackRock | 4.7 |
| Vanguard | 4.5 | Fidelity | 4.4 | Vanguard | 4.6 |
| State Street | 4.0 | State Street | 4.4 | State Street | 4.6 |
| Fidelity | 3.5 | Berkshire Hathaway | 4.3 | Barrow Hanley | 4.0 |

*Source:* José Azar, Sahil Raina, & Martin C. Schmalz, Ultimate Ownership and Bank Competition (unpublished manuscript, July 23, 2016), https://papers.ssrn.com/sol3/papers.cfm?abstract_id=2710252.
*Warrants without voting rights.

speculating that the institutional investors might provide the market discipline that the dispersed shareholders of the Berle-Means corporation could not.[20] Vanguard, for example, owns more than 6% of Delta Airlines, making it the largest single shareholder. Despite this not being anywhere near a majority stake, when Vanguard calls, Delta's CEO will answer the phone because Vanguard is Delta's largest shareholder.

Furthermore, most institutional investors (but not Vanguard) offer many managed funds that pick stocks and thus threaten to sell stock if the firms they invest in do not follow their advice. The actual role of institutional investors in governance remains the subject of debate. But the debate misses the real importance of the rise of institutional investors: that if they control the firms they own, then they can use this control for bad purposes as well as good.

Consider again table 4.1, representing ownership patterns in the US banking industry.[21] The largest owners of these banks are, almost uniformly, the same group of institutional investors. BlackRock is the largest owner of JP Morgan, with a 6.4% stake. It is also the largest owner of Citgroup and U.S. Bank, and the second largest owner of Bank of America, Wells Fargo, and PNC Bank. Vanguard is the second largest owner of JP Morgan, Citigroup, and U.S. Bank, and the third largest owner of Bank of America, Wells Fargo, and PNC Bank. This is characteristic of most other markets as well. When combined, BlackRock, Vanguard, and State Street constitute the single largest shareholder of at least 40% of all public companies in the United States and nearly 90% of public companies in the S&P 500.[22] The fraction of US public firms held by institutional investors who simultaneously hold large blocks of other same-industry firms increased from less than 10% in 1980 to about 60% in 2010 and has continued to rise since.[23]

Institutional investors constitute the latest iteration of the Red Queen problem in antitrust enforcement. Traditional antitrust enforcement aimed to prevent any single corporation from dominating an entire market. But institutional investors have enabled investors to avoid these rules by knitting together the interests of the biggest firms that dominate any particular market—and have done so throughout the economy. Indeed, institutional investors behave much as trusts did a century ago, but in subtler and less transparent ways. Yet the fact that these institutions have the potential to eliminate competition not just in one sector but in the whole economy, combined with the very obscurity of their actions, makes their control all the more pernicious.

Thus, antitrust law enforcement has not adapted to meet the latest form of concentrated economic power. For many years, economists worried about the potential effects of these ownership patterns for a variety of reasons. However, it was not until 2012 that a brilliant young economist, José Azar, put together the puzzle.[24]

### What's Wrong with Indexing?

So, what exactly did Azar argue is so wrong with the diversified holdings of institutional investors? To see the logic, we need to return to the basic theory of competition underlying antitrust law.

According to that theory, competition causes firms to struggle to please customers, in the process lowering prices and improving quality. Suppose that GM and Ford are the only two automobile manufacturers in the US market, and each controls half of it. GM will want to increase its profits by cutting into Ford's market share. It can do this by lowering the price of its cars. People who might otherwise buy cars from Ford switch to GM in order to benefit from the lower price. The problem for GM is that if it lowers the price of its cars, it will also earn lower profits on cars it would have sold anyway.

Thus, if Ford disappeared and GM became the sole firm in the market, a monopolist, it would raise its prices and reduce output because it need not fear that customers will switch to Ford. On the other hand, if hundreds of car manufacturers competed for customers, GM would need to lower prices drastically in order to prevent customers from going elsewhere. GM would charge a price that just covers its costs, known as the competitive price. When only two firms control the market, as in the original case (a duopoly), economists believe that the firms will compete moderately, lowering their prices below what a monopolist would charge but charging higher than the competitive price. As the number of firms increases, competition becomes more intense and prices fall, while quantity of output increases.

What determines how many firms exist in a market—or, in other words, the degree of "market concentration"? In some cases, a firm might grow large and beat out competition just by being the most efficient competitor. In such a case, the law tolerates or even encourages market concentration. The firm should be rewarded for its efficiency. Antitrust law is generally skeptical when market concentration intensifies because of a single firm buying up competitors, as Thales bought up olive presses from competing olive oil producers. But in the real world, matters can be more complicated. Imagine again that dozens of car manufacturers exist, and two of them—Ford and GM—decide to merge. Here, the effect of the merger on competition is likely to be small—because so many competitors exist. Moreover, the merger might create a more efficient company by allowing Ford and GM to avoid duplicative manufacturing facilities. To evaluate a merger, one must balance the market power effect (which is bad for consumers) and the economies of scale (which are good for producers and consumers).

The US government often challenges mergers on legal grounds. To provide guidance to firms that are thinking about merging, the two major antitrust agencies—the DOJ and the FTC—published the Horizontal Merger Guidelines ("Guidelines"), which establish numerical thresholds on the degree of concentration in markets and the nature of mergers that are likely to trigger investigation and intervention.[25] One of us helped with the drafting of the most recent guidelines.[26]

The analysis behind these guidelines assumes firms are owned and compete independently. But as we have seen, most firms are not independently owned—instead, they are dominated by institutional investors who own large stakes in rival firms. To see why this matters, imagine first that a single shareholder owns 100% of Ford and 100% of GM. When Ford lowers prices, it hopes to gain market share at GM's expense. But a shareholder who owns both companies would not benefit from Ford beating out GM, and would surely lose from lower prices. The shareholder would direct the CEOs of Ford and GM not to engage in price competition (or competition on costly product quality or innovation), but to act as if the two firms were merged.

Real institutional investors own only about 5–10% of the companies, but the same logic holds. Suppose Vanguard is the largest shareholder of GM and Ford, and BlackRock is the second largest shareholder. Vanguard owns 7% of each firm; BlackRock owns 6% of each firm. Each institutional investor wants GM and Ford to forgo price competition because price reductions lower profits. It doesn't matter whether their stake is 100%, or 7%, or 6%, or 0.01%. They all agree on the objective. Will the CEOs of GM and Ford therefore refuse to compete? The answer depends on whether the institutional investors are actually able to exert influence on the CEOs. There are several reasons for thinking that they can.

- An institutional investor could strategically advise a CEO that profits will increase if the firm raises prices or reduces investment. A recent paper observes exactly this sort of behavior: firms in concentrated industries with a lot of common ownership have made increasingly anemic investments in capacity and innovation.[27] Since each CEO knows the investor is likely to be talking to rival CEOs, each will guess that his rivals may also raise prices, facilitating tacit collusion. Moreover, the investor can punish a CEO who does not follow the investor's advice with adverse votes on his compensation and on the slate of board members.

- Institutional investors naturally dominate "earnings calls" and other interactions between the Chief Financial Officer (CFO) of leading corporations and their investors. It is the duty of such officers to "keep the investors happy." If pro-competitive moves by firms are met with scorn from such leading investors, and anticompetitive ones are praised, this will tend to co-opt the CFO to become an anticompetitive force within the firm.

- The institutional investor could design or promote incentive packages for CEOs to reduce their incentive to compete against rivals. CEOs can be judged by performance relative to competitors or by absolute performance. In the former case, the CEO can do well by taking market share from a rival, for example, regardless of absolute profit levels. In the absolute performance case, taking market share from a rival is not rewarded unless it raises absolute profits, softening competition. A recent study shows a strong decline in relative compensation with common ownership: more commonly owned firms have compensation practices that systematically discourage aggressive competition.[28]

- The investor could block bids by activist investors interested in aggressive competition.[29]

- Even less directly, but perhaps most perniciously, institutional investors could promote business standards, practices, and beliefs that superficially appear to be "pro-business" or "pro-shareholder," but also tend to reduce competition. Under the cover of promoting good corporate governance, institutional investors could promote initiatives to "cut the waste" by reducing investment and the number of workers and instead encourage firms to pay higher returns to shareholders or hoard cash. They could promote lobbying by firms for general "pro-business" policies such as less regulation and lower corporate taxes. Perhaps it is a coincidence, but over precisely the same period that institutional investors rose to prominence, the dominant corporate "ideology" shifted away from one emphasizing investment and innovation and toward one favoring retrenchment, lobbying, and cost-cutting.[30] Such initiatives may result in lower competition and thus higher profits for institutional investors.

On the other hand, CEOs often hold concentrated shares in the firms they manage. They therefore may be reluctant to follow instructions not to engage in price competition. While it is hard to imagine these CEOs can entirely ignore the interests of their investors, who can (in principle) fire them or reduce their pay, the outcome of this conflict is an empirical question.

The supporting evidence is supplied by the work of Azar, Martin Schmalz, and their co-authors. One study considers the airline industry.[31] It examines competition between airlines on a route-by-route basis (e.g., New York to Chicago, or Los Angeles to Houston), and finds that where institutional investors own substantial stakes in airlines, prices are higher for routes where those airlines compete than for routes where they do not. Overall, they find that airline prices are 3–5% higher as a result of the anticompetitive power of institutional investors. They cleverly exploit the merger of two institutional investors and find even clearer effects of this merger on precisely those routes one would expect to be affected, suggesting that institutional investors are so deeply involved that they can even affect pricing on individual routes.

Another study reaches a similar conclusion for the banking industry. The authors find that a measure of overlapping ownership by different institutional investors predicts the prices and terms of financial products offered by banks far better than do standard measures of concentration.[32] Where institutional investors own large stakes in banks that compete in local markets, customers receive lower interest rates for their checking accounts. And the problem is just getting worse. A third paper shows that in construction, manufacturing, finance, and services, horizontal holdings by institutional investors increased by 600%, by one measure, from 1993 to 2014.[33] In all these industries, we should therefore expect a reduction of competition over time and increases in prices over what they would be if competition were more robust.

The emerging dominance of institutional investors means not only that people face higher prices. It likely means that they receive lower wages as well. Firms compete for workers just as they compete for consumers. Like firms that collude to raise prices and reduce output, those that collude in the market for workers are likely to pay lower wages and fire workers to create greater unemployment so they can sustain these lower wages and exploit workers. This phenomenon is known as "monopsony," the reverse of monopoly. The stagnation of wages for most workers we discussed in our introduction immediately comes to mind, and recent research has shown a tight link between the rise of market power and anemic wage growth.[34]

Furthermore, if firms coordinate their political activities, they are likely to be more effective in lobbying for their interests and against regulations and taxes that serve the public interest. Political scientists Jacob Hacker and Paul Pierson have documented the rise of this phenomenon in parallel with the rise of institutional investment.[35] The logical end point of institutional investment and diversification is the coordination of all capital to extract maximum wealth from consumers and workers.

### Restoring Competition

A simple but Radical reform can prevent this dystopia: ban institutional investors from diversifying their holdings *within* industries while allowing them to diversify *across* industries. BlackRock would own as much as it wants of (say) United Airlines, but it would own no stake in Delta, Southwest, and the others. It would also own as much as it wants of Pepsi, but not Coca-Cola and Dr. Pepper. And it would own as much as it wants of JP Morgan, but none of Citigroup and the other banks. If BlackRock remains large, it would likely end up with very large stakes in the firms it owns—10–20%, or more—in various markets, as illustrated in our opening vignette.

We would also allow institutional investors to remain diversified within, as well as across, industries as long as they did not grow too large. Based on more detailed calculations in our joint work on this proposal with Fiona Scott Morton (former chief economist of the Antitrust Division of the DOJ), we think 1% is a reasonable threshold.[36] Thus, an institutional investor could own 1% of United, 1% of Delta, 1% of Southwest, and 1% of all the other airlines; and 1% each of Pepsi, Coca-Cola, and Dr. Pepper; and 1% of all the banks; and so on. Under our scheme, institutional investors face a tradeoff. They can be *small* and *fully* diversified—within as well as across industries.

Or they can be *large* and *partially* diversified—not within but only across industries. We also exempt investors that opt to be *purely passive* (that do not engage in any corporate governance activities).

Our approach can be stated as a simple rule:

> No investor holding shares of more than a single effective firm in an oligopoly and participating in corporate governance may own more than 1% of the market.

The actual operationalization of this rule is subtle (e.g., how to define "oligopoly" and an "effective firm"). Questions concern how to address firms that operate in multiple markets, among many others. Readers who are interested in the details may consult our companion study.[37] For current purposes, however, the rule should be clear.

By now, the justification for our policy should also be clear. Because institutional investors appear to reduce competition among firms they own, they should not be permitted to own firms that are rivals within a single, concentrated industry—with exceptions where institutional investors are small or passive. Yet our policy affects issues other than competition, and we now consider its likely effects on these other areas.

### GOVERNANCE

Beyond the competition benefits of our proposal, it would also greatly improve corporate governance. Commentators have noted that the current system of institutional-investor dominance harms corporate governances. In the words of law professors Ronald Gilson and Jeffrey Gordon:

> Institutional intermediaries compete and are rewarded on the basis of "relative performance" metrics that give them

little incentive to engage in shareholder activism that could address shortfalls in managerial performance; such activity can improve absolute but not relative performance [of the institution].[38]

In other words, if a large investor spends time and resources improving the performance of Firm X, the higher stock price of Firm X benefits all owners of Firm X. Because a large institutional investor owns roughly the same shares, including the shares of Firm X, as other large institutional investors, it has gained nothing *relative to its own competitors in the financial services industry*. It will still gain by increasing the overall size of the stock market, which increases the share it takes of it, and thus it will still have some incentives to engage in the sorts of corporate governance we highlighted earlier. However, these incentives are greatly dampened relative to the case in which each corporation is mostly controlled by a single institutional investor.

Our proposal addresses this problem by concentrating the interests of each institutional investor in a single firm within an industry—for example, a large stake in GM rather than smaller stakes in GM, Ford, and Chrysler. As illustrated in our vignette, this provides strong incentives for the institutional investor to monitor this firm by making the reputation and profits of the institutional investor dependent on the performance of that firm. Furthermore, our proposal could change the nature of competition between mutual funds.[39] That competition at present centers primarily on fees, services, and the illusory ability of fund managers to "pick" stocks.[40] If our proposal were put into effect, competition would instead focus on the quality of governance that institutional investors provide, leading to a market where competition between institutional investors would directly help solve the Berle-Means problem by holding institutional investors accountable for governing the companies they invest in to maximize returns.

This is not to say that our proposal has no drawbacks for corporate governance. Some, though we would guess few, index funds might choose to opt out of governance entirely (as we allow and discuss further below), which could harm governance. By creating dominant, large, concentrated shareholders, our policy might disadvantage minority shareholders, a challenge that other reforms (including applying Quadratic Voting to corporate governance) would have to deal with. Our policy would likely make it slower and more cumbersome for institutional investors to switch the firms they invest in, which could beneficially check excessive stock picking but might also make the market somewhat less liquid (though again, other policies we advocate, like a COST, would help address this). Finally, our policy would doubtless require a transitional period, to allow institutional investors to come into compliance with it, jointly with other regulations. However, the benefits of our policy for corporate governance are substantial and the challenges it creates are limited.

## DIVERSIFICATION

The major objection to our strategy is that it could limit the diversification available to investors. For example, investors in a single institution will not be quite as well diversified with only one airline firm in their portfolio instead of four. There are three reasons that this cost is much smaller than the gains from our proposal.

First, if our policy did limit diversification within an industry, the size of this effect would be small. Financial economists have found that a randomly chosen portfolio of as few as fifty stocks achieves 90% of the diversification benefits available from full diversification across the entire market.[41] The reason is that once one owns shares of a few dozen of them, the diversification gains from ownership of shares in additional corporations are small. However, our proposal would allow much greater diversification for many reasons. These include the fact that an important component of variance in individual stock returns is accounted for by an industry component, so diversifying across industries is substantially better than diversifying randomly, and that our proposal only affects holdings in concentrated oligopoly industries, not all industries.[42] Furthermore, most US institutional stock holdings are held by many small funds. These funds—holding less than 1% of any company—would not be affected by our policy. We therefore believe our proposal would preserve nearly all of the gains from diversification for typical investors, even if investors chose to hold only the funds offered by a single institution.

Second, there is no reason why our proposal need worsen diversification at all. If savers truly want that last bit of diversification, they can simply invest some of their money in many different institutional investors. Our rule would do nothing to prevent such direct diversification by individual investors.

Finally, an investor who sought maximal diversification as well as a large scale could take advantage of the index fund exception in our policy. An institutional investor could be allowed to own as much equity as it wants—within industries as well as across industries—as long as it never communicates with the operational firms; commits itself to "mirror voting," in which it votes the same as other shareholders do; and commits to a clear, verifiable investment strategy such as indexing that allows the investor no discretion in selling some stocks and buying others, and hence prevents the investor from punishing firms by selling their stock. Thus, the cost to diversification of our policy is *de minimus.*

## Law on Our Side

The legal prohibition on institutional investing patterns that lead to the monopoly problems we highlight is quite clear. The relevant portion of the law reads:

> No person . . . shall acquire, directly or indirectly, the whole or any part of the stock or . . . assets of another person . . . , where . . . the effect of such acquisition may be substantially to lessen competition, or to tend to create a monopoly.[43]

A corporation counts as a "person," so a corporation cannot buy the assets or stock of another corporation where the effect is to concentrate the market to a sufficient degree. But the statute includes an exception:

> This section shall not apply to persons purchasing such stock solely for investment and not using the same by voting or otherwise to bring about, or in attempting to bring about, the substantial lessening of competition.[44]

This provision came to be known as the passive investment defense. Thus, a corporation cannot obtain shares when doing so reduces competition; but it may obtain shares for "investment purposes." How are these provisions reconciled? In *United States v. E.I. du Pont de Nemours & Co.,* the US Supreme Court ruled that du Pont's purchase of a substantial stake in General Motors could violate Section 7.[45] "Even when the purchase is solely for investment, the plain language of Section 7 contemplates an action at any time the stock is used to bring about, or in attempting to bring about, a substantial lessening of competition."[46] So, in the end, the only question is whether the acquisition of stock does or does not reduce competition. Section 7 has been used to block numerous mergers and other asset acquisitions over the years. It has not been used against institutional investors.

Yet as the legal scholar Elhauge notes, the legal argument for applying Section 7 to institutional investors seems clear.[47] As in the case of merger-related antitrust enforcement, the plaintiff need not prove that the defendant "intended" to reduce competition; effects are what matter.[48] Moreover, the so-called passive investment defense in the statute does not apply to institutional investors because, regardless of how they choose stocks, they vote and communicate with corporations in an effort to influence their behavior, and are likely to be liable even if they only have the capacity to influence a corporation, whether or not they use it.[49] Regulators and private antitrust plaintiffs could sue the institutional investors whenever investors' stock purchases tend to lessen competition in particular industries.

If institutional investors are found to have violated the Clayton Act, they would be potentially subject to treble damages, owing three times the harm they have caused to consumers and workers. Our calculations suggest these harms total at least $100 billion *annually*, implying damages could easily run into the trillions of dollars, sums that would wipe out the entire industry.

Yet directly and indiscriminately pursuing such litigation seems an unpromising strategy for addressing the power of institutional investors for several reasons. First, while they are likely illegal, these activities have been tolerated for years and it seems capricious and unfair to bankrupt all institutional investors for behavior that is so standard to the industry, however egregious its harms. Second, the violations are so widespread and the theory around them so unsettled that courts, without external guidance, are unlikely to create a predictable legal environment that allows investors to operate inside the law without fear of litigation. This could unnecessarily disrupt the industry.

Most important, though, lawsuits of this sort are likely to be difficult to bring financially. Antitrust cases are usually brought by large firms against other large firms, or by groups of consumers, organized by lawyers, against a single firm or a small number of firms. A law firm that sued institutional investors, on the other hand, would be bringing a case against capital *as a class*. Given that institutional investors effectively control most of the corporate economy, if a law firm attempted to bring a case against institutional investors, it would run the risk of losing all work for public corporations. While the antitrust laws were designed to constrain large corporations and trusts, their sponsors never quite imagined the sort of systematic coordination of all business in the economy that institutional investors have within their grasp.

The most promising path is for the antitrust enforcement agencies to threaten broad enforcement actions, but to offer a safe harbor to any institutional investor that comes into compliance with our rule. This would use existing institutions to enforce this new rule, creating a predictable business environment. Such safe harbors are a standard tool of antitrust policy used in a variety of areas at present to provide guidance to firms as they choose their business strategies.

However, there are clear impediments to this approach at present. Any antitrust authority or government trying to adopt such a policy would face a swift and overwhelming lobbying backlash, initially from the institutional investors, but eventually from the broader class of investors.[50] Anyone who earns substantially more of their income from capital or corporate power than is average in the population would stand to lose the monopoly profits that institutional investors earn for them. This group includes most families in the top 10% of income earners, but almost none outside this group.[51]

Still, the effort is worth it. Gains from breaking the power of institutional investors could be as much as 0.5% of national income, accounting only for effects on product markets.[52] Effects on labor markets are likely of the same magnitude, and those on politics (while far less certain) should not be smaller. This would increase the gains we calculate to 1.5%. Our other antitrust proposals below, while each individually narrower, should in total account for at least a third of this and thus raise the total value to 2% of national income. Effects on inequality should be similarly large. Extrapolating from our previous analysis beyond narrow product market effects in the same manner, our proposal would transfer about 2% of national income from the owners of capital to the broader public, thereby reducing the share of income captured by the top 1% by a percentage point.[53] This would go an eighth of the way to restoring the income shares of the top 1% that prevailed in the 1970s.

## Beyond Monopolies

While our primary focus so far and in chapter 1 was on the "monopoly" problem of concentrated power among sellers of goods, we also noted that large firms pose a problem of monopsony as well with respect to workers. Monopsony was a central feature of the industrial era, when the growth of industries allowed robber barons to artificially hold down the wages of workers who could not find good jobs outside of the industry they specialized in. Growing economic evidence suggests that monopsony is at least as great a problem as the monopoly power on which antitrust enforcement usually focuses. Starting in the Progressive era and culminating with the New Deal, the government introduced laws to support labor unions and protect workers from being overworked, underpaid, and subject to inadequate safety conditions in the workplace. These institutions played a crucial role, especially in industries that are natural monopsonies (where trying to avoid monopsony would do more harm than good).

However, many industries with monopsony power are not natural monopsonies, and antitrust has a powerful role to play in preventing monopsony from establishing itself in the first place. To take an example of how antitrust might address this problem, consider two coal mines in the same part of West Virginia. Their owners want to merge the mines. Together the mines account for less than 1% of national coal production and thus such a merger would not usually concern antitrust authorities. In fact, such authorities might look positively on the tendency of such a merger to "reduce labor costs." However, it would most likely do so not by actually reducing the amount of resources used to make coal, but instead by using the new labor market power of the mines to artificially depress wages and increase unemployment. Prior to the merger, the mines had to compete for workers, buoying wages. After the merger, the joint mine would be the only game in town and could force down wages to the point where workers drop out of the labor force and/or go on disability, leaving society to effectively pay their wages.

Monopsonistic conspiracies can also take subtler forms. A famous anticompetitive trick in typical markets is called "resale price maintenance." In this scheme, a supplier of, say, clothing insists that no retailer sells the clothing below a particular price. This can help ensure that the retailers do not compete with each other on price, increasing retailer profits. The clothing supplier can take advantage of these increased retail profits to charge retailers more and increase what it earns.

Recent research by sociologist Nathan Wilmers suggests a way to pull off the same trick, but in labor markets. A large retailer, such as Walmart, can insist that none of its suppliers of (say) clothing pay workers more than the minimum wage. This lowers the wage all workers expect and thus allows each supplier to stay competitive in the labor market while paying an extremely low wage. This in turn lowers the costs and raises the profit of suppliers, even though it may drive workers out of the labor force by lowering their earning opportunities. Walmart can benefit from these increased profits by striking more favorable deals with the suppliers. Wilmers provides evidence that something like this style of monopsonistic behavior has been happening systemically in US labor markets and may account for as much as 10% of the lagging of wage growth for lower-income workers below that for higher-income workers.[54] Antitrust authorities can and should, but at present do not, prevent such employer power as vigorously as they attack the power of producers over product markets.

Antitrust laws also are underenforced in local markets. Because national (or in the case of Europe, regional) antitrust authorities are much more powerful and experienced than those at more local levels, amassing of assets or collusion in a local area are often permitted. In his 2016 landmark sociological study of urban housing in the United States, *Evicted*, sociologist Matthew Desmond suggests that landlords in poor neighborhoods often buy up enough housing to have substantial power to drive up rents by holding units vacant and artificially depressing supply.[55] Yet as far as we know, no antitrust case has ever been brought against such local but potentially devastating attempts at monopolization.

Another growing area where antitrust goes underenforced is the digital economy. Competition there often happens through the sort of "disruption" highlighted by business scholar Clayton Christensen in his 1997 classic *The Innovator's Dilemma*, where entry by a new firm or product changes the nature of the market rather than produces a better or cheaper version of an existing product.[56] For example, Facebook is currently probably the most important competitor of Google (for user attention and advertiser dollars), but began in a completely unrelated business (of social networking as opposed to search functions). Antitrust authorities, who are accustomed to worrying about competition within existing, well-defined, and easily measurable markets, have allowed most mergers between dominant tech firms and younger potential disrupters to proceed. Google was allowed to buy mapping start-up Waze and artificial intelligence powerhouse Deep Mind; Facebook to buy Instagram and WhatsApp; and Microsoft to buy Skype and LinkedIn.

While such acquisitions doubtless help accelerate a path to market for start-up products and provide badly needed financing, they also have a dark side. Economist Luís Cabral has named these mergers "Standing on the Shoulders of Dwarfs": they may crush the possibility of new firms emerging to challenge the business model of existing industry leaders, instead co-opting them to cement the dominance of those leaders.[57] To prevent this dampening of innovation and competition, antitrust authorities must learn to think more like entrepreneurs and venture capitalists, seeing possibilities beyond existing market structures to the potential markets and technologies of the future, even if these are highly uncertain.

A final and more fraught area in which we believe antitrust has a role to play is preventing the excessive concentration of political power. Fears about the political influence of large firms were a central motivation for the original antitrust laws. Economist Luigi Zingales makes a forceful case in his 2012 book, *A Capitalism for the People*, that antitrust law should be used to block mergers that result in the acquisition of political influence through the concentration of lobbying capacity in a few firms.

Given the often discretionary nature of antitrust enforcement, there is a danger that such authority could be used selectively to attack rivals of the current party in power. We would only favor adoption of such a remit of authority once objective standards for judging the risk of excess political influence develop similar to those underlying existing merger guidelines. Nonetheless, this is an area that merits more research and regulatory attention than it has received in recent years.

Markets without competition are not markets at all, just as a one-party state cannot be a democracy. Because investors earn the highest returns by creating monopolies, markets are constantly in danger of becoming concentrated, and only the government can stand in the way. This chapter has focused on the most important such form of concentration of our era—the rise of the institutional investor. Our Radical approach, in the spirit of the Progressive economists, is to put a hard ceiling on the holdings of those investors. If our approach is followed, it will not only transform capital markets and generate a great deal of wealth, but also lead to greater prosperity for the least well-off. Yet we have also admitted that new forms of market concentration will predictably arise. To misquote another Radical, eternal vigilance is the price of market competition.[58]

# 5

# Data as Labor

## VALUING INDIVIDUAL CONTRIBUTIONS TO THE DIGITAL ECONOMY

Facebook: Jayla, why is Imani always trolling Deon's posts?

Jayla: I'm a little busy today, Facebook.

Facebook: I know, but rates are double today. If you can give me ten minutes to figure this out, you'll make $15.

"Ok what's up?"

"I'm trying to figure out what's going on between Imani and Deon. They used to only interact rarely, then not at all, and now Imani is always mocking what Deon posts."

"Yeah that's what happens when romance goes astray."

"Ah, so they were romantically involved? They didn't post about it."

"Right, not everyone likes to announce their intimate engagements to the world."

"I guess it makes sense now, given some other things I saw them doing . . ."

"You shouldn't be telling me about that!"

"So, who broke up with whom?"

"Can't you tell? Deon dumped Imani! That's why she's always trying to make him out to look like a sissy in her comments. She's getting back at him and wants to make him feel like he's nothing without her."

"I get it. Could you tell that just from the posts or did you know the whole story?"

"Well, they kept it pretty quiet, but I guessed from what was going down online and then I got Imani to go to yoga with me to give me the low-down."

"Do you two often talk about private things at yoga?"

"It's kinda a private girl place, and the physicality of the workout opens you up to talking things out."

"Well, thanks for your help, Jayla. Next time I'll hopefully be able to pick up these dynamics on my own and maybe even help you notice them. In the meantime, anything you need help with today?"

"Given you used up the time I was going to spend finding gifts for my cousins, maybe you can help me fix that."

"You mean for Diwali?"

"How did you know that?"

"Well, it is coming up next week and Malik's wife is Indian, so I thought their kids might be celebrating it."

"Good call. So, the problem is, honestly, I don't know what Diwali is, or what you get for it, or what you would get kids these days."

"I think I have the perfect thing: a virtual reality game for the kids and some artisanal sweets for the whole family. $25 total, plus $2 for the work I did finding it. Or you can subscribe to my personal assistant services for $100 a year. You've already spent $75 this year and we're not even halfway through."

"You're right, I should subscribe. You can charge my credit card. But I need the presents by tomorrow morning."

"Obviously, you do; I know when you're going to see them. The price includes a delivery by then. You're usually up by 9 and don't have anything scheduled then. Alright if the drone comes by to bring the sweets around then? The game will appear on their Oculus; how long after your arrival do you want that to happen?"

"Yeah that sounds good, and maybe 20 minutes."

"All set, I'll let you get back to your day."

"Thanks for the work and help, sorry I was a little cranky."

"No need to apologize to me. Just get some sleep, you were going hard last night."

"Good idea."

You probably find the idea of Facebook prying into the details of your friends' relationships, and paying you to help it, creepy. Yet this business practice, at one remove, is already ubiquitous. Why does Google enable us to plan our trips on Google maps? It learns traffic patterns, which it can then package into services it sells to ride-sharing and public transit platforms. Why does Facebook provide us a "free" space to build our social lives? Because we reveal personal information, which enables Facebook to match us with products we might be willing to buy. Why do Instagram and YouTube offer such useful ways to share media? The images and video they host are the inputs to "machine learning" (ML) systems that power "artificial intelligence" (AI) services that they sell to customers—from face recognition to automated video editing. If you aren't aware of how much platforms know about you and profit from this knowledge, check out the account settings pages they increasingly are required to have, which display this full set of information; you may be surprised.

The primary difference between the scenario we describe above and present practice, other than some advances in chat capacities, is that in the world we imagine, Facebook is open and honest about how it uses data and pays for the value it receives with money. The user's role as a vital cog in the information economy—as *data producer and seller*—is highlighted.

Why is this important? Most people do not realize the extent to which their labor—as data producers—powers the digital economy. Consider how people think of AI. In some portraits, AIs are autonomous agents built by brilliant and possibly mad programmers like the reclusive genius in the 2014 film *Ex Machina*, who set into motion a system that runs itself. Reality is different, however, as "the inventor of virtual reality" Jaron Lanier highlights in his brilliant 2013 book *Who Owns the Future?*,[1] which inspired many of our ideas in this chapter.[2]

AIs run on ML systems that analyze piles of human-produced data. "Programmers" do not write ingeniously self-determining algorithms. Instead, they design the interaction between workers (meaning us, the users who produce data) and machines (computational power) to produce specific information or production services. Most of the difficult work is not deriving profound algorithmic designs. Instead, it involves tweaking existing models to fit the relevant data and deliver the desired service. Programmers of ML systems are like modern factory floor managers, directing data workers to their most productive outlets.

The powerhouses of the digital economy, firms like Facebook, Google, and Microsoft, exploit the lack of public understanding of AI and ML to collect for free the data we all leave behind in our online interactions. This is the source of the record profits that make them the most valuable companies in the world. Facebook, for example, pays out only about 1% of its value each year to workers (programmers) because it gets the rest of its work for free from us! In contrast, Walmart pays out 40% of its value in wages.[3] People's role as data producers is not fairly used or properly compensated. This means that the digital economy is far behind where it should be, that the income from it is distributed to a small number of wealthy savants rather than to the masses, and that many of us have a false fear of AI creating mass unemployment when humans are more necessary than ever to our digital economy.

## The Rise of "Data Work"

Data work, like "women's work" and the cultural contributions of African Americans at one time, has been taken for granted. In the case of women, the extensive labor required to raise children and manage the home was treated as "private" behavior, motivated by altruism, that was outside the economy and hence not entitled to financial compensation or legal protections.[4]

In the case of African Americans, many of the defining concepts of modern American music and dance originated in the private entertainment practices of African American communities. As depicted in films like *Show Boat*, this creativity was often exploited by white entrepreneurs for profit. At the same time, African Americans were often not paid at all, as their contributions were dismissed as idle amusements.[5] Even when they managed to receive some compensation for performances, their intellectual property rights were usually disregarded, partly because they were excluded from the American Federation of Musicians, which was central to securing artists' rights, until the 1970s. The story of data work is less familiar than these iconic historical cases, but increasingly important.

Early in the life of what is now the Internet, its designers had to choose what information to record and what to discard. Many early designs supported technologies that would have made it easier for receivers of information to automatically pay the providers. These designs used two-way links where every piece of information would effectively carry its full provenance with it.[6] At various points in the development of the web, governments and companies made attempts to direct revenue to the diffused set of individuals who contributed value to the system. In France, the pre-Internet Minitel system had a system of micropayments,[7] for example, and the America OnLine (AOL) service popular in the 1990s in the United States charged its customers a fee and used the revenue to pay for content it made available within its simplified "walled garden" interface. For a period, some Internet designers were trying to force email to carry postage stamps as a way to deter spammers from flooding inboxes with junk.

Yet, what eventually became the mainstream Internet did not start as a commercial or economic project. Instead, it was a collaborative platform within government, military, and academic circles where participants were assumed to be interested in collaboration for reasons external to commercial motivations. The World Wide Web interface of hyperlinks developed by Tim Berners-Lee and others therefore placed emphasis on lowering barriers to participation rather than on providing incentives and rewards for labor. "Information wants to be free" became a slogan for entrepreneurs and a rallying cry for activists. It especially appealed to a Silicon Valley mentality that grew from the counterculture of the 1960s.[8]

During the 1990s, venture capital poured in to commercialize the booming Internet before online services had established how they would monetize their offerings. Internet companies relentlessly pursued users under the banner "usage, revenues later" (a "backronym" for "url"). While partly driven by the dot-com stock market bubble, this strategy was also influenced by the dominant position Microsoft had established by offering its operating system at relatively low cost and in a form compatible with many hardware platforms. The "network effects" created by this strategy were widely viewed as placing Microsoft in a position to reap enormous rewards.[9] This encouraged many venture capitalists to fund services that rapidly enlarged their user base even if their business model was unclear.

As the bursting of the tech bubble cooled this euphoria, emerging tech giants like Google had to find a way to make money from their user base. Google's Sergey Brin and Larry Page initially considered user fees and paid subscriptions, while insisting they would never turn to advertising. But several factors forced them to change their minds.[10]

First, the extended period of free access to services in the late 1990s caused users to become accustomed to an Internet where payment for pure information services was infrequent. People developed a strong attachment to the idea of completely free services, an attachment that likely made this tradition hard to break later.[11] In fact, a social and business movement developed around the concept that online services *should be* free, as embodied in entrepreneur and writer Chris Anderson's 2009 best-selling book, *Free: The Future of a Radical Price.*[12]

Second, many of the services provided online were, at least initially, occasional and small, with the result that investment in the development of infrastructure that would have been needed to keep track of payments was not cost-justified. In the late 1990s and early 2000s, many start-ups tried to create systems of micropayments. For example, usability guru Jakob Nielsen led a campaign for micropayments.[13] One of these efforts eventually became the payment platform PayPal. However, in practice (at least in its early years) the overhead costs of PayPal meant it was used only for large transactions. The emergence of social networking and blogging services of "Web 2.0," where many interactions are quick and superficial, made this problem worse. Required payments would have been too small to justify the costs on platforms like PayPal.

Third, in early days the Internet was an unfamiliar Wild West populated by many sophisticated young hackers who were willing to put up with inconvenience in exchange for "freedom." In this environment, dubiously legal services, such as Napster, thrived and could muscle out more secure legal services because mainstream alternatives struggled to keep up with technology. This made charging for anything, even established forms of intellectual property such as music, challenging.

Together, these forces established an environment where users were reluctant to pay for anything and the providers of services therefore searched for alternative means of staying afloat. Desperate for some way to monetize their massive user base, Google turned to advertising to stabilize its balance sheet. Facebook, YouTube, and others followed Google's lead.

Google's insight was that advertising online could be targeted more finely to user needs than is possible in traditional advertising media, like print newspapers or television. Because Google can glean the values and preferences of users from their search history, it can minimize advertising waste and noise. The personal ecosystem offered by Facebook, far more complex than a Google search, serves a similar function. Facebook learns details about users, which allows it to match them to advertisers who seek a narrowly targeted audience, and to place advertisements in social contexts by encouraging users to share advertising campaigns with their friends. Most important, it allows Facebook to identify the most opportune moments to hit users with a "reminder" to purchase something they had previously been considering, a feature that sometimes gives users the eerie sense that the service can read their minds.

## Factories for "Thinking" Machines

The insight that *data* about users were the central assets for technology giants became increasingly salient with the explosion of interest in "big data," ML, and AI. Machine learning is a "second-generation" approach to building AI systems. The first generation, which largely died out during the 1980s, focused on building formal logical rules that represented intellectual human tasks like language or game playing. This approach had some notable successes, including the Deep Blue computer, which defeated World Chess Champion Gary Kasparov. But it failed in most commercial applications. During the 1990s and early 2000s, a new approach based on statistics and probabilistic prediction came to the forefront.

The core idea of ML is that the world and the human minds that intelligently navigate it are more complicated and uncertain than any programmer can precisely formulate in a set of rules. Instead of attempting to characterize intelligence through a set of instructions that the computer will directly execute, ML devises algorithms that train often complicated and opaque statistical models to "learn" to classify or predict outcomes of interest, such as how creditworthy a borrower is or whether a photo contains a cat.

The most famous example of an ML algorithm is a "neural network," or neural net for short. Neural nets imitate the structure of the human brain rather than perform a standard statistical analysis. In the usual methods of statistics, different input variables are assumed to have relatively simple and independent effects on the "output" variables we want to explain. Being tall, being a man, and eating a sugar-rich diet are all assumed to be predictors of a high body weight in a relatively independent manner.

Neural networks work differently. Rather than inputs directly and independently determining outputs, the inputs are assumed to combine in complex ways to create "features" of the phenomenon being studied, which in turn determine other features, which eventually determine the outcome. Such complex relationships are familiar from everyday life. If we see a number of red pixels on a computer screen, we may realize the image is predominantly red. If we see a trunk and floppy ears, we may recognize an elephant. Only once we have perceived both of these shapes, however, do we realize we are looking at a representation of the Republican party, commonly denoted by the color red and the shape of an elephant. A number of red pixels on floppy ears alone would not directly suggest "Republican"; it would be as likely to convey a wound, for example.

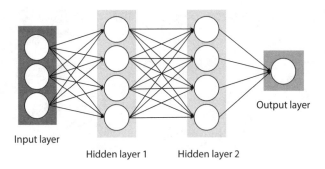

FIGURE 5.1: A stylized representation of a neural net.

A neural network is able to handle such sophisticated abstractions by learning the presence of more abstract features of data in its "hidden layers." Immediately apparent facts about an image, such as the shade of color of each pixel in an image, are represented by the activation of "neurons" or nodes in an "input layer." This input layer of neurons is then connected to a "hidden layer" meant to represent somewhat more abstract features. Neurons in this hidden layer will in turn activate when some weighted average of the inputs to that neuron surpass some "activation threshold." These activations tend to represent slightly more abstract and complex features of the image.

To achieve greater abstraction, this hidden layer is then connected to a second hidden layer, with the same properties, and so on. Eventually the last of these hidden layers yields to a final "output layer" that determines the eventual outcome of interest, such as a prediction of whether the photo is Republican campaign material. Figure 5.1 shows an example of a simple neural net with only two hidden layers.

Neural nets can, in principle, encode a very wide range of relationships, especially when the number of layers is large. Typically, each layer will encode a higher level of abstraction

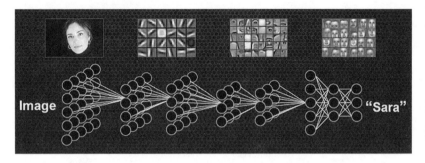

FIGURE 5.2: A facial recognition neural net. Deeper layers represent higher degrees of abstraction.

than the layer below it. Figure 5.2 represents an example. "Shallow" layers, near the input image on the left, represent relatively simple features of the image. On the far left we see a typical image input. Next, to its right, we see a shallow hidden layer. A typical set of patterns that leads to activation of this neuron is shown. This layer tends to detect lines and colors oriented in various directions, a relatively simple and concrete idea. A deeper layer, shown to its right, encodes elements of a typical face, such as eyes, ears, noses, etc. On the far right we see one of the deepest layers, closest to output. These show abstract versions of entire faces. Once a neural network reaches this level of abstraction, it is clear how it can detect faces: the firing of one or more of these deepest "facial recognition" neurons indicates that a face is present in the picture. Neural networks thus achieve astonishing intelligence through repeatedly reprocessing increasingly complex inputs into more complex ones through a series of layers, until they finally reach their desired prediction.

How does a neural network learn, from the endless possible combinations of weights at each layer, which ones are right to predict the outcome of interest (the presence of a face in this case)? There are three critical components that go into making a working neural net. First, "data," usually an extremely large collection of labeled examples; in this case, this would be a large number of photos tagged as containing or not containing a face. Second, "computation." Neural nets are usually run on large farms of servers. Last (and, as we will argue, least), "supervisors," the programmers who set up the structure of the net, help prevent it from getting stuck, and use various tricks of the trade to ensure it learns quickly and effectively.

Neural nets are nothing new. Researchers have been interested in them on and off at least since the late 1950s. However, until about a decade ago, neural nets were widely viewed as useless: in 1995 one of the founders of ML, Vladimir Vapnik, bet an extravagant dinner that by 2005 "no one in his right mind will use neural nets."[14] The problem was that "shallow" neural nets, those with few layers, could not accomplish much. Most interesting properties of objects are much more abstract than these simple, shallow nets could detect. On the other hand, attempts to train deeper nets failed for years because of the lack of data and computational power.

Without sufficient numbers of labeled examples, the space of possible representations was simply too large for the neural net to search through. It would thus end up "overfitting" to irrelevant details of particular images, such as the fact that all images containing a face might have exactly three red pixels in the picture. The problem of overfitting—that is, of trying to fit a complex model to insufficient data—is nicely illustrated by the xkcd cartoon partially reproduced in figure 5.3. If we allow a complex set of rules to predict presidential elections, there are too few examples to fit these complex rules and thus our rules can easily "overfit" to inessential features of the elections, resulting in bad predictions. The more complex the rules we

FIGURE 5.3: The problem of overfitting, illustrated by predicting presidential elections. *Source:* Excerpted from "Electoral Precedent" at https://xkcd.com/1122/.

want to fit (the deeper and more fully connected the neural net), the more data we need to avoid overfitting. Computer scientists and statisticians call the number of labeled data points needed to avoid overfitting for a problem (such as recognizing faces, or artistic styles) the "sample complexity" of the problem.[15]

Data alone, however, are insufficient to train a neural net. These data have to be stored and processed. More important, the process of actually training the net requires huge numbers of computations. Without ample computers capable of performing all these calculations, neural nets never find the right explanation of the observed data, no matter how much of it there is. The dramatic advances in computational and storage capacity on the cloud in the late 2000s were critical to allowing neural nets to be trained. The deeper and more complicated a net, the greater computation and storage required to train it. The computation and storage requirements of a net are called its "computational complexity."

The last component of making a neural net function is programming. Programmers currently play important roles in tweaking the structure of the net and the procedure by which it is trained. However, these processes are being automated through a movement called "democratizing AI" led by Microsoft.[16] The number of programmers required, unlike the amount of data and computation, does not inevitably grow with the complexity of nets. More basic research, proposing new algorithms, or training techniques, can have a greater impact, but in practice the advantages granted by such algorithmic advances are usually short-lived and quickly replicated. The crucial components of success for nets are data and computational power.

While simple, shallow nets, which can solve basic problems such as detecting whether a picture is oriented horizontally or vertically, have low complexity (both sample and computational), more complicated, deep nets, which can solve more sophisticated problems like personalized facial recognition or generating blurbs describing the action in a photo, are much more complex in terms of both the data and computation they require.

This is why neural nets were hardly used prior to the late 2000s and then, beginning around 2010, exploded to become perhaps the hottest technology of the day. It was around that time that both the volume of data collected and the speed and depth of computation became sufficient to allow applications that made a difference in users' lives. Around that time the first ML-powered personal digital assistants and dictation services emerged; Siri, Google Assistant, and Cortana became familiar features of everyday life. Even more ambitious applications are being developed, including virtual and augmented reality, self-driving cars, and drones that deliver goods to consumers at the click of a button.

Because these services have high "sample complexity," they require vast stores of data on which to train the ML systems. Thus, the vast data sets collected by Google, Facebook, and others as a by-product of their core business functions became a crucial source of revenue and competitive advantage. Companies that started as reluctantly free service providers in search of a revenue model and morphed into advertising platforms are now in the process of becoming data collectors, delivering services that lure users into providing information on which they train AIs using ML.

## Sirens and Titans

Jaron Lanier describes such platforms as "siren servers." Their allure, he explains, derives from the combination of the free services they offer because of their scale and exceptional data access. Yet Lanier worries about the social and economic consequences of their business model. Because they do not pay their users for data, they do not give their users proper incentives to supply data that are most needed.

For example, right now Facebook receives a constant flow of hundreds of millions of new photos posted each day by users. These photos are good training grounds for ML systems that Facebook is developing to automatically label and even explain photos. Yet at present, there is a mismatch between Facebook's needs and the reasons that users post photos. Users often provide little information accompanying a photo because they expect their friends to understand the context of it.

The result is that the data that Facebook receives are low-quality. Facebook tries to nudge users to provide useful labels by inducing them to write comments explaining photos or by associating emotions with them. But what Facebook really needs is the capacity to ask users simple questions about the photos and receive answers from them.

Lacking direct input of this kind, Facebook sometimes employs "crowd workers" to label the images after the fact. But these workers will rarely understand a photo as well as the person who posted it does. If, instead of hiding their ML algorithm's use of data from users, Facebook were to make users aware of the role they played, and to reward them for inconvenient but valuable contributions, ML systems would have better data to work with. This alternative world, sketched in our opening vignette, would allow them to supply better AI services to their customers and clients.

Another example is YouTube, to which 300 hours of video are uploaded every minute, according to the website. Yet the producers of this content receive minimal compensation. While the analytics are a bit complicated, a typical YouTube content creator receives roughly $2 for 1,000 views of a video. Given that an average YouTube video lasts about 4 minutes, this means that creators can expect about five hundredths of a cent per minute their videos are viewed. In contrast, Netflix pockets about half a cent per minute a typical user watches its videos, or roughly ten times as much.[17] It is not a great surprise, therefore, that Netflix has produced critically acclaimed television series like *Orange Is the New Black* and *House of Cards*, while YouTube videos are less celebrated for their cultural value. Similar calculations apply to the contrast between traditional news outlets and Twitter. These prices are all likely a small fraction of the value users derive from watching. People's time is worth more than a few percent of a cent. This phenomenon is broader than video, however; the siren servers have thrived on devaluing creative content from news to music and appropriating the value it generates for themselves rather than creators.[18]

Lanier also worries about the distributional and social consequences of the failure to pay for data and online creative production. There is widespread concern that AI systems will displace many human workers. A widely discussed engineering study found that nearly half of all jobs in the United States are likely to be automated in coming decades.[19] While skepticism is warranted, even the possibility of massive long-term job loss justifies thought about how to limit the negative distributive and social consequences. Experience with automation suggests that communities where "robots take the jobs" are usually hard hit, not just in terms of income, but also with regard to the sense of purpose of community members.[20]

Job turnover and displacement have always been unfortunate consequences of technological progress. New types of jobs regularly replace old ones: artisans were replaced by factory hands, human computers by electronic ones, buggy whips by taxi drivers. In each generation, new techniques for producing existing goods offered new kinds of jobs and new goods appeared, which required workers. What strikes many as uniquely worrisome about AI, from this perspective, is that it seems not just to make humans more productive. It holds out the possibility of entirely replacing humans in a wide range of tasks while offering no alternative role for human work.

Nor do these fears seem unwarranted by the economic data. According to one of our ongoing projects with collaborators including Lanier, the share of income going to labor in the largest tech companies is roughly 5–15%, lower than any industry other than extractive ones such as oil, and dramatically lower than service-sector companies like Walmart, where labor's share is roughly 80%.[21] Labor economists have argued that the rise of powerful companies with large monopsony power has been driving down labor's share of income.[22] Their data are too aggregated by confidentiality restrictions to determine the exact sectoral nature of these changes, but it seems plausible that the high-technology industry plays a major role in it. *If* these AI-driven companies represent the future of broader parts of the economy without something basic changing in their business model, we may be headed for a world where labor's share falls dramatically from its current roughly 70% to something closer to 20–30%.

That is a big "if." Forecasting the course of technology is notoriously difficult. Lanier's insight, however, is that even if this does come to pass, AIs are not actually the free-standing replacement for human labor they appear to be. They are trained with and learn from human data. Thus AI, just as much as fields or factories, offers a critical role for ordinary human labor—as suppliers of data, or what we will call *data as labor*. Failing to recognize data as labor could thus create what Lanier calls "fake unemployment," where jobs dry up not because humans are not useful but because the valuable inputs they supply are treated as byproducts of entertainment rather than as socially valued work. Even if AI never lives up to its hype, data as labor may offer important supplemental earning opportunities and sense of social contribution to citizens affected by rising inequality. Yet none of this will happen unless people change their attitudes toward data.

## Diamonds in the Rough

Lanier's view might strike some readers as pessimistic. In the existing system, people disclose huge amounts of data about themselves in return for the services the Internet provides—searching, mapping, digital assistance, and so on. Why is it important for people to be paid for data in money rather than in-kind in the form of valuable services?

The leading advocate of this view is Hal Varian, chief economist at Google, who has argued that data are omnipresent these days and that what is scarce are the talent and computational power needed to make sense of these data. Varian thinks that all that is needed for AI services to succeed is for nothing to stand in the way of "natural" collection of data by siren servers, and ample rewards to talented engineers and perceptive investors for their contribution to the mechanics and infrastructure. In this view, data are much more like capital than labor: they are a naturally available resource, harvested from the public domain (where they are freely available), and transformed into something useful only by the hard work of programmers, entrepreneurs, and venture capitalists who then deserve to own the data.[23]

Another way to think about this view is in relation to Adam Smith's classic "diamond-water" paradox. Smith found it paradoxical that water was so valuable in use and yet had little value in exchange, while diamonds have such limited uses and yet have great value in exchange. This diamond-water paradox was finally resolved by the "marginal revolution" of the late nineteenth century in which William Stanley Jevons, Léon Walras, and Carl Menger (the first two of whom you may recall from chapter 1) argued that the exchange value of a good is determined by the *marginal* value of the last unit of a good available,

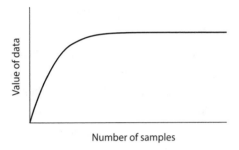

**FIGURE 5.4**: The value of data as a function of the number of observations in a standard statistical estimation problem. The marginal value declines rapidly. Thanks to Nicole Immorlica for providing this graph.

rather than the *average* value gained by its consumption. While the average value of water is high, its marginal value is low as it is so plentiful. Varian's argument is that while data may have enormous value in total or on average, *on the margin* no individual's data are worth much.

Varian's argument is persuasive if we focus on traditional uses of data in classical, pre-ML statistics. In standard statistics, the goal is to measure some parameter of interest; the simplest example would be the average of something (say, income) in a population. Under common assumptions, the marginal value of an additional individual's income in allowing you to measure the average income in the population diminishes rapidly, because the more you see, the less uncertainty you have about this average. The marginal reduction in uncertainty dies off as the 1.5 power of the number of individuals; this mathematical relationship is depicted in figure 5.4.

For example, if the marginal reduction in uncertainty from one more individual's data when there are only one hundred individuals observed is one unit, by the time we observe a million individuals, the value is a mere one one-millionth. Moreover, it is rarely useful to know a quantity extremely precisely. Most of the time knowing it roughly serves our purposes. An entrepreneur who wants to open a wealth management firm in a neighborhood wants to know whether the average income is $100,000 or $200,000, but doesn't need to know that it is $201,000 rather than $200,000. Initially collected data not only reduce uncertainty by more: those initial reductions (from huge uncertainty to reasonably bounded guesses) are more valuable than are later refinements. Thus, in a standard statistical world, data rapidly lose their value. For standard statistics, "big data" are mostly useless. Small data suffice.

The world of ML is different from the world of standard statistics for two reasons that mirror the reasons why data have so little value in the classical statistics perspective. First, the difference in approach between ML and standard statistics is how they relate to complexity. Recall that different problems of different complexity require different amounts of data. In statistics, the goal is to solve a single, simple problem. In ML, as data grow we try to teach the AI system new and more complicated things, to solve problems with increasing sample complexity.

For any one, well-defined learning task, data only tend to have marginal value for a limited range of data sizes, those close to the sample complexity of the problem. When the available data are much below the sample complexity, there are not enough data to even get started on learning. Above this size, most learning has already taken place, so additional data quickly run into the diminishing returns we highlighted above.

This pattern of data values is pictured in figure 5.5. Each vertical line represents the sample complexity of some problem in machine vision; more complex problems lie to the right.

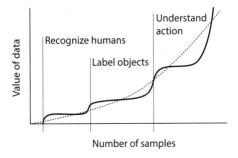

**FIGURE 5.5:** The value of data as a function of the number of observations in a typical ML domain, here machine vision. Each vertical line represents the sample complexity of a particular problem. Thanks to Nicole Immorlica for providing the graph.

Notice that, after the sharp rise around the sample complexity point, the shape of the curve, at least for a while, closely matches what we saw in classical statistics. Once we have reached enough data to make progress on a particular ML task (such as recognizing whether there is a human in a photo), this problem becomes like a classical statistics problem and additional data lose their value at a similar rate. Until we reach this point, data go through a long period of being useless for the opposite reason and then being incredibly useful over a very short range where the data teach the system what it needs to know.

However, while this pattern holds for any *given* task the ML system wants to learn, the overall learning of the system is quite different, as the figure illustrates. While at any given time the system is only in the data range of learning one or a few things, at any given time it is most likely learning *something*. In the figure, a vision system based on a third of the data (labeled photographs) that has been collected has already mastered recognizing the presence of a human, and additional labeled photographs are of little value. The system also is not yet close to having enough data to understand the nature of the action in the photograph; this is much too complex a problem. However, between these two complexities it can learn to label all discrete objects in the photograph. Thus, additional data are now useless for both the recognition and analysis problems, but very useful for the labeling problem. From this perspective, the primary determinant of the marginal value is not the statistics of a given ML problem, but rather the *distribution of complexity across different problems.*

Just as with classical statistics, there is a second critical question that determines the marginal value of data: how important it is to solve each of the problems data allow ML to tackle. If simple, early problems have much greater value than later, more complex ones, data will have diminishing value. However, if later, harder problems are more valuable than earlier, easier ones, then data's marginal value may increase as more data become available. A classic example of this is speech recognition. Early ML systems for speech recognition achieved gains in accuracy more quickly than did later systems. However, a speech recognition system with all but very high accuracy is mostly useless, as it takes so much time for the user to correct the errors it makes. This means that the last few percentage points of accuracy may make a bigger difference for the value of a system than the first 90% does. The marginal value grows to the extent that it allows this last gap to be filled.

To understand these dynamics, consider the oft-abused analogy to human learning. The analogy we are drawing is between the learning processes; we *do not* mean to say that AIs really are like humans. For learning any given skill, studying is mostly useless, then very useful, and then mostly useless again.

For example, until you are advanced enough to grasp calculus, studying math will do little or nothing to advance your understanding of calculus; it will seem impossibly complex. And once you know calculus passably well, additional study will quickly become wasted and redundant. Yet for a critical period, the study is extremely valuable in learning calculus.

At most points in a mathematics education, you will be mastering some more or less useful skill (multiplication, trigonometry, calculus, probability, etc.) and study will be valuable at acquiring that skill, but of little immediate use for other skills. Whether the marginal returns to studying math overall increase or diminish as you learn more depends on whether the more complex skills have greater or lesser value than the simpler ones. This depends on many factors, and the relationship may not always have a clear direction: multiplication may be more useful than geometry, but less useful than calculus, which you learn even later. But overall evidence on the labor market returns to education suggests that the value of additional years of schooling does not trail off very quickly: advanced degrees often boost earning power by more over what someone with a basic education earns than a basic education does over none.[24]

We suspect something similar is true of ML. While additional data may not improve some services that have matured (like selecting movies you like), the same data may improve other services that are at an early stage (virtual reality, speech translation). In many cases the more complex and sophisticated services are more valuable. This is shown in figure 5.5, where the value gained by later services is greater than the value gained from earlier services. If this is true, then data may actually have *increasing* rather than diminishing returns, as more data allow for the solution of more complicated and more valuable problems. Furthermore, since human culture is always developing in new ways, AI/ML will always need more data to keep up. Even if AIs do eventually "learn everything" and data run into diminishing returns, that day will arrive only in the distant future, once we have AI systems capable of mimicking not only an individual human intelligence but all collective human intelligence.

### Technofeudalism

Why, then, do siren servers not voluntarily pay their users to supply the high-quality data that would allow them to develop the best services? If data production is labor, why doesn't a market for data work emerge as a part of the broader labor market?

In fact, we have seen tentative first signs of markets for high-quality, labeled data. Many researchers and some companies use Amazon's Mechanical Turk (mTurk) marketplace to pay online workers to label and clean data sets, and to participate in social-science experiments. This is not entirely new. Television ratings are still determined by Nielsen, which pays households a small fee to record their viewing.

Notice, however, that the buyers of data in these settings are for the most part *not* the siren servers we have been discussing. Instead, they are smaller companies, academic researchers, and financial firms with no direct access to data. Many of these businesses have exciting prospects. Work Fusion, for example, offers a sophisticated incentive scheme to workers to help train AIs to automate business processes. Might AI firms hire workers to label maps and road images and sell the labeled data to companies producing self-driving cars?

However, the total size of these markets is tiny compared to the number of users who produce data used by the siren servers. The number of workers on mTurk is in the tens of thousands, compared to billions of users of services offered by Google and Facebook.[25] The data titans (Google, Facebook, Microsoft, etc.) do not pay for most of their data. The most important players, those who have the scale of data necessary to tackle the most complex problems, are mostly absent from these markets, instead relying on "free" data passively collected from their user base. Of course, these data are not really free; the siren servers provide services to users in exchange for receiving their data.

This arrangement, in which users take advantage of services and the company gains all the upside of the data they generate, may sound novel, but it is actually very old. Prior to the rise of capitalism, feudal labor arrangements worked similarly. Lords insulated their serfs from fluctuations in markets and guaranteed them safety and traditional rights to use the land and to keep enough of their crop to survive. In exchange, lords took all the upside of the market return on serfs' agricultural output. Similarly, today, siren servers provide useful and enjoyable information services, while taking the market value of the data we produce in exchange. We thus refer to this contemporary system as "technofeudalism."

This arrangement is far from optimal. Users who have exceptional skills or knowledge, but who are not enthusiastic about using social media, stay away and deny the value of their contributions to online social life and ML systems. So, too, do people who are poor or otherwise marginalized. Conversely, the lack of payments in the digital world makes it impossible for anyone to specialize in adding value through their data: one cannot live on the free services that Facebook and Google offer. Technofeudalism also stunts personal development, just as feudalism stunted the acquisition of education or investment in improving land. The inability to earn money in these environments undercuts the possibility of developing skills or careers around digital contributions, as technoserfs know any investment they make will be expropriated by the platforms. At best, by becoming an exceptionally active member of a digital community one can earn some kudos, badges, and recognition that one can hope to parlay into some vaguely related work offline. At worst, regardless of how much you contribute, you still receive the same digital services as anyone else.

This lack of effective incentives forces siren servers to set up their services so it is simple and convenient for the users to supply this data. Any inconvenient data labeling, or the supply of data from people not inclined to use the services provided by the siren servers, is impossible in a pure feudal system. While interaction environments can be designed to prompt users for useful information (e.g., by making available emoticons that allow users to label their interactions with their corresponding emotions), there are limits to the detail and usefulness of the tags that users will supply purely for fun in the course of entertainment and consumption.

This fact does not escape the siren servers. Most have their own crowd-sourcing platforms, which label huge sets of data they collect through other means to improve the value, reliability, and usefulness of these data. Siren servers go to extraordinary lengths to hide the role of human data work in producing their "magical" services, to the point where efforts to expose this work have become something of a social movement among Internet workers' activists,[26] as described by anthropologist Mary Gray and computer scientist Sid Suri in their upcoming book *Demanding Work*.[27] For example, Google quietly subcontracts more than 10,000 human raters to give feedback on the quality of its search results in cases where organic user feedback is insufficient, yet it took investigative reporting to uncover this practice.[28] Thus, while siren servers clearly need help from ordinary users, they wastefully contort themselves to go around the most natural channel (asking those organically interacting with their services for feedback) and make minimal payments to workers outside of this chain, hiding this practice and its importance from the public eye. At the same time, these companies have come to occupy a position of commanding influence over media and policy discussions because of their role in curating information and funding policy research.[29]

## Digital Whitewash

In ongoing work with Lanier and other collaborators, one of us is trying to explain why siren servers have tolerated this wasteful state of affairs. A useful analogy is a story from Mark Twain's *Tom Sawyer* in which Tom tries to unload his responsibility for whitewashing a fence onto his friends. His first approach is paying them, but it fails. He soon realizes that if he pretends to be enjoying the task, they will not only agree to perform the work for him but pay him for the privilege. An extensive literature in psychology has shown that, in the right social context, labor becomes leisure; work becomes entertainment.[30]

Siren servers followed in Tom's footsteps. They began collecting user data in the normal course of business, only to find that users were happily laying golden eggs for them to entertain themselves. Users of social networks provide precious labeled photographs for free to connect with their friends. Google powers its ML analysis of videos from funny YouTube posts. Very few users are paid much for their contributions, allowing the siren servers, who can sell advertising and, increasingly, AI services, to pull in large profits.

Siren servers, especially the leaders in data collection (Facebook and Google), are unlikely to begin paying for data to improve its quality or volume of their own accord. The basic problem is that there are only a few siren servers to compete for user data. Each one knows that if it starts paying for some data, competition among the services will quickly force them to pay for all the data they are currently receiving for free. Paying users, even in a relatively limited set of valuable contexts, is likely to undermine the siren server business model of exploiting free data for several reasons.

First and most basically, the market power (what economists call *monopsony* or *oligopsony* power) of siren servers means that any change to the market which causes users to be paid for their data will increase the siren servers' costs.

The importance of monopsony power in markets for data labor was first highlighted in a paper by Gray and Suri along with economist Sara Kingsley.[31] Since that time, empirical analysis by Suri and his collaborators has confirmed that task posters in mTurk have a remarkable degree of monopsony power, even if they are not very large players in the market, given the time and task-type specificity of "turkers'" interest in completing jobs.[32]

The monopsony power of the siren servers is dramatically larger. They offer a far larger fraction of all potential available work of this form. While it is difficult to quantify, it seems very likely that a majority of all valuable online and perhaps all digital data are collected by Facebook and Google; in 2015, Google's share of Internet searches (with which most browsing begins) was 64% and on average Facebook's 1.5 billion users spent 50 minutes every day on the site or app.[33] The huge fraction of the market controlled by these giants means that they would bear most of the brunt of increased prices for what are currently free data.

Given that most of the productive work to be done is not separate "crowdsourcing" that workers explicitly seek out, but rather work in the course of entertaining online interactions, competing companies would have to build up services of comparable quality and user devotion before they would be able to make productive use of querying users for valuable data. Several start-ups have adopted this model in an effort to attract users to an alternative social network (e.g., empowr) or data management service (e.g., Datacoup). However, they have attracted only a few users with an ideological attachment to the idea. Most users prefer a network that is used by most of their friends and that offers higher quality services.

One start-up that has succeeded in eliciting more useful data from users is reCAPTCHA, familiar to most Internet users as the puzzles one is often asked to solve to prove one is not a bot in order to access an online service. While the CAPT-CHAs that reCAPTCHA asks users to solve serve a security purpose, they were designed as a data source for digitizing text and increasingly as a data source for training automated text recognition and other ML-based systems. Note, however, that reCAPTCHA was successful precisely because it partnered with existing siren servers, was incorporated into their product offerings, and never offered monetary payment. After Google acquired reCAPTCHA for a reported $30 million in

2009, a Massachusetts user unsuccessfully sued Google for violating labor laws based on the theory that reCAPTCHA is unpaid labor.[34]

Most potential data labor market competitors for the siren servers would find it hard to make use of data in anywhere near as productive a way as the siren servers can. As we highlighted above, the highest-end AI services become possible only with massive computational and data capacities. These capacities are only within the grasp of a few digital titans. Of course, a start-up could gather data in the hopes of selling it to the siren servers, but they would have just as strong an interest in avoiding paying for data through the back door as they would through any other route. In short, the siren servers have occupied the central piece of real estate in a "digital commons" that has room for only a few players, and their interests are now opposed to paying technoserfs who are at present voluntarily tilling this land.

Beyond the market structure and the nature of AI technology, the nature of social media makes these sites particularly resistant to competition. Most users want to be part of a social network that includes all of their friends. These *network effects* can make it difficult for competitors to enter the market unless they have enough financial backing to subsidize users for years—and the social norms around money not changing hands makes even that strategy challenging to pull off. Many social scientists have also argued that siren servers use techniques similar to those employed by casinos to make their content addictive.[35] Together these properties raise the power of siren servers to lock users into patterns that may not serve their long-term interests.

Second, as highlighted by economist Roland Bénabou and Nobel Laureate Jean Tirole in their incisive 2003 and 2006 analyses of situations like the Tom Sawyer problem, paying for an activity often undermines *intrinsic* motivations (such as entertainment and social pressure).[36] Paying for online data provision may signal to users that the activities they currently view as entertainment are actually labor benefiting the siren servers and for which they should demand payment, undermining the entertainment value. Paying may also undermine the perceived motives of social collaboration and participation that may yield social rewards to users for "being part of an online community." On a darker side, paying may also undermine the stickiness of content as it "breaks the spell" of online entertainment by making clearer the nature of the economic relationship.

Third, despite media accounts about the data economy, most users are still unaware of the value companies harvest from their data.[37] In order to pay users for supplying the most valuable data to siren servers, servers would have to make explicit requests for labels, comments, and other user input. As users become aware of the "creepiness" of the current situation, their attitude toward online interactions is likely to change in a manner that will be both costly and disruptive to siren servers, as well as unpredictable. Publicity about Facebook's experimentation with the emotional valence of its users' newsfeeds created a public backlash, and research suggests that users who become aware of the "creepy" surveillance of technology tend to become distrustful of digital services or to use them in ways that reduce the value of their data.[38]

Finally, realizing Lanier's vision for data as labor would require building a variety of sophisticated technical systems. The architecture of many digital systems would have to be adjusted to keep track of the origin of and uses of data, so users could be rewarded at least for the average value their data create but ideally to some extent for the unique value their data may occasionally end up yielding.[39] ML systems would have to be designed to determine particularly valuable data to them; then their requests for data would need to be channeled to consumer-facing products; and finally, these products would need to be designed to query the users for extra data in a minimally intrusive way.

Another part of this problem is that users could find it burdensome to transact over the Internet on a regular basis. We imagined that Facebook would offer Jayla $15 for a few minutes of her time, but what if the actual value of the information supplied by Jayla is worth 15 cents or 15 thousandths of a cent? Personal advisor systems would have to be built to guide user choices and receive only occasional user feedback while handling all payments. Even with such systems, a basic shift in user perceptions of and social attitudes toward online interactions would be necessary.

Conversely, there would have to be a more effective way for siren servers to ensure the quality and value of the data they are receiving. Several years ago, when Microsoft experimented with paying users for their data, large numbers of bots sprang up to exploit the system and extract large amounts of money without providing value to the company. Without some way to keep track of users, which would necessarily impose further burdens on the users themselves, paying for data could easily be exploited.

The last three factors we highlight are mostly reasons that treating data as labor might also be socially undesirable. We believe these factors would be outweighed by the benefits in the medium term. However, when these factors are combined with siren servers' monopsony power, network effects, and interests in manipulating user psychology, it is unsurprising that siren servers have not yet undertaken this ambitious transition.

On the other hand, it is possible that siren servers that are poorer in data, such as Amazon, Apple, and Microsoft, could have both the scale to make competition possible and the incentive to break up this unproductive monopsony. By creating an alternative ideology to the prevailing focus on "free" stuff online, they could help break the dominant business model of their rivals and open up a chance to compete. However, it is also plausible that the structure of the industry makes it unlikely that any private entity will voluntarily and on its own shift to a more productive model. Social and regulatory pressure may be necessary to catalyze change.

## Workers' Struggle

Many aspects of the story we have told are unique to present technology and the norms that have developed around the Internet. However, the idea that monopsonistic power created by technologies with strong economies of scale would lead to undercompensated labor and thus retard both economic development and equality is not a new one. It is one of the classic themes of economic history and the central idea of the most famous economic historian of them all, Karl Marx.

A central intellectual aim of Marx's 1867 first volume of *Das Kapital* was to explain why the wealth and well-being of proletarians (workers without property) had, as of the mid-nineteenth century, improved so little since the end of feudalism.[40] Marx claimed to identify a necessary tendency of capitalists to "exploit" workers by holding their wages below the value they generated. Marx argued that these labor practices created what his collaborator Friedrich Engels called a "reserve army of the labor" (that is, a class of unemployed) whose even more squalid condition would persuade workers to do anything to maintain their jobs.[41]

As economist John Roemer showed, Marx's conclusions are extremely unlikely to prevail if employers compete for workers.[42] However, they are exactly what one would anticipate in a world where capitalists conspired with each other, or had sufficient unilateral power, to hold down wages. Beatrice and Sydney Webb, a dynamic pair of late nineteenth-century British Radicals, advocated collective bargaining by workers, arguing that it would make production more efficient by raising wages above the levels that drove workers out of the labor force.[43] John Kenneth Galbraith, the mid-twentieth-century American economist we met in chapter 2, hailed unions as a necessary form of "countervailing power" required to balance the power of monopsonists.[44]

This view has been partly vindicated by the research of subsequent economists. Economic historian Robert C. Allen shows that prior to the emergence of unions, British wages during the early process of industrialization hardly advanced at all despite improvements in technology.[45] Once unions managed to counter the monopsony power of British industrialists, not only did wages quickly increase, but the pace of overall productivity radically accelerated. Economists David Autor, Daron Acemoglu, and Suresh Naidu believe that the breaking of monopsony power through labor unions, government labor regulation, minimum wages, and other reforms was critical to the further acceleration of productivity.[46] Beyond their role in collective bargaining, unions served other functions that helped support the "Fordist" mode of assembly line–based production that prevailed in the twentieth century: they screened and guaranteed the quality of the work produced by their workers and helped them learn the skills required by a rapidly changing work environment.

To be sure, many other things were happening at the same time, making it difficult to trace clear lines of historical causation. Unions also brought many inefficiencies and rigidities, caused strikes, and may themselves have accumulated significant market power. The hostility they attracted and the extent to which they became inflexible and outmoded has led to their decline in the last several decades.

Yet even as unions have declined, some of the conditions we describe above have important resemblance to the conditions that helped stimulate their growth and benefits. The monopsony power of siren servers, we have argued, may be holding down wages for data laborers at 0 (or more precisely at the value of the services and entertainment these laborers derive from using digital services). This may suppress the productivity of the digital economy by reducing the quality and quantity of data and contribute to the maldistribution of gains from AI technologies. An individual data worker lacks bargaining power, so she cannot credibly threaten to withdraw her data from Facebook or Google unless she receives a fair reward.

Furthermore, to realize the gains from data as labor, data workers will need some organization to vet them, ensure they provide quality data, and help them navigate the complexities of digital systems without overburdening their time. These triple roles, of collective bargaining, quality certification, and career development, are exactly the roles unions played during the Industrial Age.

It may be time for "data workers of the world (to) unite" into a "data labor movement."[47] A striking feature of the data labor market is that it is an international market, one that is almost completely unaffected by borders and government regulation. Once people awaken to their role as data laborers—obtain a "class consciousness," if you will—organizations (sort of like unions) may emerge to supply data laborers with the means to engage in collective action. Imagine, for example, a data labor union that solicited members—the data laborers—by promising them higher payments for their data. Once the union obtained a critical mass, it could approach Facebook or Google and threaten a "strike" (also, effectively, a boycott because data laborers are simultaneously consumers of Facebook's and Google's services). The technical details would be complex, but we can imagine a range of possible approaches.

The union could simply call on its members to stop using Facebook or Google for a day if the companies do not negotiate. A more complicated approach could involve routing data labor through platforms set up by the union, so that the union could disrupt the supply of data if and when the Internet companies on the other side refused to pay reasonable wages. A Facebook user would reach her Facebook account through the union's platform, so that the union could enforce collective action among users by shutting down the account or providing limited access to the account for the duration of the strike. At present, an Internet Service Provider could organize such an action, though it would need to structure itself as a labor union to avoid antitrust charges.

It seems to us that these unions could be effective. Unlike traditional unions, they combine labor stoppages and consumer boycotts—because, as noted, data laborers are simultaneously consumers. During a strike, Facebook would lose not only access to data (on the labor side) but access to ad revenues (on the consumer side). It's as if autoworkers could pressure GM or Ford not only by stopping production but also by refusing to purchase cars. Also unlike traditional unions, which must struggle to maintain solidarity during strikes, the data unions could enforce the "picket line" electronically. Furthermore, the very network effects that entrench digital monopolies would work against them in this scenario: it would be embarrassing to break a Facebook strike if all your friends were striking on the same day.

Finally, a data labor union might help foster digital competition by breaking the stranglehold on data of a few of the most powerful siren servers. The unions might find it optimal to share data between many different digital companies, rather than causing it to accumulate in one place. Of course, there are downsides as well—data unions, like traditional unions, might abuse their authority. However, we believe that at the present time, in light of the absence of any market—Radical or otherwise—in data labor, the gains exceed the losses.

## A Penny for Your Thoughts

A first and necessary step before any of this is possible, however, is getting a quantitative grip on the value of data. Things that are not measured are not priced, and often once something is measured precisely, it begins to be priced organically. Systems for measuring the carbon footprint of individuals, companies, cars, and so forth have developed in the past decade. Even in the absence of legal carbon taxation, growing numbers of economic agents have begun to account for these carbon costs through voluntary offsets or by using them to guide company planning partly under social and consumer pressure and partly because of concerns about potential future regulations. In this spirit, we believe the first step toward valuing individual contributions to the data economy is measuring these (marginal) contributions.[48] The field of "active learning" within computer science considers how to optimize the search for data (possibly at some cost) and offers a rich store of ideas to build on in answering these questions.

Second, appropriate technological systems would have to be built for tracing and tracking the value created by individual users. These systems would have to balance a number of competing concerns. On the one hand, they should try to measure which users are individually responsible for what data contributions, especially when these contributions are disproportionately large and/or those individuals would be unlikely to supply and invest in the unique data that make these exceptional contributions unless they receive these monetary incentives. Creators of valuable entertainments, experts in obscure languages who can aid computer translators, specialized masters of video games who can help teach computers to expertly play them as companions in multiplayer games, wine aficionados who can help train a computer nose: these are unique skills deserving of exceptional rewards. On the other hand, trying to track every detail of the ordinary use of a Facebook post is overkill and certain classes of data should be commoditized and paid an "average price" based on meeting overall quality standards, both to reduce the burden on the system and to insulate users from unnecessary risks based on whether their data end up being valuable.

Third, users will not want to have to make a cost-benefit analysis of the monetary value versus the hassle cost of every online interaction. While it is important that users are aware of and acknowledged for the contributions they make and that the costs of services they use not be hidden from them, it would be impractical for most users to think through the financial value of every digital choice. Instead, most users will require guidance from an intelligent digital advisor that will filter and suggest opportunities that are lucrative relative to the hassle they impose—services that are worth it for users. This system will filter out "spam" that does not make sense for the user and will present the user with opportunities that do. Users can provide feedback, rating individual experiences or more likely giving comments or responses to system queries to help it learn user preferences.

Finally, a fair digital labor market would require a new regulatory infrastructure adapted to it. Minimum wage laws and related employee protections are poorly adapted to a world of flexible work where users make a variety of small contributions that supplement their main income streams. Governments would have to ensure that individual digital workers have clear ownership rights over their data, a step the European Union has moved toward with its General Data Protection Regulations, and that they have the right to freely associate to form data labor unions. Empowering users not just to be aware of their data but to be able claim the benefits of it will require allowing trusted agents to access data in appropriate formats. This sort of technically literate and creative thinking about appropriate regulations for data as labor and related flexible work in the digital age (such as driving for ride-hailing services or hosting for home sharing) is at an early stage. But competition and countervailing union power will succeed only if regulations allow the flexibility for them to help shape a productive and fair digital labor market.[49]

## A Radical Market in Data Labor

Suppose that the Internet started paying you for your data. How would this change things? The first thing to understand is that it is not a quick path to riches for the masses. Even if the entire market capitalization of Google and Facebook were divided among American citizens, each would receive only a few thousand dollars. Divide the market capitalization among billions of users throughout the world, and the amount is even less. To be sure, the system we propose would increase the efficiency of the digital economy and therefore make more value available for everyone. But in the first few years, typical users would supplement their incomes with several hundred or perhaps a few thousand dollars.

How important a source of income data labor would become after a few years depends on how important AI turns out to be. Some commentators believe that AI will automate much of the economy. If true, data labor will represent a much greater source of income and wealth in coming years than it does at present, and in fact much of the market capitalization of digital companies is based on this possibility. If this is realized, data labor may grow to become a substantial fraction of many people's income. However, it is also possible that AI will have limited applications, in which case data labor will never be more than a modest supplement to people's income.

To make a ballpark estimate of what gains we might expect, we suppose that over the next twenty years, AI that would (absent our proposal) not pay data providers comes to represent 10% of the economy. We further assume that the true share of labor if paid in this area of the economy is two-thirds, as in the rest of the economy; and that paying labor fairly expands the output of this sector by 30%, as seems quite reasonable given productivity gains accompanying fairer labor practices in the early twentieth century. Then our proposal would increase the size of the economy by 3% and transfer about 9% of the economy from the owners of capital to those of labor. Applying the same logic as in chapter 4 about the effect of such transfers, this would lower the top 1% share of income by about 3 percentage points. While this may sound small relative to the whole economy, it would be a substantial contribution to median income for a household of four, raising it by more than $20,000, as much as during the thirty years following the world wars.

Yet even if data labor does become an important source of many people's income, there is no guarantee its fruits will be evenly distributed. Some people may have idiosyncratic cultural knowledge or abilities that will be particularly valuable to ML, while others will be too ordinary for their data to have much marginal value. Some data workers may contribute a little bit to a wide range of different ML processes, while others may contribute greatly in one area (such as language learning or cultural awareness) but little or nothing in other areas. We hope that the range of opportunities such a world would offer might allow individuals to specialize across a broader range of niches than at present, some opting for diversity and a more recreational work experience and others focusing on a concentrated passion. However, it is entirely possible that large inequalities would emerge and have to be disciplined by future reforms.

Beyond the direct income implications, paying people for data may also change the social understanding of the digital economy. Rather than feeling like passive consumers of Internet services, users might see themselves as active producers and participants in the creation of value. We suspect that the term AI would gradually give way to a more accurate understanding of the sources of value in digital systems such as "collective intelligence." Users would treat the useful insights of Siri and Alexa not as advice from robots, but as assemblages of human contributions, in the way they understand an encyclopedia or the insights on their Facebook wall.

As a psychological matter, this view does not seem impossible. People living in democracies seem to feel more empowered and active in politics than people living in dictatorships, even though the contribution of one's vote to policy outcomes is very small. When we "buy American" cars, we think of ourselves as purchasing the product of the labor of our fellow citizens, even though any individual American plays at most a tiny role in producing such products.

Yet, in many ways this change in the perception of consumers may be less important than the changes seeing data as labor may create for the data laborers themselves. Paying people for their data might make them feel like more useful members of society. In recent years, economists have begun to wonder whether large segments of the population will be unable to find work in an economy that places the most value on technical work that requires advanced education. Recent research suggests that the rise of video gaming is an important cause of the decline in labor force participation among young men.[50] Given current attitudes toward such activities, it seems plausible that such young men, some of them Internet trolls or bullies, may have a less than healthy relationship to the broader society.

Most people derive a sense of self-worth from making a contribution to society. In a world where individual digital contributions were appropriately valued by society, many video gaming young men could convert their enjoyment of gaming into a productive skill. Given the trend toward the "gamification" of many productive tasks, it is not hard to imagine that the skills these young men have acquired in their life as gamers might help them earn a living if data were treated as labor. The untapped capacity of expert gamers deserves more respect, and more attempts at harnessing it for the social good, than it receives today. This would encourage gamers to develop their ability in a more socially valuable manner, yielding a sense of both personal dignity and political responsibility.

# Conclusion

## GOING TO THE ROOT

Laissez faire (in its full true meaning) opens the way to the realization of the noble dreams of socialism.

—HENRY GEORGE, *PROGRESS AND POVERTY*, 1879

When Dinh Tuyên finally drove her tuk-tuk to the scrap dealer, the time was right. She had to kick it back to life three times on the voyage. Yet each kick felt like it was delivered to her gut. Yes, maybe she would have had to buy another in any case. Yes, the city and the web were filled with a thousand other opportunities. But the rhythm of those wheels bumping along the streets of Hanoi seemed to perfectly mirror the rhythm of blood through her veins, the same blood that had pumped through her father's veins as it knocked along to that rhythm before her.

But she'd never feel that rhythm again. Even if her dividend check was enough to afford taking one of the

damn contraptions that had destroyed her life, their ride
was too perfect, their surface too gleaming to even give
her a hint of her lost world. It was a world she would not
let go. She knew there were dozens, thousands, millions
like her who would not stand for it. They would hear her
scream. The world would hear her scream.

She found them. Social media, in the squares. The
English of her school years came in handy. Meaning filled
her life again through the marches, in virtual reality cafes
and hard pavement streets. A lonely middle-aged spinster
from a corner of Asia was soon the voice of those who
spurned the robots and apps, the visa papers and the voice
credits. She was the sound of a homeland, a life lost.

Yet for all the attention she received, Tuyên was
disappointed by the narrowness of the response and the
jeering her movement received. Why couldn't the others
see that teaching a computer to cook *phở* or keeping tabs
on robots at some Korean self-driving car factory were
not the jobs they had grown up dreaming of, grown up
with a right to deserve? Some had initially responded, but
the moment that American markets began to sneeze, even
Tuyên's neighbors became jittery about her protests. Why
did she have to risk all of their dividends?

So Tuyên began to travel around the country and
world looking for pockets of fellow travelers unwilling to
sell their soul to the demons of data and commonly
owned capital. She found her compatriots online and
rallied a hundred local victories from Winnipeg to
Tashkent. Her "Defend our World" (DoW) movement
became a paradox: fiercely localist, tied to the soil and
traditions, almost every meeting relied on automated
translation and virtual reality telepresence. Too few

citizens were willing to join to create a critical mass of solidarity beyond a few pockets. Yes, they won a local council seat in many small towns, and when by luck enough of their members were in or had ties to Novosibirsk they even won a mayoralty.

But as they started to build outward, in each case, the liberals (rich and poor) always got wind of it and flocked in to buy up more votes than DoW could ever muster. So DoW became more like entertainment, a social network and a talking shop, rather than a political movement with real legs.

As it did, Tuyên found her life changing. She realized after a few years that all that time she never had taken one of the jobs she resented, and yet she was earning more than she ever did as a driver and most of it from precisely the sources she had sworn to avoid. She had become a global celebrity. Her virtual re-creations of the world of her and so many other fathers were racking up millions of uses and hundreds of billions of dong (tens of millions of dollars). Her unique experience and the global, sometimes morbid, fascination with her movement made the value of reporting on her and monitoring her every move worth many times more than that. Soon she was one of the wealthiest women in Vietnam.

She realized, too, that in many ways her new cause, fighting to get her old life back, had given her more meaning and not just greater wealth than the past she idealized. She started to wonder what else might supply that meaning and whether her whole movement was not ultimately some sort of self-serving charade. She came to see herself as a hypocrite, gave most of her accumulated wealth to establish a charity to aid Vietnamese people displaced by technology, and disbanded her movement.

She devoted her remaining years to learning each new generation of virtual reality technologies and traveling the world helping others like her build memorials to the lost life of the early twenty-first century. She was soon able to employ so many of those displaced workers, who carried with them vivid dreams that were now, partly because of Tuyên's political caché, the height of retro chic. Her movement had been doomed as a rebellion, but succeeded as a cause, as it both saved so many of those she identified with and created one of the great brands of the late twenty-first century.

The proposals we have made in earlier chapters stand on their own, and should be evaluated accordingly. But thinking about the proposals together allows one to see how they reflect a common vision that clarifies the paradox posed by our epigraph from George. Laissez-faire is often taken to refer to unrestrained market competition. At least in George's day, socialism aimed at the "noble dream" of replacing the dominance of private property and private goods with a significant degree of common ownership and public goods while dramatically reducing inequality. Our analysis shows how these ideas are not opposed to each other, as popular discussion implies, but instead are mutually reinforcing. In this conclusion, we lay out this common vision, organizing the integration of our ideas around the four topics of economy, politics, international affairs, and society. We also discuss, in a highly speculative and idealistic vein, how adopting the full set of proposals might allow each to be extended to new domains. We do so not because we think such extensions are justified at the present time, but because they help reveal the logic and limits of our approach, and because we hope to stimulate further debate.

## Economy

Concerns about the economic challenges facing wealthy countries fall into two categories that are usually treated as opposed to one another. On the one hand, the "techno-optimists" argue that technological progress based on artificial intelligence and biotechnology will accelerate and displace workers at ever increasing rates, creating large-scale social dislocation.[1] Robots will replace waiters, drones will replace delivery workers and, perhaps, robots will even serve as lovers, as in Spike Jonze's 2013 film *Her*. But this means workers will be displaced. Thus, techno-optimists are optimistic about productivity growth, but are pessimistic about employment, which they expect to decline and become a central source of social tension.

"Techno-pessimists" take the opposite perspective.[2] They expect that productivity and economic growth will continue to decline and that the standard of living will stagnate. They are doubtful about the value of recent technological advances beyond the spheres of entertainment and communications and they are skeptical that Artificial Intelligence (AI) will replace human workers on a large scale. They contrast the sweeping social changes created by electrification to the incremental entertainment supplied by smartphones; the enormous advances in human longevity produced by sanitation and antibiotics to the still-unrealized promise of stem cell research; and the fundamental change in production technology created by the assembly line to the limited impact thus far of 3D printing. Thus, while they are pessimistic about growth, they are much less concerned than techno-optimists about job displacement and changes in the labor market.

Much of this debate concerns technical feasibility and creative breakthroughs by scientists and engineers about which we have little to say. Yet, the perspective we have developed in this book contrasts with both of these poles.

We reject the assumed tradeoff between productivity and employment underlying the debate. Market power is fundamental to our view of the economy and market power simultaneously retards productivity and depresses employment.[3] Hoarding of property away from its most productive uses creates unemployment but also reduces economic growth. Monopsony power, whether created by institutional investors or by natural monopsony in data economies, induces artificial unemployment to hold down wages and devalue work. Exclusion of the workers of poor countries from the opportunities in rich ones lowers global productivity and may reduce work opportunities overall by spurring automation. Anemic employment and low productivity growth result from institutional failure rather than changes in technology.

Thus, we see economic, political, and social institutions as central to the course that the economy will chart. Liberal reforms that ended serfdom and slavery were as important as the steam engine to igniting the industrial revolution. Antitrust reform, the labor movement, and the welfare state undergirded the productive and high-employment period in wealthy countries following World War II. Neoliberal reform and globalization, and not just advances in computer technology, were critical in spreading this growth to poor countries in the last three decades. With appropriate institutional changes, we may be able to avoid the perils of large-scale unemployment and slow growth. Without them, both of these problems are likely to worsen.[4]

As we explained in chapter 1, the COST will improve the efficiency of the economy by reducing monopoly power. Because goods will move more quickly to their most valued use, economic growth will pick up. Because the prices of assets will decline, harming wealthy people at the margin and helping poorer people, inequality will decline. This more efficient method of raising revenue will make it cheaper to fund public goods that benefit people and to offer a social dividend to people whose talents are not valued by the market. Restrictions on institutional investing will also reduce the role of market power in the economy.

QV will magnify these positive effects. One of the greatest sources of inefficiency in the economy is the primitive way that public goods are selected. In the current system, revenues raised from the general public often get funneled to special interests or are recycled in the form of inefficiently designed entitlements for the majority. By "marketizing" the political system, QV will help ensure that public goods reflect the preferences of the public at large rather than subsets of it.

Our proposals for migration and treating data as labor could dramatically reduce under-employment. Both proposals expand labor markets and empower workers. The migration proposal turns passive consumer/laborers in wealthy countries into entrepreneurs who see migrants as an economic opportunity rather than labor competition. The data proposal turns passive consumers in the digital economy into data laborers who demand compensation for their services. The two proposals expand labor markets across borders and into the digital sphere.

Our proposals together are powerful enough to address stagnequality for quite some time. Combining our estimates in the individual chapters, our proposals would reduce the share of national income captured by the top 1% to well below its midcentury trough. They would also end disparities of wealth as a significant source of interpersonal inequality, as the returns of wealth would largely be shared equally by a COST. A Radical Market would allow only inequality traceable to differences in natural abilities to persist.

To see this, consider how a COST on wealth and the social dividend it funds would respond to technological change. If labor was increasingly replaced by AI and humans turn out not to have as important a role in data labor as we suggest, capital's share of income would grow dramatically. Suppose it reached as high as 90%: the revenue raised by our COST would then increase to 60% of national income (as it is designed to capture two-thirds of capital's share) and fund generous lifestyles for all citizens. Even at current levels of national income, for example, and assuming that such a tax replaced all American taxes, such a policy would provide a family of four with an income of almost $90,000 a year. But if labor remained important, our social dividend would remain modest enough that most would still want to work, supply valuable data to AI, and host migrant workers to supplement their income. The more egalitarian distribution of the benefits of these activities, as we described above, would ensure continued equality.

Our proposals would also combat the problem of stagnation. Together (totaling our estimates from each chapter), they would increase the size of the global economy by a third. This would be sufficient to restore growth to roughly its level of the immediate postwar period for a generation. Along with the reduction in inequality, this would double the living standards of median households while only reducing the absolute well-being of the top 1% of earners by roughly a third. This growth in median household income is similar to that of the golden age from 1945 to 1975. Of course, only continual innovation would ensure further growth beyond this horizon, but our ideas hold out the prospect of such further improvements if applied in concert with one another and further technological progress, as we now illustrate.

Consider a very radical extension of the COST: to human capital. Human capital refers to a person's education and training; it's a bit like physical capital (land, factories, etc.) because it enables the holder to obtain additional profits on a given investment of effort. But it's also fundamentally different, for reasons that will become clear.

To understand how a COST on human capital might work, imagine that individuals were to self-assess a value of their time, pay a tax on this self-assessed value, and stand ready to work for any employer willing to pay this wage. Consider a surgeon, for example, who announced that she would perform a gallbladder surgery for $2,000. She would pay a tax based on that amount, and be required to perform an operation on anyone who offered that amount. The tax would discourage her from overvaluing her time and thus denying her talents to a needy community, while the need to be on-call at that wage would avoid her setting too low a wage.

In principle, a COST on human capital would be immensely valuable. Indeed, it would address the single biggest threat to equality and productivity that we have not addressed—the ability of the most talented people (the top scientists, lawyers, accountants, entertainers, financial whizzes) to withhold their services unless paid a monopoly price. A COST on physical capital simply does not address this problem, which is one of the major sources of the rise in inequality over the last half century. Once most other sources of inequality are addressed by our other proposals, this could well become a leading source of social tension, especially as genetic engineering and cybernetics redefine the idea of investing in human capacities.

Furthermore, a COST on human capital would eliminate the need for one of the largest deterrents to work at present: taxes on income. By replacing taxes on income with taxes on the underlying human capital that generates income, a COST would encourage rather than discourage work. It would also be fairer and more legitimate. Those without great talents would still have a lower potential income than the most talented people would, but would never risk falling into poverty as they would receive a large social dividend based on the taxes levied on the talented. Talented people would have greater opportunities to be rich than the less talented, but at the cost of bearing the risk of falling into poverty (through taxation of their social dividend) if they refuse to make use of these talents. A COST on human capital might turn out to be politically popular because it penalizes the highly resented educated class and lazy people of all types, while rewarding ordinary workers for their labor.

Despite these potential benefits, a COST on human capital is premature. There are two major problems. First, technology is simply not ready. A COST on human capital would need to take account of all the ways in which people enjoy or do not enjoy their work. People care about how much they work, where they work, who they work with, the conditions under which they perform their work, and much else—none of which could be captured by a COST on human capital unless accompanied by technological means for measuring all these factors. Conceivably, a COST on human capital associated with a technologically integrated form of labor—like data input, which is constantly monitored by computers—would work, but it is hard to say.

Second, a COST on human capital might be perceived as a kind of slavery—incorrectly in our view, at least if the COST were properly designed. Still, we can see the problem. Imagine that a surgeon simply decides one day that he has had enough of surgery. Under a COST, he would self-assess at a high level so that no one would purchase his services—paying a large tax in return for retirement. But people could find themselves in a position where it is not practical to do so, or they simply do not want to work anymore, whatever commitment they have made in the past. While design tweaks could avoid the coercive elements of the system, society is not yet ready for such a Radical revision in its understanding of labor.

It would be a mistake, however, to think that the current system is not coercive. In our current system, there is a wide gulf between educated elites whose native or acquired talents are highly marketable and those who have been left behind by changes sweeping the economy. The talented enjoy a kind of freedom, as they can select from among a variety of appealing jobs. These jobs allow them to quickly accumulate capital that they can depend on as they age, if they do not like the jobs that are available, or pick and choose among different levels of labor (part-time, enjoyable or rewarding but low-paying jobs in the nonprofit sector, etc.). Those with fewer marketable skills are given a stark choice: undergo harsh labor conditions for low pay, starve, or submit to the many indignities of life on welfare. Yet the waste of social resources when a talented person fails to realize her potential are far greater, and arguably their failure to work should be punished more harshly.

A COST on human capital would ameliorate this form of unequal freedom by requiring the talented people to pay a tax if they do not want to work in a job that is most efficient for society. A reasonable tax will not reduce them to starvation or a welfare-style existence, but will put them under more pressure to work for the benefit of society, just as the poor must at present, while alleviating the corresponding pressure on those with less talent in our present society. Perhaps a society more accustomed to a COST on wealth and other checks on market power, and where the talented use genetic engineering to give their children clearly unfair advantages, would come to see monopolies over talents as pernicious. Thought experiments in stories like the *Handmaid's Tale* and *X-Men* suggest that societies that mismanage unique talents either by enslaving them (in the first case) or allowing complete self-ownership (in the latter) are likely to end poorly.

## Politics

Together a COST and QV would radically transform politics by breaking down artificial boundaries between public and private life. A COST would give everyone a stake in the success of companies and assets managed by others. By giving every citizen a share of national wealth, a COST could make voters attend to the consequences of policies for a nation's wealth and create a more cooperative spirit across class lines. At the same time, by aligning the interests of migrant workers from poor countries and citizen hosts in wealthy countries, VIP would defuse some of the conflict around migration and globalization that lies at the heart of many populist movements.

QV would make the public sphere more responsive to public demands, thereby creating greater trust in public and collective institutions and increasing reliance on them. It should reduce political frustration and alienation, foster a richer political dialogue, reduce gridlock, and enhance public satisfaction with democracy. At present, unequal but reasonably efficient markets govern private goods, while reasonably egalitarian but extremely inefficient one-person-one-vote rules govern politics. Radical Markets would create equality and efficiency in both politics and economics, making the two spheres more harmonious.

Our proposal on antitrust would also have important political effects that would help smooth the way for our more ambitious reforms. Money or "capital" can damage politics in many ways beyond the usual concerns about corruption and campaign contributions. When an industry is highly concentrated, it can present a united front to regulators and thwart reformers.[5] During the Gilded Age, monopolies interfered with politics in many ways; indeed, the Sherman Antitrust Act, and the reforms undertaken by the Progressives, were motivated as much by the political dangers posed by monopolies as their economic costs. In the middle part of the twentieth century, lobbyists for different firms in an industry in the United States would often be at one another's throats, each fighting for advantage and often canceling out the efforts of the others. But by the late 1970s, businesses had consolidated their influence and worked in concert to lower taxes, reduce regulations that constrained their profits, and increase regulations that protected them from competition. This consolidated influence allowed these interests to more effectively influence policy and helped shut out consumer groups.

The resulting loss of morale damages politics in the same way that concentrated economic power can harm the economy. Our antitrust proposal, by weakening the power of concentrated capital, should help cure the sense of political helplessness that has contributed to the stagnation of the public sphere and clear away the outsized influence of capital that is likely to be the strongest impediment to the success of our more radical proposals.

In a more speculative vein, we can imagine ways that QV could be extended, in connection with the COST. The COST, and the social dividend it produces, would not create a perfectly egalitarian society but would reduce the enormous wealth disparities that hamper political cooperation today. In such a society, a QV that used money rather than credits would generate further gains for the public.

For example, imagine that a town holds a vote on whether to build a public park. People could pay $1 to cast one vote for or against, $4 to cast two votes, $1 million to cast 1,000 votes, and so on. The money that is collected is added to the pool used for funding the social dividend from the COST. A moderate step toward this system, beginning with the version of QV we described in chapter 2, would be to allow the wealthy to buy some additional voice credits at a high price meant to maximize the revenue raised, which could then be used to raise the social dividend. As a COST made society increasingly equal, the people buying these extra vote credits would no longer be the wealthy and the price could thus be lowered to the point where most voice credits were purchased rather than being given out.

Monetizing QV would obviously allow greater influence, even in an egalitarian society, to whoever happened to be earning more. Of course, this is very much a feature of our present society, as we highlight above. In tandem with monetized QV, QV itself could be used to reduce the influence of money on politics. Small political contributions could be matched and large ones taxed according to a rule suggested by the logic of QV: a political campaign should receive an amount proportionate to the square root of the amount contributed.[6] Such a system would reduce the influence of wealth on politics while preserving freedom of expression.[7]

The benefit of monetized QV would be to allow people to express their preferences for public goods in a very precise way—since they would give up their ability to spend money on themselves in return for the power to influence a public decision. Such a system would also be fairer than the version of QV we suggested in chapter 2, because citizens for whom public issues are more important than private ones would be able to fully express themselves rather than being stuck with a fixed budget of voice credits. While the system gives those with high incomes more power than an ideal, nonexistent egalitarian system, it gives them less power than in real-world systems, where they exercise influence through donations. Moreover, in the QV system the rich pay the poor for political influence—since the money is redistributed—rather than pay politicians.

The monetized version of QV would overthrow many taboos, including the taboo against money in politics, and, as we acknowledge, would be unpopular in a society with high inequality.[8] But these taboos reflect intuitions that developed in our primitive one-person-one-vote system, which itself relies on outdated technology, and in our highly unequal society, which our other proposals would help us move beyond. The real contribution of monetized QV would be to create a unified market of private and public goods, generating better outcomes for people across all dimensions of their lives.

## The Global Stage

In chapter 3 we noted an imbalance that has arisen in the global order. Capital, including (to some extent) human capital and private goods, flows freely across borders. But most workers reside within national jurisdictions, and nearly all public goods are generated within nations. Globalization of international trade and capital flows has likely exhausted most of the gains from the first group of activities.

In contrast, extension of both migration and public goods provision could generate further welfare gains for people around the world. Let's start with public goods provision. Advanced countries are effective at producing public goods within their borders—for example, clean air and water, through enforcement of environmental regulations. But cross-border public goods provision is more difficult. That is why countries have struggled for decades to agree to a climate treaty. Even less daunting technological challenges, like maintaining fisheries in international waters, have frequently defeated international cooperation.

The problem is that populations in different countries often don't trust each other, or foreign leaders, or even their own leaders. Leaders who cooperate internationally are often accused by populists of selling out to foreigners. In recent years, a backlash to globalization has erupted. International terrorism, financial contagion, migration crises, and trade disputes have fueled the rise of populist groups around the world. A central question of our time is how to further gain from international cooperation while managing the conflicts that are inherent in cross-border activity.

The VIP could help address this problem, even beyond its direct economic benefits and ability to resolve political conflicts over migration that plague many countries. The increase in migration would ease tensions between rich and developing nations by contributing, through remittances and improvement in skills, to the development of poor countries. The warm relations between the Gulf Cooperation Council nations and the South Asian governments that send labor to them, despite all the failings of their labor regulations, illustrate what is possible. Combining our calculations above, the VIP—if adopted by all rich countries—would reduce international inequality by more than the reduction that occurred from the 1980s to the 2000s.[9] As poor countries develop, their citizens will be less inclined to migrate, while those countries will be less vulnerable to civil strife, which often spills across borders. Moreover, greater availability of competitive labor through migration in wealthy countries would reduce the pressure to outsource jobs and would likely even create well-paying jobs for natives who are needed to manage foreign unskilled workers—the foreman of the construction crew, the manager of the restaurant.[10]

A world with greater international migration of workers would create new international governance challenges. We have already seen this with trade and investment. Free trade is not just a matter of lowering tariffs; it also requires adjudicators and other governance institutions to resolve disputes between countries—for example, over whether apparently neutral regulations have the actual effect of blocking trade from foreign countries, just like tariffs. International investment likewise has generated demand for judicial institutions to resolve disputes—when, for example, a country enacts health and safety laws that investors believe are designed to expropriate their investment. Similarly, a world with greatly increased migration flows would generate disputes about how migrant workers should be treated, and whether they have been treated in conformity with international commitments. Countries have recognized these problems and entered into bilateral labor agreements to address them, but this legal regime is at an early stage and would not be able to handle the problems that would arise if migration were more common.

QV offers some hope in the face of the checkered past of international governance. The recurrent problem in the design of international institutions is that large countries refuse to yield influence—and hence typically demand veto rights—while small countries resent their diminished influence. To navigate this deadlock, international bodies often allocate power to "impartial" bureaucratic elites, but these elites are not always impartial, and have generated a nationalist backlash. Furthermore, when veto rights exist, as they almost always do, international institutions can quickly become gridlocked. QV, as we have explained, offers hope against gridlock by making voice more continuous and divisible. Large countries would need to be given credits in proportion to their power, but they would not be given the right to veto. This would ensure that large countries can exert influence in proportion to their power but small countries would have influence over issues that are of the utmost importance to them.[11]

This raises the possibility that QV voice credits could be a common currency that countries use to trade influence across different legal regimes—trade, investment, migration, the environment, and so on. Imagine, for example, that countries are given credits in proportion to some combination of their wealth, population, and military power. That means, of course, that large, wealthy, powerful countries exert more influence over international relations than other countries do, but that's just the way things are—currently and in the foreseeable future—and we need to ground our proposal in a realistic assessment as to the way things are. QV would not directly eliminate these power asymmetries (though our other proposals might help mitigate them) but it would make it easier for countries to cooperate across issue areas where cooperative gains are possible.

Large country X will continue to dictate most of the policies of the WTO, the IMF, the Law of the Sea Authority, and the UN Security Council. But where small country Y cares enough about a particular policy—let's say a fishery that lies near its shore—it can use its credits to cast enough votes to affect policy on the margin. This simply substitutes for the extraordinarily cumbersome method by which countries cooperate today—mostly through bilateral negotiations where concessions in different areas are laboriously stitched together ("linkages" in the jargon) or multilateral bodies where a consensus must be reached.

More broadly, many of the benefits of our proposals for domestic politics could gradually spill outward into the international sphere. Precisely how is hard to predict, but we now speculate on some pathways.

*QV.* Most countries, even liberal democracies, give few political rights to migrants until they have undertaken the arduous and time-consuming process of becoming citizens—which in many countries is nearly impossible for all but the very wealthy or lucky. There are minor exceptions here and there—for example, resident aliens might be allowed to vote in school board elections in a locality. Many people regard this state of affairs as regrettable, and maybe it is, but it is also understandable: native citizens do not want to yield political influence to people who may be more loyal to their home countries than to the country in which they happen to hold a job. The vote is sacred, and only given to people who have proven their worth (or been born to it).

One of the virtues of QV is that it breaks down the "vote" into a system of continuous voice, allowing participants to exert influence to a greater or lesser degree. Resident aliens could receive a small number of credits in order to give them marginal rather than decisive influence wherever they reside. This would allow them to use political voice to protect their strongest interests without allowing them to determine the character of a place in which they do not have roots. As migration became more common, people might start seeing themselves as loyal to multiple countries, in which they exert partial influence through QV. For example, hosts and migrants could even trade voice credits from their respective countries. In such a world, there might be more pressure against military conflict. And if QV gives migrants more control over political decisions in host countries that affect them, it would make labor migration more desirable and hence more common, further enhancing its economic benefits.

*The COST.* A COST on capital might allow a significant extension of our migration ideas, which are still in important ways based on restrictions on entry. A main goal of the VIP is to share the gains from migration throughout host countries rather than concentrating them in the hands of businesses and the wealthy. However, in a society where a COST was enacted, benefits to companies and capital would *automatically* flow to the broader society through a social dividend. In such a society, every citizen would have an interest in seeing the value of companies and land increase, something unlimited migration is very effective in achieving. Thus, a COST might make citizens favor increasing the number of visas allowed under the VIP so they can benefit from the capital gains and not just the direct value they get from hosting.

Additionally, suppose that wealthy countries, in lieu of providing foreign aid to poor countries as grants as they do today, agreed to a scheme among themselves and with poor countries in which all countries agree to share a portion of COST revenues with each other. In such a scenario, at any given time the wealthy countries would send aid to the poor countries. However, if poor countries developed and became richer, this transfer would even out and the payments in each direction would be equal. This would give citizens of rich countries an incentive to develop poor countries, as well as giving citizens of poor countries a reason not to resent too much the prosperity of wealthy countries. Together these two features would help tilt the scales of opinion in wealthy countries in favor of opening migration further to aid the development of poor countries.

A COST might also revive the possibility of significant additional gains from international trade. The structure of a COST deepens the way markets work by breaking private monopoly power over assets. If international agreements could be struck to allow these benefits to accrue across countries—to allow Americans the right to buy French assets at their self-assessed values and vice versa—the gains from international investment treaties might be revived.

## Society

Markets of the last two centuries, for all their limitations, have been spectacular engines of economic progress. Their social effects have been equally profound, upending traditional communities and values, while fostering the growth of large cities full of diverse lifestyles. They have created an international consumer culture full of foods, fashions, and music that combine traditions from different civilizations.

Yet the cultural consequences of capitalism have not all been for the better. Some commentators believe that markets foster selfish individualists who are indifferent to the public good. One theory is that by reducing so much of social exchange to impersonal monetary terms, markets undermine the close connection that people in traditional communities felt toward those they know closely and interact with on a daily basis. By supplanting the moral values upon which such communities are founded with the pursuit of personal ambition and profit, markets tend to reduce social solidarity.[12]

Moreover, some scholars have argued that by encouraging selfishness, markets undermine the trust that is necessary for markets to function.[13] Competition in impersonal commodity markets creates associations between commerce and bargaining, market power, and jockeying for advantage at the expense of others in the marketplace.[14] Markets focus attention on private goods rather than public goods, fostering hostility to collective action.

Yet at the same time, markets have fostered newer forms of trust, solidarity, and cultural openness. In markets, individuals can gain from exchanging with others even if they do not have close personal relationships. This gives each individual a stake in others' prosperity and, when markets function successfully, a reason to trust others and to act in a trustworthy manner toward others.[15] This spirit is most clearly on display in well-functioning urban settings, where people live among numerous strangers and near-strangers. Urbanist Jane Jacobs describes the "modicum of responsibility" city dwellers take for each other "even if they have no ties to each other." The critical benefit of "light" trust over the deep connections of tight-knit communities displaced by markets, Jacobs emphasizes, is that it allows for greater diversity and makes "city streets equipped to handle strangers."[16] The sociological spirit of the market is that of the city.

While all speculation about social change is fraught, we believe Radical Markets have the potential to greatly strengthen these sociological benefits of markets.[17] The COST would strengthen solidarity by breaking down the barriers created by the system of private property. By making every asset currently held by others more easily accessible, it would reduce the distinction between "my" possessions and the possessions of "others." Everyone would benefit from the expansion of everyone's wealth. Transactions between individuals would be more common, fostering the feeling of mutually beneficial exchange, while haggling and hucksterism would be discouraged.[18] Our other economic proposals, by undermining the power of monopolies, would reduce the feelings of exploitation and passivity in relation to the economic system experienced by most citizens.

QV would play a special role. By making the market work as powerfully to provide public as private goods, QV would undermine the association of markets with individualism. Markets would no longer be seen as opposed to public action but as the mechanism through which public action takes place.

Radical Markets would also advance social tolerance. By promoting mutually beneficial commerce, markets have been powerful forces for breaking down stereotypes about, and for easing conflict between, people with different religions, languages, sexualities, or backgrounds. By promoting competition, markets have helped to gradually drive out discrimination against the able but despised.[19] It is no coincidence that the greatest progress along these dimensions has occurred in the most active market societies, such as (the large cities in) the United States, UK, and Sweden.

Yet markets have achieved this progress very slowly. Private property allows people to discriminate by refusing to sell goods to those they dislike. A thick layer of government regulation blocks the most egregious forms of discrimination but not all of it, and the regulation, which is often costly to comply with, has generated considerable resentment. In contrast, nondiscrimination is built into the structure of the COST. One-person-one-vote rules have allowed majorities to oppress un-popular minorities. QV would be a powerful tool for their self-emancipation. Limits on migration have preserved the most persistent sources of prejudice: those across national frontiers. By enhancing migration and tying together the inter-ests of hosts and migrants, we reduce this prejudice as well.

Capitalism undermined the social and political divisions that prevailed earlier in history, but has thrown up new ones, based largely on wealth. Radical Markets would take the next step, and help break down privileges based on wealth and eco-nomic advantage as well.

## Beyond Our Sketch

In this chapter, we have allowed our imaginations to run wild, but we want to conclude with some words of caution. Our pro-posals are grounded in economic theory and the history of ideas, but human nature has a way of defeating the best thought-out schemes, both through stubbornness and through its occasionally extreme malleability. It is notoriously difficult to predict when human cultural adaptation to new social insti-tutions will undermine or support those institutions, or turn utopian designs into dystopias.

As we have emphasized in earlier chapters, the proposals should be implemented as small-scale experiments first, not as a society-wide revolution. QV can be used in small groups that make collective decisions. The COST can be applied initially to existing administrative property regimes, like grazing rights within a specific geographic area. Migrant labor sponsorship could be implemented as a modest extension of the J-1 visa, with a limited number of visas in a special economic zone made available for a carefully monitored test run. The limits on institutional investment can start at a level that would require relatively little divestment by the big institutional investors; if financial disruption is small, the screws could be tightened. Payment for data labor merely needs to await technological developments and social organizations that seem to be in process.

What could go wrong? One possibility is that people will not be able to handle the additional burdens that these schemes would impose on them. All of them, in one way or another, require people to give more thought to activities that they currently take for granted or disregard. This is a natural consequence of the extension of markets, so different from the passivity with which people confront government or corporate bureaucracy. It is a cliché that freedom implies responsibility; by expanding freedom our proposals also increase individual agency and responsibility.

Yet we should not be afraid of the burden of such responsibility. After all, we live in the age of the computer intermediary. As we have explained in earlier chapters, many of the decisions can be automated. And the institutions themselves can be designed to put a greater or lesser cognitive burden on the people who use them. We are familiar with this problem from existing markets and government institutions, which are constantly being tweaked in ways that increase or reduce cognitive burdens. The introduction of Social Security, for example, made life a lot easier for many people who no longer needed to worry about calculating retirement savings. The introduction of tax subsidies for defined-contribution retirement plans had the opposite effect, requiring people to make saving and investment decisions of immense complexity. This in turn stimulated various imaginative reforms, like opt-out rules, which weakened the cognitive burden without eliminating it altogether.[20] Both the COST and QV—our most important proposals—can be designed with more or less complexity. The proper level of complexity is a design question that can be answered only with experience.

The opposite problem is that our proposals can be gamed by sophisticated people, who figure out ways to undermine them. QV is, at least in principle, vulnerable to various forms of sophisticated collusion, and a legal regime and social norms would need to be put in place to ban them. The COST might be evaded by sophisticated citizens who can hide wealth. It is important to understand, however, that sophisticated forms of gaming are endemic in our existing institutions. Stock markets are manipulated, tax rules are arbitraged, campaign finance restrictions are evaded, legislative districts are gerrymandered. We see no reason to believe that QV and the COST would be more vulnerable to manipulation than the institutions that they replace and many reasons why they would be less so.

As at present, laws and social norms are needed to curtail strategic behavior. At present, social norms encourage people to vote and, along with the law, deter them from vote-trading and other forms of manipulation. Under QV, law and norms would be needed to deter collusion. At present, the law gives people incentives to sue corporations that sell hazardous products; under a COST the incentive to profit by taking underpriced assets from the wealthy would create an army of private tax enforcers. Yet the full set of the vulnerabilities of these proposals, and appropriate social responses, can be discovered only through testing and implementation.

Even if some of these proposals ultimately prove unworkable in testing, we hope that the Radical spirit behind our ideas will take broader root. Our society is replete with opportunities beyond those we have discussed to break down the power of established privileges to increase wealth and equality together. In fact, many of Vickrey's more modest ideas have been on the public agenda for years: for example, liberalizing zoning restrictions, encouraging equity to replace debt in financing education, and taxing road congestion. Other ideas even more powerful than those we have proposed are surely yet to be born. Our aim in this book is to show that the familiar lines of economic and political debate are artifacts of poor imagination and stale assumptions. To build a better world, we must move beyond the self-defeating conflict of right and left.

## A Square Deal

Any new and radical proposal will be greeted by skepticism, even scorn. Yet all of the institutions that we take for granted today—the free market, democracy, the rule of law—were at one time radical proposals. At a time of "stagnequality"— vicious inequality, economic stagnation, and political turbulence—there is nothing safe about well-worn ideas, and the greatest risk is stasis. If we aspire to prosperity and progress, we must be willing to question old truths, to get at the root of the matter, and to experiment with new ideas. This is what we have tried to do.

# After Markets?

> The market process . . . may be considered as a computing device of the pre-electronic age.
>
> —OSKAR LANGE, "THE COMPUTER AND THE MARKET," 1967

Throughout this book we advocate the transformative power of Radical Markets. But why exactly are markets so powerful? In this epilogue, we ask this question from the reverse direction: we ask, what are the limits of markets? Doing so allows us to speculate about a time when markets may be replaced by a more efficient method of economic organization.

## Markets as Miracles

As we saw in chapter 1, many economists who were committed to the market economy also considered themselves "socialists." Yet in the early twentieth century, socialism became identified with central planning, thanks to the role of Marxism and the French Revolution in inspiring and justifying the economic policies of the Soviet Union. Central planning also received a boost from World War I, where national control of the economy for the purpose of war production was more successful than advocates of laissez-faire could ever have imagined. This led to a heated debate about whether central planning should be used in peacetime as well.

In the popular imagination, central planning could not succeed because it provided individuals with no incentives to work. People needed the prospect of riches, or at least wages, to get them out of bed in the morning. Yet incentives were quite strong in the Soviet Union, stronger, in many ways, than they are in capitalist countries. While there was less chance under Communism to grow rich, any prisoner of the Gulag knew the fate of those who "malingered."

Another popular argument against central planning was advanced by Nobel Laureate Friedrich Hayek in 1945. Hayek argued that no central planner could obtain information about people's tastes and productivity necessary to allocate resources efficiently.[1] The genius of the market was the way that the price system could, in disaggregated fashion, collect this information from everyone and supply it to those who needed to know it, without the involvement of a government planning board.

A related version of this argument, less well-known than Hayek's but actually more compelling, was made a few decades earlier. The brilliant economist Ludwig von Mises argued that the fundamental problem facing socialism was not incentives or knowledge in the abstract but *communication* and *computation.*[2] To see what Mises meant, consider an illustrative parable proposed by Leonard Read in his 1958 essay, "I, Pencil."[3]

Read tells the "life story" of a pencil. Such a simple thing, one would at first think. And yet as you begin to reflect, you realize the enormously complex layers of thought and planning it would require to make a pencil from scratch. The wood must be chopped, cut, shaped, polished, and honed. The graphite must be mined, chiseled, and shaped. The ferrule—the collar that connects the wood shaft and the eraser—is an alloy of dozens of metals, each of which must be mined, melted, combined, and reformed. And so forth.

Yet what is most remarkable about the pencil is not its complexity but the complete lack of understanding that anyone involved in the manufacture of the eventual pencil has about any of these steps in the process. The lumberjack knows only that there is a market for his wood and some price that induces her to buy the needed tools, cut down trees, and sell lumber down the line of production. The lumberjack may never even know that the wood is used for a pencil. The pencil factory owner knows only where to purchase the needed intermediate materials and how to run a line assembling them. The knowledge and planning of the pencil's creation emerge organically from the process of market relations.

Now suppose that we were to try to replicate the market relationships with a central planning board. The board would determine how much wood to chop and when, the number of workers to employ at each stage of production, the correct places and times to produce, ship, and build. Yet, to do this effectively the board would have to understand a great many things. It would have to learn from each of these specialized producers the unique knowledge of her domain of expertise that allows her to earn a living—for example, whether the lumber would have a more valuable use elsewhere in the economy (to build houses or ships or children's toys) than as an input for pencils. Absorbing all this information and constantly receiving and processing the necessary updates to keep abreast of evolving conditions in each of these steps of the process, would overwhelm the capacity of even the most skilled managers.

And even if the board somehow had an unlimited capacity to absorb this information, it would still have the unmanageable problem of trying to act on this sea of data. Prices, supply and demand, and production relations in markets arise through a complex interplay of individuals each helping to optimize a tiny part of a broad social process. If, instead, a single board had to plan this entire dance, it would force a small number of individuals to contemplate an endless sequence of choices and plans. Such elaborate calculations are beyond the capacity of even the most brilliant group of engineers.

Mises wrote decades before the rise of the fields of computer science and information theory and lacked any way to formalize these intuitive ideas. Many of Mises's arguments were dismissed by mainstream economists, whose increasingly narrow mathematical approach to the field Mises disdained. Mises's critics, including Oskar Lange, Fred Taylor, and Abba Lerner, argued that the market mechanism was but one of many ways (and far from the most efficient way) to organize an economy. They viewed the economy purely mathematically, rather than computationally, and saw no difficulty *in principle* with solving a (very large) system of equations relating the supply and demand of various goods, resources, and services.

In a simplified picture of the economy, ordinary people perform dual functions as producers (workers, suppliers of capital, etc.) and consumers. As consumers, people have preferences regarding different goods and services. Some people like chocolate, others like vanilla. As producers, they have different talents and capacities. Some people are good at doing math, others at mollifying angry customers. In principle, all we need to do is figure out people's preferences and their talents, and assign jobs to people who do them best, while distributing the value created by production in the form of goods and services that people really want. Rewards and penalties need to be determined to give people incentives to reveal their preferences and talents, and to ensure that they actually do what they are supposed to do. All of this can be represented mathematically and solved. That's why socialist economists viewed the economy as a math problem the solution of which only required a computer.

Yet the later development of the theory of computational and communication complexity vindicated Mises's insights. What computational scientists later realized is that even if managing the economy were "merely" a problem of solving a large system of equations, finding such solutions is far from the easy task that socialist economists believed. In an incisive computational analysis of central planning, statistician and computer scientist Cosma Shalizi illustrates how utterly impossible "solving" a modern economy would be for a central planning board. As Shalizi notes in his essay, "In the Soviet Union, Optimization Problem Solves *You*," the computer power it takes to solve an economic allocation problem increases more than proportionately in the number of commodities in the economy.[4] In practical terms, this means that in any large economy, central planning by a single computer is impossible.

To make these abstract mathematical relationships concrete, Shalizi considers an estimate by Soviet planners that, at the height of Soviet economic power in the 1950s, there were about 12 million commodities tracked in Soviet economic plans. To make matters worse, this figure does not even account for the fact that a ripe banana in Moscow is not the same as a ripe banana in Leningrad, and moving it from one place to the other must also be part of the plan. But even were there "merely" 12 million commodities, the most efficient known algorithms for optimization, running on the most efficient computers available today, would take roughly a thousand years to solve such a problem exactly once. It can even be proven that a modern computer could not achieve even a reasonably "approximate" solution—and, of course, today there are far more goods, services, transport choices, and other factors that would go into the problem than there were in the Soviet Union in the 1950s. Yet somehow the market miraculously cuts through this computational nightmare.

## Markets as Parallel Processors

But all of this raises a question. If the problem is so hard to solve, how is it possible for the market to solve it? Consider Lange's quote from our epigraph.[5] The market is just a set of rules enforced by the government—not much different from a computer algorithm, although a very complex one. It's true that no single person invented the market. Yet the rules of the market are well understood, and economists are constantly telling people to implement them. Imagine that a new country is created, and its leaders ask a western economist how best to create an economy. The economist will tell them how to set up a market—the rules of contract and property law, for example. (Indeed, economists have been running around the halls of government of developing countries and the floors of start-ups for decades doing just this.) Aren't the economists just supplying a kind of computer program to the leaders, who by implementing it are engaging in a style of centralized planning?

To understand how the market solves the "very large system of equations," you need to know the key ideas of *distributed computing* and *parallel processing*. In these systems, complicated calculations that no one computer could perform are divided into small parts that can be performed *in parallel* by a large number of computers *distributed* across different geographic locations. Distributed computing and parallel processing are best known for their role in the development of "cloud computing," but their greatest application has gone unnoticed: the market economy itself.

While the human brain is wired differently from a computer, computational scientists estimate that a single human mind has a computational capacity roughly ten times greater than the most powerful single supercomputer at the time of this writing.[6] The combined capacity of all human minds is therefore tens of billions of times greater than this most powerful present-day computer. The "market" is then in some sense a giant computer composed of these smaller but still very powerful computers. If it allocates resources efficiently, it does so by harnessing and combining their separate capacities.

Adopting this perspective, we must ask how the market is "programmed" to achieve this outcome. The economy consists of a variety of resources and human capacities at a range of locations, along with a system for transmitting data about these resources among individual human beings. A standard approach in parallel processing is to take information local to one location in, say, a picture or puzzle and assign this to one processor, integrating these inputs on still other processors in a hierarchical fashion. Now apply this image to the economy. In every place, we take one of the computers (humans) available to us and assign it to collect information about that location's needs and resources and report some parsimonious "compressed" summary of all that data to other computers. For example, there might be a hierarchical arrangement of computers, with those responsible for particular locations on the ground reporting to a higher "layer" that integrates local areas and then upward from there.

Consider the following example. A person works on a farm and is in charge of ensuring that the farm is productive and that her family is happy. This person sends information about the farm and her family, not in its full richness and complexity, but in broad strokes, to district managers. One manager specializes in understanding the resources that farms need to operate—seeds, fertilizer—while another understands the resources that people living on farms need in order to be happy, including food and clothing. These managers would then aggregate these data and convey them to the next layer, perhaps a national wheat distributor or a regional supplier of products for use on farms. At every level of this chain, some information would need to be lost for the parallel processing to remain parallel and tractable: the farm manager could not detail every way in which a slightly better paved road would help in conveying goods to market or how slightly cleaner water would protect her crops. But at least she could report the largest and most important needs and hope that the loss of information only slightly reduces the efficiency of the resulting solution.

This arrangement has a flavor of central planning but also resembles a market economy. People specialize in different parts of the production chain and operate under limited information, yet are able to coordinate their behavior because the information takes a certain form. While people are experts on local conditions, they know little about economic conditions elsewhere. They know that grain prices are high and tractor prices are low, but not why this is the case. When they buy a tractor or sell grain, they don't tell the vendor or purchaser their life story, all the conditions on their farm, and so forth. They just place an order or offer so much grain at the going price.

This "price system" thus greatly simplifies communication between different parts of the economy. In fact, economists have shown that prices are the minimum information that a farmer needs to plan her operations effectively. So long as every important way that the farm could benefit or draw down resources from the outside world has a price attached to it, this is all the information the farmer needs to make economic decisions. Any greater information would be a waste, from a purely economic efficiency perspective, though it might be interesting from time to time to develop personal relationships. Conversely, if these prices were not available, there would be no way for a farmer to know whether it pays to use new tractors or rely instead on more labor, nor would she know how many seeds to plant for next season. The farmer without such prices could easily produce too little or waste resources on a tractor that could be better used for more labor, seed, or even consumption.

In this sense, prices are the "minimum" information necessary for rational economic decision-making.[7] No other system of distributed computing can be equally productive and yet require less communication.

Markets elegantly exploit distributed human computational capacity. In doing so they allocate resources in ways that no present computer could match. Von Mises was right that central planning by a group of experts cannot replace the market system. But his argument was mistakenly taken as implying that the market is "natural" rather than a human-created program for managing economic resources. In fact, there is nothing natural about market institutions. Human beings create markets—in their capacity as judges, legislators, administrators, and even private business people who frequently set up organizations that create and manage markets.

Markets are powerful computers, but whether they produce the greatest good or not depends on how they are programmed. We advocate "Radical Markets" because we believe that in the present stage of technological and economic development, when cooperation has grown too large to be managed by moral economies, the market is the appropriate computer to achieve the greatest good for the greatest number. If we see it as such, we can fix the bugs in the market's code and enable it to generate more wealth that is distributed more fairly.

By sharpening our understanding of the role and value of markets, the computational analogy clarifies our claim that the solutions we propose are based on extending the reach of markets. The COST on wealth radicalizes markets as it puts greater responsibility on individuals to articulate their values and gives them greater ability to claim things they value highly. QV does the same in the political sphere. Our ideas on migration give individuals more scope for determining the best path for where they live and work. Our proposals on antitrust and data valuation break up centralized power and place greater responsibility on individuals and small firms to compete, innovate, and make rational economic choices to allow for the distributed computation of optimal economic allocations. But all these proposals raise the question: if the market is just a computer program that harnesses the power of individual human intellects, will it still be necessary as computer power increases?

### Markets as Antiquated Computers?

In a response to Hayek, Lange said, "Let us put the simultaneous equations (governing the market) on an electronic computer and we shall obtain the solution in less than a second."[8] The seed of truth in this claim had been identified just six months before Lange's death in 1965 by technology entrepreneur Gordon Moore.

Moore observed that the density of microchips and the computing power that could be achieved for a given cost doubled roughly every eighteen months. While this "Moore's Law" was a wild extrapolation rather than a well-founded principle, it has largely held up. Because of this rapid development of computational capacity, the dream of a computer network that can achieve the complexity of the human mind is no longer out of reach. Most engineers believe that in the near future, probably the 2050s, the total capacity of digital computers will exceed that of all human minds.

When this point has been reached, the computational critique aimed at Lange will no longer hold. In principle, the market could be replicated in silicon—replacing the distributed, parallel flesh-and-blood system that we are familiar with. The computers would tell people what to produce—distributing rewards and meting out sanctions as necessary—and distribute to people whatever they should consume. The technological problem in aggregating information can be solved. The public attention currently given to the rise of robots—as workers, servants, and lovers—has focused overwhelmingly on the micro level, the human-to-computer interactions that could result in physical or emotional harm. But if robots can drive cars, they can also make purchase orders, accept deliveries, gauge consumer sentiment, plan economic operations, and coordinate this activity at the level of the economy. At this macro level, the role of artificial intelligence in reshaping social organization has—bizarrely—received little attention. Whether such a system would work as intended, or its centralized authority be horribly abused, is of far more significance than the hot topic of whether a robot driver should be programmed to sacrifice a single passenger to save two pedestrians.

Meanwhile, behind-the-scenes information technology plays an increasing role in business planning. While our economy remains primarily driven by the interplay of markets, an increasing number of businesses organize logistics, production schedules, distribution channels, and supply chains in automated ways. These vast, successful corporations engage in the type of technical calculations that Lange envisioned for the central planner, albeit at a smaller scale. Walmart grew to be one of the most valuable enterprises in the world through its mastery of automated logistics and pricing, and yet is quickly being outstripped by the even further automated and centralized planning of Amazon. Uber directs a large part of the flow of transportation services in many cities. In short, vast corporations—islands of centralized planning in the ocean of the market economy—produce a significant amount of economic value by exploiting computational power.

### Can Computers Plan You?

Despite its eventual defeat in the Cold War, the Soviet Union managed many impressive feats of development that eluded other countries. From the end of World War II until the early 1970s, the Soviet economy grew at an impressively high rate.[9]

In the famous 1959 Nixon-Khrushchev debate in a mock-up of an American kitchen, Vice President Nixon conceded the United States had fallen behind the Soviets in important areas of rocketry and science, but many observers nonetheless felt Nixon had prevailed in illustrating the diversity of choice offered by the capitalist system and its responsiveness to consumer preferences. The Soviet system, on the other hand, was legendary for the drab homogeneity of its cars, homes, food, and entertainment.

The problem for the central planner is that, while it knows that most people want cars, home, food, and entertainment, and can supply these things to them, it cannot estimate people's wants beyond a basic level. Mary wants a car that goes fast, Joe wants one that is safe, Manuel cares about handling, Naomi needs storage space for her sports equipment. The central planner, unable to distinguish among these and thousands of other preferences, gives everyone the same car, disappointing nearly everyone. The problem is reproduced for work as well: people have many different preferences about work conditions and types of work. Without knowing what these are, the central planner offers only the same basic amenities that it can reasonably assume nearly everyone wants, which undermines morale and raises the cost of production. Many economists believe that it was this inability to respond to, supply, and innovate for consumer (and worker) desires that made the Soviet system unsustainable.

And yet, recent developments in algorithms and computation that we discussed in chapter 5 have challenged these assumptions. Today, machines learn from the statistical patterns in human behavior, and may be able to use this information to distribute goods (and jobs) as well as, or possibly better than, people can choose goods (and jobs) themselves. We are very far from this point, but we can see the outlines of the route that we might travel. Let us start with an increasingly familiar phenomenon: machine learning–based recommendation systems drawing on existing market behavior. How does Netflix guess what movies you are likely to enjoy? Roughly, it finds people who are like you—who watch many of the movies you watch— and gives those movies ratings similar to your ratings. It then infers that you will enjoy movies you have not yet seen that your hidden doppelgangers have seen and rated highly. Pandora and Spotify take a similar approach in recommending music. Facebook and Apple's news services use similar methods to help guide consumers to the information they want to consume. Google uses related algorithms to determine the information, and product placements, most appropriate not just to your search query but to all the other things it knows about you. Amazon triangulates consumer preferences to suggest additional items to buy.

A central planning machine obviously could not rely on market behavior—markets would, by hypothesis, be gone! But it could derive information from people's behavior—as well as from their physical and psychological attributes, to the extent these are observable—and how it does this may well resemble what Netflix or Amazon does today.

To see how, start with a more homely example. In the medical systems in most advanced countries, even the United States, market choices have been eliminated or greatly curtailed. In a national health system, like the UK's, people do not receive whatever medical treatment they want, but must persuade government agents—doctors—that they suffer from conditions that warrant such treatment. The doctors verify patients' complaints through highly intrusive, physical (and often psychological) examinations. In the United States, most people use HMOs and other insurance systems. While they still have market choice among those systems, for all practical purposes they are in the same positions as British patients because Americans must persuade doctors of their complaints if they are to rely on their insurance, as most of them must.

It is predictable that in the near future all routine medical functions will largely be determined by machines. Doctors who currently perform these functions will be replaced by medical assistants who act as administrative interfaces between patients and machines. Diagnoses will be statistical estimates derived from data about the patient's body and behavior—which just means that people's "preferences" for medical treatment are derived from data rather than from choices made in a market setting. The underlying assumption is that people want "health," and the planner will give it to them within the limits of medical technology; patient "choice" in any conventional sense plays no role, except of course that people are allowed to refuse treatment if they don't want it.

Combine the Netflix/Amazon example with Britain's National Health Service, and one can imagine how a planner might act in other economic sectors. Some people want fast cars, others want safe cars, and still others want cars with large storage capacity (or, as we expect, car services rather than actual cars). In the old-style Soviet system, the planner might know only a few things—that a person needs to live far from work in an area devoid of public transportation, for example. In a more sustainable system, the planner needs to know consumer preferences about speed, color, handling, storage space, vehicle size, and so on, and how these preferences change over time and across place. How would the planner estimate a person's preferences along these dimensions?

Like Netflix or Amazon, it would need to draw on the data traces the person has left in the world, deriving estimates of preferences based on how people who have produced similar data traces have acted in similar conditions. This is the domain of machine learning. If people's phones show they are physically active, prone to call their parents, and enthusiastic about taking photos; their Netflix account shows that they like animated movies and romantic comedies; and their search record shows an interest in climate regulation and other liberal causes, then it may turn out that a Prius is the car for them, and they do not even know it. When it shows up at their door, they are grateful that, unlike their great-great-grandparents, they were not required to delay their purchase until after reading *Consumer Reports*, test driving fourteen different models, and debating the merits of tail fins with their friends. People will not make choices but simply accept goods and services sent to them by computer programs.

Or consider entertainment. Spotify and Pandora already allow people to request a stream of music that they will like, making choices on a case-by-case basis unnecessary. People like these services because the traditional method for deciding whether to purchase music—which involves listening to a lot of stuff you don't like, reading reviews, talking to music store clerks, and engaging in other time-consuming and not always enjoyable activities—is so cumbersome. But Spotify is the dark ages compared to the future of consumption. Suppose that it were possible, based on tracking the movements of the eyes of a viewer, for an algorithm to determine which parts of a movie appealed to him in what ways; technologies like this are, in fact, already in use for marketing purposes.[10] Further, suppose that, based on cross-referencing these eye movements to those of other viewers, it were possible to determine which other movies might interest him. Finally, suppose that these inferences were so reliable and accurate that the viewer, while initially skeptical, came to rely on them so implicitly that he almost always chose to watch the first video presented to him by the artificial intelligence system.

In this scenario, we could say that the viewer is "choosing" his future consumption based on the way he chooses to move his eyes when watching the film and that other viewers are simply giving him advice through their eye movements about what he might like. But choice seems like a metaphor rather than a phenomenologically accurate term for the relevant behavior. Eye movements are largely subconscious and rarely feel subjectively like choices. The pathways through which the viewing activity of other people led to the delivery of a particular movie to a particular person would be obscure to everyone. The automated process would form a consumption pattern out of the collective intelligence created by digital computation and dispersed human sensory perceptions fused together. At some point, "market" may no longer seem to be the right word for economic organization, though central planning might not, either.

Could such processes guide major life decisions—what house to buy, what career to embark on? Would they guide political judgments and romantic involvements as well? Would people be freed to live more meaningful lives or deprived of the ability to do so?

Like most long-term predictions about the future, these questions are beyond the ability of scientific analysis to answer. Certainly, such a world, characterized by the combination of massive computer power and big data supplied by a voluntary (or possibly legally mandated) system of continuous surveillance, poses obvious dystopic risks. No individual or small group of individuals could be trusted to direct such a system, as the temptation to abuse would be overwhelming. But whether it would be possible to govern it in some (Radically) democratic manner, in an auditable algorithmic way, or according to a quasi-decentralized form of distributed computing, is far from certain. It is also unclear whether technology will ever advance to the point where computers outstrip human minds or whether human minds may themselves advance faster and maintain the present equilibrium favoring the market.

While we leave such speculation to the writers of science fiction, we remain confident that for at least a few generations, markets—Radical Markets, that is—will remain the best method of large-scale social organization.

# NOTES

## Preface. The Auction Will Set You Free

1. Mason Gaffney, Warm Memories of Bill Vickrey (1996), http://www
.wealthandwant.com/auth/Vickrey.html. Gaffney suggested that God replied, "Bill,
that's how we've always done it here; but thank you for urging folks to have my will
done on earth as it is in Heaven."

2. Juan Camilo Castillo, Daniel T. Knoepfle, & E. Glen Weyl, Surge Pricing Solves
the Wild Goose Chase (2017), https://www.microsoft.com/en-us/research/wp
-content/uploads/2017/06/ECabstract.pdf.

3. Janny Scott, After Three Days in the Spotlight, Nobel Prize Winner Is Dead,
*New York Times*, October 12, 1996.

## Introduction. The Crisis of the Liberal Order

1. Francis Fukuyama, *The End of History and the Last Man* (Free Press, 1992).

2. Marion Fourcade-Gourinchas & Sarah L. Babb, The Rebirth of the Liberal
Creed: Paths to Neoliberalism in Four Countries, 108 *American Journal of Sociology*
533 (2002); Fourcade et al., The Superiority of Economists, 29 *Journal of Economic
Perspectives* 89 (2015).

3. Marion Fourcade, *Economists and Societies: Discipline and Profession in the
United States, Britain, and France, 1890s to 1990s* (Princeton University Press, 2010).

4. Thomas Piketty, Emmanuel Saez, and Gabriel Zucman, Distributional National Accounts: Methods and Estimates for the United States, *Quarterly Journal of
Economics* (Forthcoming).

5. Thomas Piketty & Gabriel Zucman, Capital Is Back: Wealth-Income Ratios in
Rich Countries 1700–2010, 129 *Quarterly Journal of Economics* 1255 (2014).

6. Council of Economic Advisers, Benefits of Competition and Indicators of Market Power (April 2016), https://obamawhitehouse.archives.gov/sites/default/files
/page/files/20160414_cea_competition_issue_brief.pdf; *The Economist*, In the Sha-
dow of Giants (February 17, 2011), http://www.economist.com/node/18182262.

7. Simcha Barkai, Declining Labor and Capital Shares (2017), http://home
.uchicago.edu/~barkai/doc/BarkaiDecliningLaborCapital.pdf.

8. Jan de Loecker & Jan Eeckhout, The Rise of Market Power and Macroeco-

nomic Implications (2017), http://www.janeeckhout.com/wp-content/uploads/RMP.pdf.

9. Chad Syverson, Challenges to Mismeasurement Explanations for the US Productivity Slowdown, 34, *Journal of Economic Perspectives* 165 (2017).

10. OECD, The Future of Productivity (2015), https://www.oecd.org/eco/OECD-2015-The-future-of-productivity-book.pdf.

11. Christine Lagarde, Reinvigorating Productivity Growth (April 3, 2017), https://www.imf.org/en/News/Articles/2017/04/03/sp040317-reinvigorating-productivity-growth.

12. Stephen Nickell, Luca Nunziata, & Wolfgang Ochel, Unemployment in the OECD since the 1960s. What Do We Know?, 115 *Economic Journal* 1 (2005).

13. Chad Syverson, What Determines Productivity?, 49 *Journal of Economic Literature* 326 (2011).

14. Chang-Tai Hsieh & Peter J. Klenow, Misallocation and Manufacturing TFP in China and India, 124 *Quarterly Journal of Economics* 1403 (2009).

15. Raj Chetty et al., The Fading American Dream: Trends in Absolute Income Mobility Since 1940 (April 24, 2017), http://science.sciencemag.org/content/early/2017/04/21/science.aal4617/tab-pdf.

16. In the case of Greece, which is now only a marginally wealthy country, Syriza, a leftist populist movement, came to power in 2015 in the midst of the Greek financial crisis but then moderated its policies.

17. Zachary Crockett, Donald Trump Is the Only US President Ever with No Political or Military Experience (updated January 23, 2017), https://www.vox.com/policy-and-politics/2016/11/11/13587532/donald-trump-no-experience.

18. Matt Golder, Far Right Parties in Europe, 19 *Annual Review of Political Science* 477 (2016); Katherine Cramer Walsh, Putting Inequality in Its Place: Rural Consciousness and the Power of Perspective, 106 *American Political Science Review* 517 (2013); David Autor, David Dorn, Gordon Hanson, & Kaveh Majlesi, A Note on the Effect of Rising Trade Exposure on the 2016 Presidential Election (2017), https://gps.ucsd.edu/_files/faculty/hanson/hanson_research_TrumpVote-032017.pdf.

19. Matthew Gentzkow, Jesse M. Shapiro, & Matt Taddy, Measuring Polarization in High-Dimensional Data: Method and Application to Congressional Speech (National Bureau of Economic Research, Working Paper No. 22423, 2016); David Autor, David Dorn, Gordon Hanson, & Kaveh Majlesi, Importing Political Polarization? The Electoral Consequences of Rising Trade Exposure (National Bureau of Economic Research, Working Paper No. 22637, 2016).

20. For example, in a poll conducted by PRRI and *The Atlantic* after the election, two-thirds of Trump voters described his election as "the last chance to stop American decline," https://www.prri.org/research/prri-atlantic-poll-post-election-white-working-class/, and a poll by Lord Ashcroft found that by 16 percentage points, those favoring Brexit believed life was worse in Britain than it was 30 years ago, while those favoring "Remain" had the opposite view by 46 percentage points, http://lordashcroftpolls.com/2016/06/how-the-united-kingdom-voted-and-why/.

21. Arlie Hochshild, *Strangers in Their Own Land: Anger and Mourning on the American Right* (New Press, 2016).

22. Adam Smith, *The Wealth of Nations*, Part I, 56 (Collier, 1902).

23. The distinction we are drawing is famously associated with the 1893 work of the great sociologist Émile Durkheim, *The Division of Labour in Society* (Simon & Schuster, 1997).

24. See Michael J. Sandel, *What Money Can't Buy: The Moral Limits of Markets* (Farrar, Straus and Giroux, 2012); Samuel Bowles, *The Moral Economy: Why Good Incentives Are No Substitute for Good Citizens* (Yale University Press, 2016) for a contemporary defense of moral economies.

25. As highlighted in Gareth Stedman Jones, *Karl Marx: Greatness and Illusion* (Harvard University Press, 2016), Marx actually abandoned these ideals toward the end of his life, and thus we describe them as "Marxism" rather than as the views of Marx himself.

26. John Stuart Mill, *On Liberty* (John W. Parker and Sons, 1859).

27. Adam Smith, *Theory of Moral Sentiments*, 296 (Wells and Lilly, 1817) (emphasis added).

28. Smith, *Wealth of Nations*, 137.

29. While accepted by most applied economists who interacted with policymakers, economic theorists who were often far removed from practical policy discussions continued to question this view. For a discussion, see Anthony B. Atkinson, The Mirrlees Review and the State of Public Economics, 50 *Journal of Economic Literature* 770 (2012).

30. Joan Robinson, *The Economics of Imperfect Competition* (Palgrave Macmillan, 1932).

31. William Cronon, *Nature's Metropolis: Chicago and the Great West* (W. W. Norton, 1992).

## Chapter 1. Property Is Monopoly

1. Hyperloop Tests Magnetic Levitation At 192 mph, NPR Morning Edition, August 4, 2017, available at http://www.npr.org/2017/08/04/541538743/hyperloop-tests-magnetic-levitation-at-192-mph.

2. William J. Bernstein, *A Splendid Exchange* (Grove Press, 2008).

3. Robert C. Allen, Engels' Pause: Technical Change, Capital Accumulation, and Inequality in the British Industrial Revolution, 46 *Explorations in Economic History* 418 (2009).

4. Henry George, *Progress and Poverty* 1–5 (Robert Schalkenbach Foundation, 1997).

5. Alexander Gray, *The Socialist Tradition: Moses to Lenin* (Longmans, Green, 1947).

6. Philip T. Hoffman, Institutions and Agriculture in Old Regime France, 16 *Policy & Society* 241 (1988).

7. The number comes from the economist Chad Syverson, who found that as a result of dramatic misallocation of resources to low-productivity firms, output is reduced by as much as 25% annually. Chad Syverson, Market Structure and Productivity: A Concrete Example, 112 *Journal of Political Economy* 1181 (2004); Syverson, Product Substitutability and Productivity Dispersion, 86 *Review of Economics and Statistics* 534 (2004); Syverson, What Determines Productivity, 49 *Journal of Economic Literature* 326 (2011). Not all of this misallocation is due to the monopoly problem in its simplest form. However, as we discuss below, many other problems that cause misallocation (adverse selection, endowment effects, and credit constraints) are also addressed by partial common property. We thus believe much of this misallocation can be addressed by a COST and related reforms.

8. Gareth Stedman Jones, *Karl Marx—Greatness and Illusion* (Belknap Press, 2016).

9. Michael Kremer, *The O-Ring Theory of Economic Development*, 108 *Quarterly Journal of Economics* 551 (1993), provides a definitive account of how large-scale enterprises typically must overcome monopoly problems.

10. R. H. Coase, The Nature of the Firm, 4 *Economica* 386 (1937).

11. W. Stanley Jevons, *The Theory of Political Economy* xlvi (Macmillan and Company, 5th ed., 1957).

12. Léon Walras, *Studies in Social Economics* 224–225 ( Jan van Daal & Donald A. Walker, trans., Routledge, 2010).

13. The term "social dividend" seems to have been coined by Oskar Lange, The Economic Theory of Socialism, 4 *Review of Economic Studies* 1 (1936), but he attributed the concept to Walras. We will see more about Lange's ideas below.

14. Walras, *Studies in Social Economics*, 234.

15. George, *Progress and Poverty*, 223.

16. George, *Progress and Poverty*, 244.

17. http://landlordsgame.info/.

18. George R. Geiger, *The Philosophy of Henry George. Introduction by John Dewey* xxii (MacMillan Co., 1933).

19. Garrett Hardin, The Tragedy of the Commons, 162 *Science* 1243 (1968).

20. Harold Schiffrin, Sun Yat-sen's Early Land Policy: The Origin and Meaning of "Equalization of Land Rights," 16 *Journal of Asian Studies* 549, 555 (1957).

21. Joseph A. Schumpeter, *Capitalism, Socialism and Democracy* (Harper & Brothers, 1942).

22. Oskar Lange & Fred M. Taylor, *On the Economic Theory of Socialism* (Benjamin E. Lippincott, ed., 1938); Abba P. Lerner, *The Economics of Control: Principles of Welfare Economics* (Macmillan, 1944).

23. Ludwig von Mises, *Economic Calculation in the Socialist Commonwealth* (S. Alder trans., Ludwig von Mises Institute, 2012); Frederich A. Hayek, The Use of Knowledge in Society, 35 *American Economic Review* 519 (1945). See also Samuel Bowles, *Microeconomics: Behavior, Institutions and Evolution* 475–476 (Princeton Uni-

versity Press, 2006) for a discussion of the midcentury debates. We return to these debates in our epilogue.

24. These critiques would eventually lead modern socialist thinkers to advocate various hybrid economic relationships like workers' cooperatives, which would have placed production under greater democratic control, and stronger economic rights, which would make workers less dependent on their employers. See Samuel Bowles & Herbert Gintis, *Democracy and Capitalism: Property, Community, and the Contradictions of Modern Social Thought* (Basic Books, 1986); Alec Nove, *The Economics of Feasible Socialism Revisited* (Routledge, 2d ed., 1991).

25. Friedrich Hayek, *The Road to Serfdom* (Routledge, 1944).

26. Some limited empirical work confirms the lawyer's intuition that bargaining can be extremely difficult, especially in the sorts of examples that Coase preferred. See Hoyt Bleakley & Joseph Ferrie, Land Openings on the Georgia Frontier and the Coase Theorem in the Short and Long-Run (2014) at http://wwwpersonal.umich.edu /~hoytb/ Bleakley_Ferrie_Farmsize.pdf and Ward Farnsworth, Do Parties to Nuisance Cases Bargain after Judgment? A Glimpse Inside the Cathedral, 66 *University of Chicago Law Review* 373 (1999). Even in highly competitive environments, economic evidence corroborates these findings. See Bradley Larsen, The Efficiency of Real-World Bargaining: Evidence from Wholesale Used-Auto Auctions, NBER Working Paper 20431 (2014).

27. Coase originally wanted to show that it's not always best to regulate the person who seems to cause a problem (here, the music teacher); it might make more sense to let the parties reach an agreement.

28. This can be seen in the three major textbooks on law and economics. All three books give great weight to the investment problem as a justification for private property: if private property did not exist, then people would not invest in improving property since they could not be sure that they would profit from the returns on the investment. See Steven Shavell, *Foundations of Economic Analysis of Law* 11–19 (Harvard University Press, 2004); Robert Cooter & Thomas Ulen, *Law & Economics* 76–80 (Pearson, 6th ed., 2012); Richard A. Posner, *Economic Analysis of Law* 40–42 (Aspen Publishers, 9th ed., 2014). The textbooks give only passing attention to the monopoly problem. While they acknowledge that holdout problems, and related problems of strategic behavior, can interfere with the transfer of property, they largely consider these problems as confined to cases where the use of property affects many people, as in the case of factory pollution.

29. See Benjamin Edelman, Michael Ostrovsky, & Michael Schwarz, Internet Advertising and the Generalized Second-Price Auction: Selling Billions of Dollars' Worth of Keywords, 97 *American Economic Review* 242 (2007); Hal R. Varian, Position Auctions, 25 *International Journal of Industrial Organization* 1163 (2007).

30. R. H. Coase, The Federal Communications Commission, 2 *Journal of Law and Economics* 1 (1959); Thomas W. Hazlett, Assigning Property Rights to Radio Spectrum Users: Why Did FCC License Auctions Take 67 Years?, 41 *Journal of Law and Economics* 1 (1959).

31. Paul Milgrom, Putting Auction Theory to Work, 108 *Journal of Political Economy* 245 (2000).

32. Roger B. Myerson & Mark Sattherwaite, Efficient Mechanisms for Bilateral Trading, 29 *Journal of Economic Theory* 265 (1983).

33. Peter Crampton, Robert Gibbons, & Paul Klemperer, Dissolving a Partnership Efficiently, 55 *Econometrica* 61 (1987); Ilya Segal & Michael D. Whinston, A Simple Status Quo that Ensures Participation (with Application to Efficient Bargaining), 6 *Theoretical Economics* 109 (2011).

34. One might think this case is natural, if the two partners have shares in proportion to the work they have put into the project, as the best partner to take over is likely the one who has put most effort into the company. However, if the partners' shares reflect not only their effort ("sweat equity") but also financial investment ("cash equity"), or if the commitment to the company has shifted over time, this may not be the case.

35. E. Glen Weyl & Anthony Lee Zhang, Depreciating Licenses (2017), https://ssrn.com/abstract=2744810.

36. Demosthenes, *Against Phaenippus* (c. BCE 359), discussed in George C. Bitros & Anastasios D. Karayiannis, *Creative Crisis in Democracy and Economy* 20 (Springer, 2013).

37. Christopher D. Hall, Market Enforced Information Asymmetry: A Study of Claiming Races, 44 *Economic Inquiry* 271 (1986).

38. Antonio Cabrales, Antoni Calvó-Armengol, & Matthew O. Jackson, *La Crema*: A Case Study of Mutual Fire Insurance, 111 *Journal of Political Economics* 425 (2003).

39. Emerson Niou & Guofu Tan, An Analysis of Dr. Sun Yat-sen's Self-Assessment Scheme for Land Taxation, 78 *Public Choice* 103 (1994).

40. Yun-Chien Chang, Self-Assessment of Takings Compensation: An Empirical Study, 28 *Journal of Law, Economics, and Organizations* 265 (2012).

41. Arnold C. Harberger, Issues of Tax Reform for Latin America, in *Fiscal Policy for Economic Growth in Latin America* (Johns Hopkins University Press, 1965).

42. Maurice Allais, *L'Impôt sur le Capital et la Réforme Monétaire* (Hermann, 1988). Saul Levmore, a law professor, helped revive interest in it among academics. Saul Levmore, Self-Assessed Valuation Systems for Tort and Other Law, 68 *Virginia Law Review* 771 (1982).

43. This fact helps allay two potential objections to a COST: that possessors may wish to "sabotage" the appeal of their goods to others to avoid their interest in taking the good, and that predatory outsiders may maliciously take goods just to harm a possessor. Notice that neither of these are possible if possessors always set prices above the minimum they would be willing to accept, because in this case the possessor is happy when her possessions are taken: she still profits, just not as much as if she set a monopoly price. Thus "predation" will be nearly as welcome as would be the "predation" of someone offering you out of the blue an extravagant sum for your home and you would never wish to sabotage your possessions as this would reduce the chance

of such an exceptional opportunity. Only individuals who fraudulently report extremely low values and try to dramatically sabotage their goods would be open to predation, but so they should, and such individuals are likely to be caught by others before too much sabotage is possible.

44. Weyl & Zhang, Depreciating Licenses.

45. Thomas W. Merrill, Property and the Right to Exclude, 77 *Nebraska Law Review* 730 (1998).

46. Of course, this is also true of an ordinary property tax, and many other legal restrictions on the use of private property.

47. To make our account vivid we discuss some examples of personal possessions of individuals, like homes and cars, but the reader should keep in mind that most assets are owned by businesses and thus much of the participation in and benefits from a COST would be through business assets.

48. For further details, see Eric A. Posner & E. Glen Weyl, Property Is Another Name for Monopoly, 9 *Journal of Legal Analysis* 51 (2017).

49. Note that this would create a highly liquid market in home refinancings.

50. A team of researchers led by Nikhil Naik is already using image analysis to conduct automated property assessments for real estate, so this idea is not as far-fetched as it may at first sound.

51. George A. Akerlof, The Market for "Lemons": Quality, Uncertainty and the Market Mechanism, 84 *Quarterly Journal of Economics* 488 (1970); Michael Spence, Job Market Signaling, 87 *Quarterly Journal of Economics* 355 (1973).

52. Richard Thaler, Toward a Positive Theory of Consumer Choice, 1 *Journal of Economics, Behavior, and Organizations* 39 (1980).

53. John A. List, Neoclassical Theory versus Prospect Theory: Evidence from the Marketplace, 72 *Econometrica* 615 (2004); Coren L. Apicella, Eduardo M. Azevedo, Nicholas A. Christakis, & James H. Fowler, Evolutionary Origins of the Endowment Effect: Evidence from Hunter-Gatherers, 104 *American Economic Review* 1793 (2014).

54. For a review of the many ill effects of an economy based on debt, especially from a macroeconomic viewpoint, see Atif Mian & Amir Sufi, *House of Debt: How They (and You) Caused the Great Recession and How We Can Stop It from Happening Again* (University of Chicago Press, 2014).

55. J. R. Hicks, Annual Survey of Economic Theory: The Theory of Monopoly, 3 *Econometrica* 1, 8 (1935).

56. Weyl & Zhang, Depreciating Licenses.

57. Chad Syverson, What Determines Productivity?, 49 *Journal of Economic Literature* 326 (2011).

58. Milgrom, Putting Auction Theory to Work.

59. Paul Milgrom, E. Glen Weyl, & Anthony Lee Zhang, Redesigning Spectrum Licenses, 40 *Regulation* (2017).

60. Jacqueline D. Lipton, Beyond Cybersquatting: Taking Domain Name Disputes Past Trademark Policy, 40 *Wake Forest Law Review* 1361 (2005).

61. Hope King, Owner of ClintonKaine.com wants $90,000, CNN Money ( July

27, 2016), http://money.cnn.com/2016/07/27/technology/clinton-kaine-website /index.html.

62. Lauren Cohen, Umit G. Gurun, & Scott Duke Kominers, The Growing Problem of Patent Trolling, 352 *Science* 521 (2016).

63. It is increasingly popular to refer to such a universal refundable tax credit as a "universal basic income" (UBI). We resist this description because a UBI is typically described as being indexed to some notion of an income required to live a decent life, a notion that we consider ill-defined and which, in any case, is not the aim of our proposal. Our social dividend would be proportioned to the total self-assessed wealth of a country and not to some notion of basic needs.

64. David P. Hariton, Sorting Out the Tangle of Economic Substance, 52 *Tax Lawyer* 235 (1999); David A. Weisbach, Ten Truths about Tax Shelters (John M. Olin Program in Law and Economics Working Paper No. 122, 2001).

65. Note that the nominal principal does not fall; it is the value of the claim against this principal that falls.

66. Piketty et al., Distributional National Accounts.

67. Tyler Cowen, *The Complacent Class: The Self-Defeating Quest for the American Dream* (St. Martin's Press, 2017).

68. Leaf Van Boven and Thomas Gilovich, To Do or to Have? That Is the Question, 85 *Journal of Personality and Social Psychology* 1193 (2003).

69. More recent exponents of this view are, for example, Robert H. Frank, *Choosing the Right Pond: Human Behavior and the Quest for Status* (Oxford University Press, 1987), and Juliet B. Schor, *The Overspent America: Why We Want What We Don't Need* (Harper Perennial, 1999).

70. Saumitra Jha, Financial Asset Holdings and Political Attitudes: Evidence from Revolutionary England, 130 *Quarterly Journal of Economics* 1485 (2015); Markku Kaustia, Samuli Knüpfer, & Sami Torstila, Stock Ownership and Political Behavior: Evidence from Demutualizations, 62 *Management Science* 945 (2015).

71. Francis Fukuyama, *Trust* (Free Press, 1995); Paola Sapienza, Anna Toldra-Simats, & Luigi Zingales, Understanding Trust, 123 *Economic Journal* 1313 (2013).

## Chapter 2. Radical Democracy

1. Mogens Herman Hansen, *The Athenian Democracy in the Age of Demosthenes: Structure, Principles, and Ideology* 6 (J. A. Crook, trans., Basil Blackwell, 1999).

2. Xenophon, *Hellenica* bk. 1, ch. 7, §§ 1–35 (Carlton Brownson trans., 1921) and Hansen, *Athenian Democracy*.

3. Andrew Lintott, *The Constitution of the Roman Republic* (Oxford University Press, 1999).

4. See Goronwy Edwards, Presidential Address, *The Emergence of Majority Rule in the Procedure of the House of Commons*, 15 *Transactions of the Royal Historical Society* 165 (1965).

5. John Gilbert Heinberg, Theories of Majority Rule, 26 *American Political Science Review* 452, 456 (1932).

6. Melissa Schwartzberg, *Counting the Many: The Origins and Limits of Supermajority Rule* 52–58 (Cambridge University Press, 2013); Heinberg, Theories of Majority Rule, at 456.

7. Thomas Hobbes, *Leviathan* (Penguin Classics, 1986) (originally published in 1651).

8. US Declaration of Independence, para. 3 (1776).

9. The Federalist No. 51, at 323 (James Madison) (Clinton Rossiter, ed., 1961).

10. US Constitution, article II, § 2.

11. US Constitution, article I, §7.

12. US Constitution, article V.

13. See Robert A. Dahl, *How Democratic Is the American Constitution?*, 12–18 (Yale University Press, 2d ed., 2003).

14. In fact, many advocates for minority groups victimized by such laws have recognized the limits of the legitimacy of such judicial intervention and called for giving greater voice in voting on crime issues to those directly affected. William J. Stuntz, *The Collapse of American Criminal Justice* (Harvard University Press, 2011), and Lisa L. Miller, *The Perils of Federalism: Race, Poverty, and the Politics of Crime Control* (Oxford University Press, 2010).

15. Spanish mathematician and philosopher Ramon Llull had anticipated many of Condorcet's later ideas in the thirteenth century, but his manuscripts were lost from the time of his life until the early part of the new millennium and thus he had very little impact on the subsequent development of ideas about voting.

16. Kenneth Arrow, *Social Choice and Individual Values* (Yale University Press, 1970) (originally published in 1951).

17. Witness, for example, the frequent citation of this theorem in a recent poll of economists asking whether an ideal voting system exists. IGM Forum, Primary Voting (March 7, 2016), http://www.igmchicago.org/surveys/primary-voting. However, this view is somewhat misleading. Arrow's Theorem also applies to market allocations and conversely the positive results about markets also apply to collective decisions (because of QV). The failures of collective decision-making relative to markets for private goods concern more specific features of existing institutions (which we turn to below), not these broad possibilities covered by Arrow's Theorem.

18. "Sur les assemblées provinciales" in *Oeuvres de Condorcet*, 8:214–216, 268–271, "Ésquisse" in *Oeuvres de Condorcet*, 6:176–177.

19. See Gary W. Cox, *Making Votes Count: Strategic Coordination in the World's Electoral Systems* (Cambridge University Press, 1997).

20. This most famous pathology of strategic voting is known as Duverger's law. See Maurice Duverger, *Political Parties: Their Organization and Activity in Modern States* (Wiley, 1954).

21. Richard J. Evans, *The Coming of the Third Reich* (Penguin, 2004).

22. Ivan Ermakoff, *Ruling Oneself Out: A Theory of Collective Abdications* (Duke University Press, 2008).

23. See Richard D. McKelvey, Intransitivities in Multidimensional Voting Models and Some Implications for Agenda Control, 12 *Journal of Economic Theory* 472 (1976).

24. Martin Niemöller, "First They Came" (c. 1945), American Holocaust Memorial Museum, https://www.ushmm.org/wlc/en/article.php?ModuleId=10007392.

25. Élie Harlévy, *A History of the English People in the Nineteenth Century: The Triumph of Reform: 1830–1841* (E. I. Watkin, trans., Barnes & Noble, 1961).

26. Jeremy Bentham, Article on Utilitarianism, in *The Collected Works of Jeremy Bentham: Deontology Together with a Table of the Springs of Action and Article on Utilitarianism* (Amnon Goldworth ed., Oxford University Press, 1983; originally published in 1829).

27. John Stuart Mill, *Considerations on Representative Government* (Parker, Son, and Bourn, 1861).

28. Paul A. Samuelson, The Pure Theory of Public Expenditure, 36 *Review of Economics and Statistics* 387 (1954).

29. Mancur Olson, *The Logic of Collective Action: Public Goods and the Theory of Groups* (Harvard University Press, rev. ed., 1971).

30. See William Vickrey, Counterspeculation, Auctions and Competitive Sealed Tenders, 16 *Journal of Finance* 8 (1961); William Vickrey, Automobile Accidents, Tort Law, Externalities, and Insurance: An Economist's Critique, 33 *Law and Contemporary Problems* 464 (1968).

31. See Edward H. Clarke, Multipart Pricing of Public Goods, 11 *Public Choice* 17 (1971); Theodore Groves, Incentives in Teams, 41 *Econometrica* 617 (1973).

32. Theodore Groves & John Ledyard, Optimal Allocation of Public Goods: A Solution to the "Free Rider" Problem, 45 *Econometrica* 783 (1977); Aanund Hylland & Richard Zeckhauser, A Mechanism for Selecting Public Goods When Preferences Must Be Elicited (Kennedy School of Government, Harvard University, Discussion Paper 51, 1980).

33. For a more detailed exposition of this graphical analysis, see Nicolaus Tideman & Florenz Plassmann, Efficient Bilateral Taxation of Externalities, 172 *Public Choice* 109 (2017).

34. Economists Jacob Goeree and Jingjing Zhang independently discovered a more specific version of the idea only a few months after Weyl posted the first version of his work, "Quadratic Voting Buying," online in 2012. Their paper was published in 2017. Jacob Goeree & Jingjing Zhang, One Man, One Bid, 101 *Games & Economic Behavior* 151 (2017).

35. This is an artifact of the discretized numerical example, not a feature of the model. The voter gains the marginal benefit from casting a vote times the number of votes cast ($MB * v$), and pays the square of the number of votes cast ($v^2$). Setting marginal benefit equal to marginal cost, $v^* = MB/2$. Accordingly, the number of votes that a voter casts will be proportionate to her marginal benefit. The result is driven by the fact that the derivative of a quadratic relationship is linear.

36. Mathematical investigations by Weyl and co-authors suggest that this "chance of being pivotal" will be quite similar in a wide range of circumstances across most individuals, especially when the number of voters is large, implying that the approximation is quite accurate. In fact, after investigating a wide range of cases, these analy-

ses could not find an example where QV loses more than 5% of potential welfare; 1p1v can easily lose 100% in cases where the majority imposes its weak interests on a minority of people who have very strong interests. This does not mean QV is perfect, any more than the imperfectly competitive markets our previous chapter sought to address are. Future innovators surely will further refine QV, as we have tried in the previous chapter to refine capitalist markets. Yet QV represents a powerful step toward functioning markets for collective decisions. See Steven P. Lalley & E. Glen Weyl, Quadratic Voting: How Mechanism Design Can Radicalize Democracy, *American Economic Association Papers and Proceedings* (Forthcoming); Steven P. Lalley & E. Glen Weyl, Nash Equilibria for Quadratic Voting (2017) at https://arxiv.org/abs/1409.0264; Bharat K. Chandar & E. Glen Weyl, Quadratic Voting in Finite Populations (May 21, 2017) at https://ssrn.com/abstract=2571026; E. Glen Weyl, The Robustness of Quadratic Voting, 172 *Public Choice* 75 (2017).

37.　Louis Kaplow & Scott Duke Kominers, Who Will Vote Quadratically? Voter Turnout and Votes Cast Under Quadratic Voting, 172 *Public Choice* 125 (2017).

38.　E. Glen Weyl, The Robustness of Quadratic Voting, 172 *Public Choice* 125 (2017).

39.　There are important subtleties in defining the notion of equal voice, because the definition of issues available for voting and their relative cost may advantage or disadvantage some citizens. See Daniel Benjamin, Ori Heffetz, Miles Kimball, & Derek Lougee, The Relationship Between the Normalized Gradient Addition Mechanism and Quadratic Voting, 172 *Public Choice* 233 (2017). We are collaborating with several other scholars to probe these questions more deeply.

40.　Philosophers such as Ronald Dworkin have argued that the ideally just model of distribution of resources is a competitive equilibrium beginning from a position of equal incomes. See, e.g., Ronald Dworkin, What Is Equality? Part II: Equality of Resources, 10 *Philosophy & Public Affairs* 283 (1981); Ronald Dworkin, *Sovereign Virtue: The Theory and Practice of Equality* (Harvard University Press, 2000).

41.　Rensis Likert, A Technique for the Measurement of Attitudes, in *Archives of Philosophy* No. 140, 5–55 (R. S. Woodworth, ed., 1932).

42.　Sendhil Mullainathan & Eldar Shafir, *Scarcity: The New Science of Having Less and How It Defines Our Lives* (Picador, 2014).

43.　David Quarfoot, Douglas von Kohorn, Kevin Slavin, Rory Sutherland, David Goldstein, & Ellen Konar, Quadratic Voting in the Wild: Real People, Real Votes, 172 *Public Choice* 283 (2017).

44.　There is still one anomaly in the QV distribution: a dip at 0. This results from a weakness in the weDesign software: we only allow "whole" votes on issues. This may make it impossible to vote a bit more on something you are passionate about once you have already put several votes on this issue, because you may only have a few credits left. Most participants become so engaged that they want to use up all their credits and thus end up using the last few to move issues they otherwise would have given 0 to 1 in either direction. While this further indicates participant engagement, we hope to fix this "bug" as we iterate the software.

45. Alisha Holland, Square Miles: The Spatial Politics of Mass Infrastructure, American Political Science Association Working Paper, 2017.

46. Liran Einav, Chiara Farronato, & Jonathan Levin, Peer-to-Peer Markets, 8 *Annual Review of Economics* 615 (2016).

47. Chris Nosko & Steven Tadelis, The Limits of Reputation in Platform Markets: An Empirical Analysis and Field Experiment (National Bureau of Economic Research, Working Paper No. 20830, 2015).

48. Andrew Quentson, Can Ethereum-Based Akasha Revolutionize Social Networks? *Cryptocoins News*, January 29, 2017, https://www.cryptocoinsnews.com/can -ethereum-based-akasha-revolutionize-social-networks/.

49. See Eric A. Posner & E. Glen Weyl, Quadratic Voting as Efficient Corporate Governance, 81 *University of Chicago Law Review* 251 (2014), for more on the application to corporate governance.

50. For a more detailed elaboration of these ideas, see Eric A. Posner & E. Glen Weyl, Voting Squared: Quadratic Voting in Democratic Politics, 68 *Vanderbilt Law Review* 441 (2015); Eric A. Posner & Nicholas Stephanopoulos, Quadratic Election Law, 172 *Public Choice* 265 (2017).

51. Note that there are systems somewhat closer to 1p1v that also avoid this, such as the rule devised by Condorcet, the Approval Voting system proposed by Steven Brams in the late 1970s, and the "Range Voting" system of Warren Smith. See Steven J. Brams & Peter C. Fishburn, *Approval Voting* (Birkhauser, 2d ed., 2007); Warren D. Smith, Range Voting (unpublished manuscript, November 28, 2000). Available at http://rangevoting.org/WarrenSmithPages/homepage/rangevote.pdf. Unfortunately, these systems do not have the other benefits of QV and in particular in binary referenda institute majority rule.

52. In joint work with computer scientists Nicole Immorlica and Katrina Ligett, one of us is working to prove formally that this logic implies, under reasonable conditions, that QV will always lead to the election of the candidate achieving the greatest happiness for the greatest number, in the sense we discussed above.

53. Michel Balinski & Rida Laraki, Majority Judgment vs Majority Rule, Working Paper (2016). We took a Likert-based survey they used and assumed that each point on the scale corresponded to a number of votes. This likely understates the strength of the result under QV, given the censoring of extremes we discuss in chapter 2. Under this method, Kasich is the only candidate with an average net positive score (.12), followed by Sanders (-.11), Cruz (-.22), Clinton (-.32), and Trump (-.69).

54. Daron Acemoglu, Suresh Naidu, Pascual Restrepo, & James A. Robinson, Democracy Does Cause Growth, *Journal of Political Economy* (Forthcoming).

55. QV also offers the possibility of helping break free of the twin bonds of "political correctness" and costless online vitriol by offering a rich and costly but anonymous way for citizens to express their political convictions.

56. John Kenneth Galbraith, *The Affluent Society* 187 (Mariner Books, 1958).

## Chapter 3. Uniting the World's Workers

1. For an excellent long-term history of trade, see William J. Bernstein, *A Splendid Exchange: How Trade Shaped the World* (Grove Press, 2009).

2. Edgar S. Furniss, *The Position of the Laborer in a System of Nationalism. A Study in the Labor Theories of the Late English Mercantilists* (Houghton Mifflin Company, 1920).

3. We benefited from discussions with Michael Clemens, who shared some of his unpublished research with us. See also Michael Clemens, Economics and Emigration: Trillion Dollar Bills on the Sidewalk?, 25 *Journal of Economic Perspectives* 3 (2011).

4. Barry Baysinger, Robert B. Eckelund, Jr., & Robert D. Tollison, Mercantilism as a Rent-Seeking Society, in Roger D. Congleton, Arye L. Hillman, & Kai A. Konrad, eds., *40 Years of Research on Rent-Seeking 2: Applications: Rent-Seeking in Practice* (Springer, 2008).

5. Furniss, *Position of the Laborer in a System of Nationalism.*

6. François Bourguignon & Christian Morrisson, Inequality Among World Citizens: 1820–1992, 92 *American Economic Review* 727 (2002).

7. Technically this measure is only an approximation, as the actual measure uses continuously compounded percentage increases, so that this interpretation is accurate only for relatively modest changes. The formal measure is the difference between the natural logarithm of average income and the average value of the natural logarithm of income.

8. Because the mean logarithmic deviation uses continuous compounding, this calculation is not quite right. In this case the mean logarithmic deviation is actually 2.76 logarithmic points. For less dramatic changes in income, however, this approximation is a good way of thinking about what the mean logarithmic deviation corresponds to.

9. For a thoughtful overview, see Branko Milanovic, *Global Inequality: A New Approach for the Age of Globalization* (Belknap Press, 2016).

10. Richard J. Evans, *The Pursuit of Power: Europe 1815–1914* (Penguin, 2016).

11. Letter from Karl Marx to Sigfrid Meyer & August Vogt (April 9, 1870).

12. Matthew Annis, Henry George, John Stuart Mill, and Solving the "Knotty Labor Question" (October 26, 2011), https://thechinesequestion.wordpress.com/tag /john-stuart-mill/; Edward Alsworth Ross, *The Old World in the New* (Century Company, 1914).

13. Migration Policy Institute, U.S. Immigrant Population and Share over Time, 1850–Present, http://www.migrationpolicy.org/programs/data-hub/charts/immi grant-population-over-time.

14. Steven Best, *The Global Industrial Complex: Systems of Domination*, ix (Lexington Books, 2011).

15. Niels Boel, Eduardo Galeano: The Open Veins of McWorld, 54 *UNESCO Courier* 4 (2001).

16. Pierre-Olivier Gourinchas & Olivier Jeanne, The Elusive Gains from International Financial Integration, 73 *Review of Economic Studies* 715 (2006).

17. Jonathan D. Ostry, Prakash Loungani, & Davide Furceri, Neoliberalism: Oversold?, 53 *IMF Finance and Development* 38 (2016).

18. John Gibson & David McKenzie, Eight Questions about Brain Drain, 25 *Journal of Economic Perspectives* 107 (2011), and Frédéric Docquier & Hillel Rapoport, Globalization, Brain Drain, and Development, 50 *Journal of Economic Literature* 681 (2012).

19. Obviously, these calculations are exceedingly rough and neglect many factors, such as the changes in wages for migrants such large-scale migration would cause. However, the most rigorous studies by economists nearly uniformly find that gains to global welfare from fully liberalizing migration would range from 50% to 150%, so gains of 20% are actually quite modest by the standards of the literature. See Clemens, Economics and Emigration.

20. Wolfgang F. Stolper & Paul A. Samuelson, Protection and Real Wages, 9 *Review of Economic Studies* 58 (1941).

21. George J. Borjas, The Labor Demand Curve Is Downward Sloping: Reexamining the Impact of Immigration on the Labor Market, 118 *Quarterly Journal of Economics* 1335 (2003).

22. George J. Borjas, *Issues in the Economics of Immigration* (Princeton University Press, 2001).

23. David Card, Is the New Immigration Really So Bad?, 115 *Economic Journal* F300 (2005); Gianmarco I. P. Ottaviano & Giovanni Peri, Rethinking the Effect of Migration on Wages, 10 *Journal of the European Economic Association* 152 (2012).

24. National Academy of Sciences, Engineering, and Medicine, *The Economic and Fiscal Consequences of Immigration* (National Academies Press, 2016).

25. Dane Stangler & Jason Wiens, The Economic Case for Welcoming Immigrant Entrepreneurs (2015). http://www.kauffman.org/what-we-do/resources/entrepreneurship-policy-digest/the-economic-case-for-welcoming-immigrant-entrepreneurs.

26. National Academy, *Economic and Fiscal Consequences of Immigration*.

27. Christian Dustmann & Tommaso Frattini, The Fiscal Effects of Immigration to the UK (2014), 24 *Economic Journal* F565 (2016).

28. Joel S. Fetzer, *Public Attitudes Toward Immigration in the United States, France and Germany* (Cambridge University Press, 2000).

29. For a systematic study of the nonenforcement of laws as a policy tool see Alisha Holland, *Forbearance as Redistribution: The Politics of Informal Welfare in Latin America* (Cambridge University Press, 2017).

30. Gary S. Becker, *The Challenge of Immigration: A Radical Solution* (Institute of Economic Affairs, 2011).

31. See *The Economist*, Immigration Systems: What's the Point?, July 7th, 2016, for a review.

32. A few studies, relying on anecdotal data, do document some instances of abuse, but the problem is that existing programs are not structured as guest worker

programs. See Janie A. Chuang, The U.S. Au Pair Program: Labor Exploitation and the Myth of Cultural Exchange, 36 *Harvard Journal of Law and Gender* 269 (2013); Daniel Costa, Guestworker Diplomacy, Economic Policy Institute Briefing Paper No. 317 (July 14, 2011), http://www.epi.org/files/2011/BriefingPaper317.pdf. Instead, they are structured as cultural exchange programs, which then are manipulated by employers and private intermediary institutions who arrange for migration. The abuse arises from this mismatch; a properly structured guest worker program would have more protections.

33. E. Glen Weyl, The Openness-Equality Trade-Off in Global Redistribution, *Economic Journal* (Forthcoming), https://papers.ssrn.com/sol3/papers.cfm?abstract _id=2755304. The rest of the material in this section is based on empirical results from this paper.

34. Michael Clemens, *The Walls of Nations* (Columbia University Press, forthcoming).

35. Douglas S. Massey, Jorge Durand, & Nolan J. Malone, *Beyond Smoke and Mirrors: Mexican Immigration in an Era of Economic Integration* (Russell Sage Foundation, 2002).

## Chapter 4. Dismembering the Octopus

1. Aristotle, *Aristotle's Politics* (Carnes Lord, ed. & trans., University of Chicago Press, 2d ed., 2013) (350 BCE).

2. Claude Menard, Three Forms of Resistance to Statistics: Say, Cournot, Walras, 12 *History of Political Economy* 524 (1980).

3. Léon Walras, *Studies in Social Economics* 157 (Jan van Daal & Donald A. Walker, trans., Routledge, 2d ed., 2010) (1896).

4. 15 U.S.C. §§ 1–7 (1890).

5. Ransom E. Noble, Jr., Henry George and the Progressive Movement, 8 *American Journal of Economics & Society* 3 (1949).

6. Renato Crillo, Léon Walras and Social Justice, 43 *American Journal of Economics & Society* 1 (1984).

7. *Standard Oil Co. of N.J. v. United States*, 221 U.S. 1 (1911).

8. For a short history, see William E. Kovacic & Carl Shapiro, Antitrust Policy: A Century of Economic and Legal Thinking, 14 *Journal of Economic Perspectives* 43 (2000).

9. Einer Elhauge, Horizontal Shareholding, 109 *Harvard Law Review* 1267 (2016).

10. Lewis Carroll, *Through the Looking-Glass* 50 (Henry Altemus, 1897).

11. 15 U.S.C. § 18 (amend. 1950).

12. David Gerber, *Law and Competition in Twentieth-Century Europe: Protecting Prometheus* (Clarendon Press, 2001).

13. See Peter L. Bernstein, *Capital Ideas: The Improbable Origins of Modern Wall Street* (Wiley, 1992), for a history.

14. A classic statement of this theory is Burton G. Malkiel, *A Random Walk Down Wall Street: The Time-Tested Strategy for Successful Investing* (W.W. Norton & Company, 10th ed., 2012).

15. Robert J. Shiller, *Irrational Exuberance* (Princeton University Press, 3d ed., 2015).

16. As of 2010, institutional investors held common stock worth $11.5 trillion. In the same year, index funds held about $1.4 trillion. Marshall E. Blume & Donald B. Keim, Institutional Investors and Stock Market Liquidity: Trends and Relationships, 5 (working paper, Wharton School, University of Pennsylvania, 2012), http://finance.wharton.upenn.edu/~keim/research/ChangingInstitutionPreferences_21Aug2012.pdf.

17. Business Insider's Global Macro Monitor, Q3 2012; http://www.business insider.com/who-owns-the-us-equity-market-2013-1.

18. Joseph A. McCahery, Zacharias Sautner, & Laura T. Starks, Behind the Scenes: The Corporate Governance Preferences of Institutional Investors, 71 *Journal of Finance* 2905 (2016).

19. OECD Institutional Investor Statistics, 2008–2015. See also José Azar & Martin C. Schmalz, Common Ownership of Competitors Raises Antitrust Concerns, 8 *Journal of European Competition Law & Practice* 329 (2017), for a more detailed discussion of issues in Europe.

20. This view was widespread in the 1990s. See, e.g., Bernard S. Black, Agents Watching Agents: The Promise of Institutional Investor Voice, 39 *UCLA Law Review* 811 (1992); Mark J. Roe, A Political Theory of American Corporate Finance, 91 *Columbia Law Review* 10 (1991). For some early criticisms, see Edward B. Rock, The Logic and (Uncertain) Significance of Institutional Shareholder Activism, 79 *Georgetown Law Journal*. 445 (1991); John C. Coffee, Jr., The SEC and the Institutional Investor: A Half-Time Report, 15 *Cardozo Law Review* 837 (1994).

21. From José Azar, Sahil Raina, & Martin C. Schmalz, Ultimate Ownership and Bank Competition (unpublished manuscript, July 23, 2016), https://papers.ssrn.com/sol3/papers.cfm?abstract_id=2710252.

22. Jan Fichtner, Eelke M. Heemskerk, & Javier Garcia-Bernardo, Hidden Power of the Big Three? Passive Index Funds, Re-Concentration of Corporate Ownership, and New Financial Risk, 19 *Business and Politics* 298 (2017); José Azar, Portfolio Diversification, Market Power, and the Theory of the Firm (IESE Business School, Working Paper No. 1170-E, 2017), https://papers.ssrn.com/sol3/papers.cfm?abstract_id=2811221.

23. Jie He & Jiekun Huang, Product Market Competition in a World of Cross-Ownership: Evidence from Institutional Blockholdings, 30 *Review of Financial Studies* 2674 (2017).

24. Azar first wrote about these issues in his 2012 PhD thesis. See José Azar, A New Look at Oligopoly: Implicit Collusion Through Portfolio Diversification () (unpublished PhD dissertation, Princeton University May 2012), http://www.princeton.edu/~smorris/pdfs/PhD/Azar.pdf. He has since transformed that work into papers, including José Azar, Portfolio Diversification, Market Power, and the Theory of the

Firm (IESE Business School, Working Paper No. 1170-E, 2017), https://papers.ssrn .com/sol3/papers.cfm?abstract_id=2811221, and his joint work cited in notes 21 and 31.

25. Based largely on the legal authority of Section 7 of the Clayton Act, 15 U.S.C. § 18 (1996).

26. See U.S. Department of Justice & Federal Trade Commission, Horizontal Merger Guidelines (2010), https://www.ftc.gov/sites/default/files/attachments /merger-review/100819hmg.pdf; Sonia Jaffe & E. Glen Weyl, The First-Order Approach to Merger Analysis, 5 *American Economic Journal: Microeconomics* 188 (2013).

27. Germán Guitérrez & Thomas Philippon, Investment-less Growth: An Empirical Investigation (National Bureau of Economic Research, Working Paper No. 22897, 2016). Also, Schmalz reports a conversation with a fund manager, in which the manager admitted to Schmalz that he does not tell his portfolio firms to compete harder against his other portfolio firms since market share is zero sum. Martin Schmalz, Anti-Competitive Effects of Common Ownership (presentation at Columbia Law School, November 3, 2016).

28. Miguel Antón, Florian Ederer, Mireia Giné, & Martin C. Schmalz, Common Ownership, Competition, and Top Management Incentives (Ross School of Business, Paper No. 1328, 2017).

29. Martin C. Schmalz, One Big Reason There's So Little Competition Among U.S. Banks, *Harvard Business Review* (June 13, 2016), https://hbr.org/2016/06/one -big-reason-theres-so-little-competition-among-u-s-banks.

30. Sociologists of business refer to this shift as the "Finance-dominated" or "post-Fordist" business model. See William Lazonick & Mary O'Sullivan, Maximizing Shareholder Value: A New Ideology for Corporate Governance, 29 *Economics & Society* 13 (2000), for a review of the early history of this move. See also Engelbert Stockhammer, Some Stylized Facts on the Finance-Dominated Accumulation Regime, 12 *Competition & Change* 184 (2008), for an update.

31. See José Azar, Martin C. Schmalz, & Isabel Tecu, Anti-Competitive Effects of Common Ownership, *Journal of Finance* (Forthcoming).

32. Azar, Ultimate Ownership and Bank Competition.

33. See Antón et al., Common Ownership.

34. David Autor, David Dorn, Lawrence F. Katz, Christina Patterson, & John Van Reenen, The Fall of the Labor Share and the Rise of Superstar Firms (MIT Working Paper, 2017), https://economics.mit.edu/files/12979; and De Loecker & Eeckhout, The Rise of Market Power.

35. Jacob S. Hacker & Paul Pierson, *Winner-Take-All Politics: How Washington Made the Rich Richer—And Turned Its Back on the Middle Class* (Simon and Schuster, 2011).

36. Eric A. Posner, Fiona M. Scott Morton, & E. Glen Weyl, A Proposal to Limit the Anti-Competitive Power of Institutional Investors, 81 *Antitrust Law Journal* 669 (2017).

37. Posner et al., A Proposal to Limit the Anti-Competitive Power of Institutional Investors.

38. Ronald J. Gilson & Jeffrey N. Gordon, Agency Capitalism: Further Implications of Equity Intermediation 7 (Columbia Law and Economics Working Paper No. 461, 2014). See also Ronald J. Gilson & Jeffrey N. Gordon, The Agency Costs of Agency Capitalism: Activist Investors and the Revaluation of Governance Rights, 113 *Columbia Law Review* 863 (2011).

39. We tread speculatively in this paragraph. The industry is complex, fluid, and poorly understood.

40. See Ali Hortaçsu & Chad Syverson, Product Differentiation, Search Costs, and Competition in the Mutual Fund Industry: A Case Study of S&P 500 Index Funds, 119 *Quarterly Journal of Economics* 403 (2004); John C. Coates IV & R. Glenn Hubbard, Competition in the Mutual Fund Industry: Evidence and Implications for Policy, 33 *Journal of Corporate Law* 151 (2007).

41. John Y. Campbell et al., Have Individual Stocks Become More Volatile? An Empirical Exploration of Idiosyncratic Risk, 56 *Journal of Finance* 1 (2001).

42. Karen K. Lewis, Why Do Stocks and Consumption Imply Such Different Gains from International Risk Sharing?, 52 *Journal of International Economics* 1 (2000).

43. 15 U.S.C. § 18 (1996).

44. 15 U.S.C. § 18 (1996).

45. 353 U.S. 586 (1957).

46. 353 U.S. 586, 597–98 (1957).

47. See Elhauge, Horizontal Shareholding.

48. Thus, our argument does not depend on conscious coordination across firms, as some readers have suggested.

49. Elhauge, Horizontal Shareholding, at 1305–1308.

50. In fact, institutional investors have funded at least one publication to sow doubt about the academic research. See Daniel P. O'Brien & Keith Waehrer, The Competitive Effects of Common Ownership: We Know Less than We Think (February 23, 2017), https://papers.ssrn.com/sol3/papers.cfm?abstract_id=2922677. The authors state in their first footnote that they received funding from the Investment Company Institute, an association of investment companies that engages in lobbying and related activities.

51. Thomas Piketty, Emmanuel Saez, & Gabriel Zucman, Distributional National Accounts: Methods and Estimates for the United States (National Bureau of Economic Research, Working Paper No. 22945, 2016).

52. Posner et al., Proposal to Limit the Anti-Competitive Power of Institutional Investors.

53. Ibid.

54. Nathan Wilmers, Wage Stagnation and Buyer Power: How Buyer-Supplier Relations Affect U.S. Worker Wages, 1978-2014, *American Sociological Review* (Forthcoming).

55. Matthew Desmond, *Evicted: Poverty and Profit in the American City* (Broadway Books, 2016).

56. Clayton M. Christensen, *The Innovator's Dilemma: When New Technologies Cause Great Firms to Fail* (Harvard Business Review Press, 2016).

57. Luis Cabral, Standing on the Shoulders of Dwarfs: Dominant Firms and Innovation Incentives (2017), http://luiscabral.net/economics/workingpapers/innovation%202017%2007.pdf.

58. Not Patrick Henry, nor Thomas Jefferson. Apparently from the abolitionist Wendell Phillips in 1853. See http://www.bartleby.com/73/1073.html.

## Chapter 5. Data as Labor

1. Jaron Lanier, *Who Owns the Future?* (Simon & Schuster, 2013).

2. While Lanier's work provided the direct inspiration for our work, the themes he raises appeared roughly simultaneously in other scholarship. See, for example, Lilly C. Irani & M. Six Silberman, Turkopticon: Interrupting Worker Invisibility in Amazon Mechanical Turk, *CHI'13 Proceedings of the SIGCHI Conference on Human Factors in Computing Systems* (2013), and Trebor Scholz, ed., *Digital Labor: The Internet as Playground and Factory* (Routledge, 2013).

3. Imanol Arrieta-Ibarra, Leonard Goff, Diego Jiménez-Hernández, Jaron Lanier & E. Glen Weyl, Should We Treat Data as Labor? Moving Beyond "Free," *American Economic Association Papers and Proceedings* (Forthcoming).

4. For an entertaining and artistic if exaggerated attempt to draw a connection between women's work and data work, see http://wagesforfacebook.com/. For a more scholarly analysis of the analogy, see Kylie Jarrett, The Relevance of "Women's Work": Social Reproduction and Immaterial Labor in Digital Media, 15 *Television & New Media* 14 (2014).

5. Marc Anthony Neal, *What the Music Said: Black Popular Music and Black Public Culture* (Routledge, 1999).

6. Lanier, *Who Owns the Future?*.

7. Julien Mailland & Kevin Driscoll, *Minitel: Welcome to the Internet* (MIT Press, 2017).

8. Franklin Foer, *The World Without Mind: The Existential Threat of Big Tech* (Penguin, 2017).

9. Richard J. Gilbert & Michael L. Katz, *An Economist's Guide to* U.S. v. Microsoft, 15 *Journal of Economic Perspectives* 25 (2001).

10. Sergey Brin & Lawrence Page, *The Anatomy of a Large-Scale Hypertextual Web Search Engine*, 30 *Computer Network & ISDN Systems* 107 (1998).

11. Richard Thaler, Toward a Positive Theory of Consumer Choice, 1 *Journal of Economic Behavior & Organization* 39 (1980).

12. Chris Anderson, *Free: The Future of a Radical Price* (Hyperion, 2009).

13. Jakob Nielsen, *The Case for Micropayments*, Nielsen Norman Group (January 25, 1998), https://www.nngroup.com/articles/the-case-for-micropayments/.

14. Daniela Hernandez, Facebook's Quest to Build an Artificial Brain Depends on this Guy, *Wired* (2014), https://www.wired.com/2014/08/deep-learning-yann-lecun/.

15. "Complexity" is often used in academic parlance to refer to the difficulty of a problem in the worst case. Often these worst-case bounds are very "conservative" in the sense that they dramatically overstate the requirements in typical real-world ap-

plications. With a slight abuse of nomenclature, we use complexity to refer to what a problem requires in a typical or "average" case in practice rather than what it can be proven to require in the worst case.

16. https://news.microsoft.com/features/democratizing-ai/.

17. A monthly Netflix subscription is $10 and a typical subscriber in 2015 watched 1.5 hours daily according to Netflix's publicly released statistics.

18. Foer, *World Without Mind.*

19. Carl Benedikt Frey & Michael A. Osborne, The Future of Employment: How Susceptible Are Jobs to Computerisation?, 114 *Technological Forecasting & Social Change* 254 (2017).

20. Daron Acemoglu & Pascual Restrepo, *Robots and Jobs: Evidence from US Labor Markets* (National Bureau of Economic Research, Working Paper No. 23285, 2017).

21. Arrieta-Ibarra et al., Should We Treat Data as Labor?

22. David Autor et al., The Fall of the Labor Share and the Rise of Superstar Firms (National Bureau of Economic Research, Working Paper No. 23396, 2017).

23. Julie E. Cohen, The Biopolitical Public Domain: The Legal Construction of the Surveillance Economy, *Philosophy and Technology* (Forthcoming).

24. Colm Harmon, Hessel Oosterbeek, & Ian Walker, The Returns to Education: Microeconomics, 17 *Journal of Economic Surveys* 115 (2003).

25. Ming Yin et al., *The Communication Network Within the Crowd* (Proceedings of the 25th International Conference on World Wide Web 1293, 2016), https://www.microsoft.com/en-us/research/wp-content/uploads/2016/07/turker_network1.pdf.

26. Irani & Silberman, Turkopticon; and Mary L. Gray & Siddharth Suri, The Humans Working Behind the AI Curtain, *Harvard Business Review*, January 9, 2017.

27. Mary L. Gray & Siddharth Suri, this project is currently untitled, but is under contract from Houghton Mifflin Harcourt. (Forthcoming).

28. Annalee Newitz, Raters of the World, Unite—The Secret Lives of Google Raters, *Ars Technica* (April 27, 2017), https://arstechnica.com/features/2017/04/the-secret-lives-of-google-raters/.

29. For example, a controversy raged in 2017 over Google's role in the firing of a policy researcher critical of their business practices.

30. See Roland Bénabou & Jean Tirole, Intrinsic and Extrinsic Motivation, 70 *Review of Economic Studies* 489 (2003), for a survey of this literature.

31. Sara Constance Kingsley et al., Accounting for Market Frictions and Power Asymmetries in Online Labor Markets, 7 *Policy & Internet* 383 (2015).

32. Arindrajit Dube, Jeff Jacobs, Suresh Naidu, & Siddharth Suri, Monopsony in Crowdsourcing Labor Markets (Columbia University Working Paper, 2017).

33. https://www.nytimes.com/2016/05/06/business/facebook-bends-the-rules-of-audience-engagement-to-its-advantage.html?mcubz=0&_r=0.

34. David L. Harris, Massachusetts Woman's Lawsuit Accuses Google of Using Free Labor to Transcribe Books, Newspapers, *Boston Business Journal* (January 23, 2015), https://www.bizjournals.com/boston/blog/techflash/2015/01/massachusetts-womans-lawsuit-accuses-google-of.html.

35. For a review of this research, see Adam Alter, *Irresistible: The Rise of Addictive Technology and the Business of Keeping Us Hooked* (Penguin, 2017).

36. Bénabou & Tirole, Intrinsic and Extrinsic Motivation; Roland Bénabou & Jean Tirole, Incentives and Prosocial Behavior, 96 *American Economic Review* 1652 (2006).

37. Aaron Smith, *What Internet Users Know about Technology and the Web*, Pew Research Center (November 25, 2014), http://www.pewinternet.org/2014/11/25/web-iq/.

38. Lisa Barnard, The Cost of Creepiness: How Online Behavioral Advertising Affects Consumer Purchase Intention, https://cdr.lib.unc.edu/indexablecontent/uuid:ceb8622f-1490-4078-ae41-4dc57f24e08b (unpublished PhD dissertation, University of North Carolina at Chapel Hill, 2014); Finn Brunton & Helen Nissenbaum, *Obfuscation: A User's Guide for Privacy and Protest* (MIT Press, 2015).

39. For proposals on how this could be done, see Lanier, *Who Owns the Future?*; Butler Lampson, *Personal Control of Data*, Microsoft Research ( July 13, 2016), https://www.microsoft.com/en-us/research/video/personal-control-of-data/.

40. Karl Marx, *Capital: A Critique of Political Economy* (Ben Fowkes, trans., Penguin Classics, 1992) (1867).

41. Friedrich Engels, *The Condition of the Working Class in England* (David McLellan, ed., Oxford University Press, 2009) (1845).

42. John E. Roemer, *A General Theory of Exploitation and Class* (Harvard University Press, 1982).

43. Beatrice & Sydney Webb, *Industrial Democracy* (Longmans Green and Co., 1897).

44. John Kenneth Galbraith, *American Capitalism: The Concept of Countervailing Power* (Houghton Mifflin, 1952).

45. Robert C. Allen, Engels' Pause: Technical Change, Capital Accumulation, and Inequality in the British Industrial Revolution, 46 *Explorations in Economic History* 418 (2009).

46. This is the subject of work in progress by these authors, but was discussed by Acemoglu in a presentation he gave in 2016 at Microsoft Corporation. Daron Acemoglu, *The Impact of IT on the Labor Market* (September 2016), https://economics.mit.edu/files/12118.

47. In a variety of settings and with various collaborators, one of us is working to quanitfy the marginal value of data.

48. The first paper in this project is Azevedo et al., 2017, "A/B Testing," but this only relates to a narrow aspect of the use of data for testing new products and suggesting ideas for them. While this is one important component of the value of data labor, it is far from being the main one. In 2018, Weyl, in collaboration with Lanier, Imanol Arrieta Ibarra, and Diego Jiménez Hernández, will be working to build more broadly useful systems for empirically calculating the value of data in various ML settings.

49. See, e.g., Lawrence F. Katz & Alan B. Krueger, The Rise and Nature of Alternative Work Arrangements in the United States, 1995–2015 (National Bureau of Economic Research, Working Paper No. 22667, 2016); Jonathan V. Hall & Alan B.

Krueger, An Analysis of the Labor Market for Uber's Driver-Partners in the United States (National Bureau of Economic Research, Working Paper No. 22843, 2016); Gray & Suri, untitled book project.

50. Mark Aguiar, Mark Bils, Kerwin Kofi Charles, & Erik Hurst, Leisure Luxuries and the Labor Supply of Young Men (NBER Working Paper, 2017).

## Conclusion. Going to the Root

1. The most prominent recent exponents of the techno-optimist within economics have been Erik Brynjolfsson and Andrew McAfee in their 2014 book, *The Second Machine Age: Work, Progress and Prosperity in a Time of Brilliant Technologies* (W. W. Norton & Company). More broadly, the most prominent techno-optimist is Ray Kurzweil, in a series of books.

2. The most prominent techno-pessimistic perspective is offered by Robert J. Gordon in his 2016 book, *The Rise and Fall of American Growth: The U.S. Standard of Living since the Civil War* (Princeton University Press).

3. This view is increasingly prevalent among economists. We cannot list the large group of papers published in recent years that document the large and rising importance of market power, but we refer the reader to an excellent blog, http://www .promarket.org, for a comprehensive set of resources.

4. It is perhaps surprising that this view of the economic future is not more broadly held, given that it is central to many economists' understanding of economic history. For example, according to a 2016 presentation by economist Daron Acemoglu entitled "The Impact of IT on Labor Markets" to the Toulouse Network for Information Technology, the fears of technological displacement of workers by the Luddites in early nineteenth-century Britain turned out to be "wrong," not because untamed capitalism drove up the price of labor but because radical institutional change (labor unions, universal schooling, etc.) helped workers catch up economically.

5. See Jacob S. Hacker & Paul Pierson, *Winner-Take-All Politics: How Washington Made the Rich Richer—and Turned Its Back on the Middle Class* (Simon & Schuster, 2011) for an account of the increasing concentration of political power by cooperating firms in past decades.

6. Such a tradeoff would probably violate the First Amendment as it is currently interpreted, but we think that courts would eventually accommodate political developments that are socially beneficial.

7. Eric A. Posner & Nicholas Stephanopoulos, Quadratic Election Law, 172 *Public Choice* 265 (2017).

8. See Ben Laurence & Itai Sher, *Ethical Considerations on Quadratic Voting*, 172 *Public Choice* 195 (2017); Josiah Ober, Equality, Legitimacy, Interests, and Preferences: Historical Notes on Quadratic Voting in a Political Context, 172 *Public Choice* 223 (2017, for a detailed discussion of these concerns.

9. Milanovic, *Global Inequality*.

10. Margaret E. Peters, *Trading Barriers: Immigration and the Remaking of Globalization* (Princeton University Press, 2017).

11. Eric A. Posner & Alan O. Sykes, Voting Rules in International Organizations, 15 *Chicago Journal of International Law* 195 (2014).

12. Émile Durkheim, *The Division of Labour in Society* (Simon & Schuster 1997; originally published in 1893).

13. The classic and perhaps most carefully developed version of this critique is by Fred Hirsch, *The Social Limits to Growth* (Harvard University Press, 1976), but similar themes are developed more recently by Michael J. Sandel, *What Money Can't Buy: The Moral Limits of Markets* (Farrar, Straus and Giroux, 2012), and Samuel Bowles, *The Moral Economy: Why Good Incentives Are No Substitute for Good Citizens* (Yale University Press, 2016).

14. A. O. Hirschman, Rival Interpretations of Market Society: Civilizing, Destructive, or Feeble?, 20 *Journal of Economic Literature* 1463 (1982).

15. Durkheim, *Division of Labour in Society*.

16. Jane Jacobs, *The Death and Life of Great American Cities* (Random House, 1961).

17. Marion Fourcade & Kieran Healy, Moral Views of Market Society, 33 *Annual Review of Sociology* 285 (2007), highlight that the most powerful visions of markets have been inherently moralizing and not just economic. We hope some readers will find this moral vision an important component of the project of Radical Markets.

18. Some may wonder whether individuals might not come to fear others taking their possessions. However, under the optimal COST rate, individuals would price their possessions above the amount they would be willing to accept and thus a purchase would still be mutually beneficial, just not in as imbalanced a manner as at present. Some individuals might severely understate asset values and try to hide or degrade them to avoid forced sales, but such antisocial strategies could and should be socially sanctioned, just as tax avoidance is; see below in the text.

19. Gary Becker, *The Economics of Discrimination* (University of Chicago Press, 2d ed., 2010).

20. See Richard H. Thaler & Cass R. Sunstein, *Nudge: Improving Decisions About Health, Wealth, and Happiness* (Penguin, 2009).

## Epilogue. After Markets?

1. F. A. Hayek, The Use of Knowledge in Society, 35 *American Economic Review* 519 (1945).

2. Ludwig von Mises, *Economic Calculation in the Socialist Commonwealth* 19–23 (S. Adler trans., Ludwig von Mises Institute, 1990) (1920).

3. Leonard E. Read, I, Pencil (Foundation for Economic Education, 2010) (1958), https://fee.org/media/14940/read-i-pencil.pdf.

4. Cosma Shalizi, In Soviet Union, Optimization Problem Solves You, *Crooked*

*Timber* (May 30, 2012), http://crookedtimber.org/2012/05/30/in-soviet-union -optimization-problem-solves-you/.

5. Oskar Lange, The Computer and the Market, in *Socialism, Capitalism and Economic Growth: Essays Presented to Maurice Dobb* (Cambridge University Press, C. H. Feinstein, ed., 1967).

6. *Global Computing Capacity*, AI Impacts (February 16, 2016), http://aiimpacts .org/global-computing-capacity/#easy-footnote-bottom-7.

7. J. S. Jordan, The Competitive Allocation Process Is Informationally Efficient Uniquely, 28 *Journal of Economic Theory* 1 (1982); Noam Nisan & Ilya Segal, The Communication Requirements of Efficient Allocations and Supporting Prices, 129 *Journal of Economic Theory* 192 (2006).

8. Lange, The Computer and the Market, at 157.

9. The Soviet Union: GDP Growth, Nintil (March 26, 2016), https://nintil .com/2016/03/26/the-soviet-union-gdp-growth/.

10. See, for example, Modiface's eye-tracking–based advertising analytic system described at http://www.mobilemarketer.com/news/modiface-eye-tracking-app -increases-smashbox-conversions-by-27/447825/.

# INDEX

Italic page numbers indicate figures and tables

abortion, 27, 112–13, *116*
Acemoglu, Daron, 240, 316n4
activism, 3, 124, 140, 176–77, 188, 193, 211, 232
Adachi, Kentaro, 80–81, 105–8
Africa, 136, 138
African Americans, 24, 89, 209–10
Airbnb, 70, 117
airlines, 171, 183, 189–91, 194
Akerlof, George, 66–67
algorithms, 208, 214, 219, 221, 281–82, 289–93, 307n7
Allen, Robert C., 240
Amazon, 112, 230–31, 234, 239, 248, 288, 290–91
American Constitution, 86–87
American Federation of Musicians, 210
American Tobacco Company, 174
America OnLine (AOL), 210
Anderson, Chris, 212
antitrust: Clayton Act and, 176–77, 197, 311n25; landlords and, 201–2; monopolies and, 23, 48, 174–77, 180, 184–86, 191, 197–203, 242, 255, 262, 286; resale price maintenance and, 200–201; social media and, 202
Apple, 117, 239, 289
Arginoussai Islands, 83
aristocracy, 16–17, 22–23, 36–38, 84–85, 87, 90, 135–36
Aristotle, 172
Arrow, Kenneth, 92, 303n17
Articles of Confederation, 88
artificial intelligence (AI), 202, 257, 287; Alexa and, 248; algorithms

and, 208, 214, 219, 221, 281–82, 289–93; automated video editing and, 208; Cortana and, 219; data capacities and, 236; Deep Blue and, 213; democratization of, 219; diminishing returns and, 229–30; facial recognition and, 208, 216–19; factories for thinking machines and, 213–20; Google Assistant and, 219; human-produced data for, 208–9; marginal value and, 224–28, 247; Microsoft and, 219; neural networks and, 214–19; payment systems for, 224–30; recommendation systems and, 289–90; siren servers and, 220–24, 230–41, 243; Siri and, 219, 248; technofeudalism and, 230–33; techno-optimists and, 254–55, 316n2; techno-pessimists and, 254–55, 316n2; worker replacement and, 223
Athens, 55, 83–84, 131
Atwood, Margaret, 18–19
auctions, xv–xxi, 49–51, 70–71, 97, 99, 147–49, 156–57, 300n34
au pair program, 154–55, 161
Australia, *10*, 12, *13*, 159, 162
Austrian school, 2
Autor, David, 240
Azar, José, 185, 189, 310n24

Bahrain, 158
banking industry, 182–84, *183*, 190
Bank of America, *183*, 184
Becker, Gary, 147

## A NOTE ON THE TYPE

This book has been composed in Adobe Text and Gotham. Adobe Text, designed by Robert Slimbach for Adobe, bridges the gap between fifteenth- and sixteenth-century calligraphic and eighteenth-century Modern styles. Gotham, inspired by New York street signs, was designed by Tobias Frere-Jones for Hoefler & Co.